Object-Oriented Project Management with UML

Object-Oriented Project Management with UML

Murray Cantor

WILEY COMPUTER PUBLISHING

John Wiley & Sons, Inc.

New York • Chichester • Weinheim • Brisbane • Singapore • Toronto

Publisher: Robert Ipsen
Editor: Theresa Hudson
Assistant Editor: Kathryn A. Malm
Managing Editor: Micheline Frederick
Electronic Products, Associate Editor: Mike Sosa
Text Design & Composition: SunCliff Graphic Productions

Library of Congress Cataloging-in-Publication Data

Cantor, Murray, 1947–
    Object-oriented project management with UML / Murray Cantor.
        p.   cm.
    Includes bibliographical references and index.
    ISBN: 0-471-25303-0 (cloth : alk. paper)
    1. Object-oriented methods (Computer science)   2. Computer
software--Development.   3. UML (Computer science)   I. Title.
QA76.9.O35C36   1998
005.1'17--dc21   98-16413
                                                            CIP

Printed in the United States of America
10 9 8 7 6 5 4 3

With love and gratitude to my wife,
Judi Taylor Cantor, and my son, Michael

ABOUT THE AUTHOR

Dr. Murray Cantor has over ten years experience managing object-based systems. He is currently employed by Rational Software as a member of its Worldwide Services Organization. Before joining Rational, Cantor was a program manager at TASC, a subsidiary of Litton Industries, where he directed complex software development programs. Prior to joining TASC, Dr. Cantor was a development manager at IBM, where he oversaw the development of high-end graphics and multimedia systems.

CONTENTS

CHAPTER 3

Choosing a Development Lifecycle Model   81

CHAPTER 4

Planning Object-Oriented Projects   109

Part two

Managing Through the Lifecycle   163

CHAPTER 7

Managing the Construction Phase   237

CHAPTER 8

Managing the Transition Phase   283

Part three
Measuring Progress and Success

CHAPTER 9
Tracking and Oversight

APPENDIX
The Web Page

BIBLIOGRAPHY

INDEX

ACKNOWLEDGMENTS

This book would not have been written without the help of many people. Some helped directly, others by sharing insight and knowledge throughout the years. One of the side benefits of writing a book is the opportunity to say thank you.

First, I want to thank my wife Judi. She provided valuable advice, support, and insight throughout the writing. Also, she did more than her share. Next time, it is her turn.

I also want thank the TASC management for their support while I was writing. Frank Serna, the simulations system Business Unit director, as well as my manager, deserves special thanks for his encouragement and valuable discussions throughout the writing of the book. In addition, this book is the result of many conversations with colleagues, staff, and students. I especially want to thank David Alvey, Roger Blais, Pat Durante, Robert McCarron, Hal Miller, William Myers, Michael Olson, David Pierce, and Ralph Vincigeurra. Martin Svedlow and Todd Withey deserve special thanks, too, for their support and enthusiasm in applying the book's techniques. Thanks are also due to Martha Dionne, the TASC Librarian, and her staff, Audrey Palmieri and Margaret Ouzts, for their invaluable research assistance. Thanks also to Jan Lapper and Pauline Parziale in helping me stay organized.

Much of this book is based on my valuable experience at IBM. I especially thank Khoa Nguyen (now at Videoserver), who guided me through my early days in project management. I also learned a great deal from working with Robert Swann and Fred Scheibl.

I am especially grateful to the editors at John Wiley. Thanks to Theresa Hudson for her belief and support of the book, and to Sandra Bontemps and Kathryn A. Malm for their patient efforts in shaping the text.

INTRODUCTION

This book is a practical guide to modern software development. It grew out of a course I regularly teach at TASC, which itself began as happenstance. I had been asked to appraise an online course on managing object-oriented development. I hated it. It was a rehash of the old, discredited waterfall methods of software development. They replaced the design and code steps plus some object jargon. When I expressed this opinion, TASC management threw down the gauntlet, essentially saying, "If you are so smart, then you teach the course."

While preparing the course, I realized a few things: The first is that we in the industry really do know how to manage software development. There is no reason for software development to be a risky, high-stress business. On the other hand, most programs do not seem to benefit from what we have learned over the last few years. Second, a lot of material must be covered when teaching software management, most of which is not commonly taught in universities. And because developers are still the best source of software managers, it is important that a book be available to teach the trade. As of this writing, I know of no other book that covers the material that I feel is essential for any project manager.

The third realization is that the use of objects and object design languages such as the Unified Modeling Language (UML) can improve not only the technical quality of the development: It can also facilitate the task of the project managers. I believe that all new software development projects should adopt object methodology and be managed according to the techniques in this book.

Goals

Based on my experience, the available literature, and conversations with my colleagues, staff, and students, this text describes the effective management of software development projects using object-oriented methodology. I describe not only what the project manager should do through all phases of the project, but explain why the techniques work. To that end, the book covers the planning, staffing, organization, development, and delivery of object-based software. The day-to-day activities of the project manager are covered in depth, providing leadership and management to your team. I include enough theoretical background so that you come to understand the why as well as the how. The theory will help you apply the techniques to your particular situation.

As a project manager, you should have a library of books, because no one can cover all you need to know as you broaden your skill base. Although this book covers a lot of ground, I leave such topics as maturing the organization and quality management to other books, and only peripherally cover others. I provide references for those who want to learn more about the topics of secondary importance to this book.

Who Should Read This Book

The book's primary target is software project and program managers, neophytes, and experts, as well as those developers who have an interest in how their roles fit into the overall development process, or even better, who aspire to project management. So, too, the managers of project managers should read the book, to develop an appreciation of what your project manager is doing and thereby have a basis for providing oversight. The same goes for those who contract software.

I have strived to make the book applicable to developers of small programs, as well as to development teams working on large programs. The techniques described can be applied to research and development projects, internal tool development, contracted software, and shrink-wrapped products. To a great degree, this book is self-contained. I assume the reader has some experience with software development and some notion of software objects. I also assume the reader has at least participated in a software development project and can read a Gantt chart.

How This Book Is Organized

The book has three parts. The first lays the foundation for the rest of the book. In order to succeed at software project management, you need to understand some important principles. These underlying principles are introduced in Chapter 1. This is followed by an introduction to the Unified Modeling Language (UML) and its use in software development in Chapter 2. Chapter 2 also provides an overview of object-oriented design and the UML for the project manager. Anyone familiar with the UML can skim this chapter. However, there is some managerial advice on managing complexity that even the UML expert may find of use. Chapter 3 completes the foundation with a discussion of software development lifecycle models.

The second part of the book discusses the application of the concepts inherent in the software development phases. All the phases and activities of UML software development are covered in detail. Chapter 4 details how to plan and organize your project. Chapters 5 through 8 describe the software development lifecycle in detail, how to manage throughout the phases: activities, exit criteria, and special managerial and communication issues.

The third part consists only of Chapter 9; it tells you how to assess and report your project's status, and it provides the means, budget, and development metrics to verify whether your project is on track. Chapter 9 also outlines a format for the program manager to use to succinctly report status and project health to upper management and/or the customer.

In addition to the body of the book, an ongoing example of a software development project—a manned cockpit simulator for a stealth fighter—is presented in sidebar format throughout. The example, while detailed, is fictional and is not based any real project. It was written to be sufficiently complicated to show how the book's methods work. The example is intended to help you to understand how plans are set, teams are organized, risks are managed, and code is developed and delivered, not how to actually build a simulator. I reviewed the simulator architecture with some developers who tell me it is reasonable, however, I'm not sure I would actually use it in a real program.

On the Web Site

Because one of the goals of this book is to help you in your day-to-day program management, the publisher, John Wiley & Sons, Inc., has established a Web site, **www.wiley.com/compbooks/cantor**, where you can download material that you might find useful as you apply some the techniques in the book. Among the site's features are:

- A sample project file for the simulator example, including a work breakdown structure (WBS) for a software development program described in Chapter 4.
- A database template for managing use cases described in Chapter 5.
- A Svedlow diagram for tracking development during the construction phase found in Chapter 7.
- A development artifact status template from Chapter 9.

In addition, the site contains links to other useful Web sites. You can also use the site to write me to comment on the ideas in the book and to share your experience. In keeping with the nature of all Web sites, the content will change from time to time.

From Here

The value of the book lies in the application of the ideas and technique, so read it and make use of the Web page. Try out the ideas. They work for me; I think they will for you. Thank you for reading the book. I hope you enjoy it.

Object-Oriented
Project Management
with UML

Part one

PRINCIPLES FOR OBJECT-ORIENTED PROGRAM MANAGEMENT

1 OBJECT-ORIENTED DEVELOPMENT AS A MANAGEMENT TOOL

If you know the enemy and know yourself, you need not fear the result of a hundred battles. If you know yourself but not the enemy, for every victory gained you will also suffer a defeat. If you know neither the enemy nor yourself, you will succumb in every battle.

Sun Tzu, Chinese general. *The Art of War*, Chapter 3, Axiom 18, c. 490 B.C.; (ed. by James Clavell, 1981).

The days of bringing a bunch of hackers together to build a large system are over. This method of organizing a project, although quick, results in chaos; such development programs are often in a continual crisis and programmers burn out quickly. For software organizations to thrive, they must be productive over the long term. Today's programming challenges call for large teams of programmers to collaborate to develop large complex programs without reeling from crises to crises.

As computers have become more powerful, two complementary phenomena have emerged:

- Increasingly large and complex programs, whose development requires teams of programmers, are in demand.

- Better software design packages that automate tools for programming higher-order languages are being developed.

3

These two trends call for methods that enable teams of programmers to develop robust, manageable code quickly and efficiently. Perhaps the most important trend to emerge, however, is the change of focus from the machine to the person. Early programming languages were designed to reflect the limitations of the machine. The programmer had to focus on how the machine processed data. We revered those who were good at this and labeled them with the exalted title of hacker. The resulting programs, known today as *spaghetti code*, had fatal deficiencies: No one could follow it. No one could fix it. No one could extend it. Even the original programmer, after some time away from the code, had no idea how it worked. It was difficult to unravel and brittle, fixing one bug was likely to introduce another. Attempting to extend the functionality of such code was futile, and reuse was out of the question. In fact, changing the format of the date fields in this code to accommodate years beyond 1999 has proven to be so daunting there is discussion of international economic catastrophe.

To be fair, the machines of that period were so expensive and resource-limited, it made sense to write tight programs that used the machines efficiently. Now, the economics are quite different. Modern languages accommodate human limitations; machine resources are cheap; labor is expensive. The entire focus of modern programming methodology has shifted from conserving machine resources to making teams of programmers efficient.

There are two responses to "humanizing" software development: improved software design paradigms with the associated programming languages and project management approaches that better reflect how teams collectively solve problems. If people are to collaborate, they need to be confident that they are "on the same page." Objects make it possible for humans to deal with the complexity of modern software systems.

Almost all software projects become a battle because the project manager is often faced with a schedule and budget that are rigidly fixed, while the actual effort it will take to deliver to a satisfactory release is at best an educated guess (I will discuss estimation methods later). The goal of every project manager is to somehow deal with the cost and schedule uncertainty while meeting the customer's needs. Victory is claimed with customer acceptance of a project delivered on time and within budget. But as in all battles, formidable enemies stand between you and your victory. Therefore, this chapter begins with an introduction to the enemies and how they conspire to prevent us from delivering the right product on time. In addition, I will cite some useful ways to help you understand the enemies so that you can defeat them with a minimum of effort. The chapter continues with a brief discussion of the chief weapons you can use in object-oriented projects to defeat the enemies. These include the standard object concepts and modern concurrent team-based development techniques. (Later chapters focus on addressing enemies and achieving victory using object-oriented technology.)

> **NOTE**
>
> As promised in the Introduction, the techniques in this book are applied to a real-world object development example, which begins in this chapter. Follow the project as it progresses through the book to learn how you can apply the techniques to your own projects.

Meet the Enemies

Every software project is besieged by at least one of these enemies:

- Inadequate and unstable requirements
- Inadequate customer communications
- Poor team communications
- Unnecessary complexity
- Ineffective team behavior

Though object technology may be directly applied to attack these enemies, it is only by understanding their nature and how object technology provides the necessary weapons that you can successfully apply the book's techniques to your particular program. Let us get to know the enemies better.

Inadequate and Unstable Requirements

Software projects derive from a customer's need. Someone must want you to deliver something useful or that person would not be willing to pay for its development. These needs are captured as requirements, or the specifics of what the system must do. For example, despite the complexity of bridge building, it is comparably easy to specify its requirements: a bridge needs to connect point A to point B, withstand storms, and be able to carry a certain volume of traffic. Barring any geological surprises, it is possible to completely specify a bridge that fully meets requirements.

Software projects, too, are governed by a list of requirements. Unlike the requirements for a bridge, however, which do not change often, specifications for building a piece of software are frequently added and changed throughout the development cycle. Establishing stable software requirements and communicating them effectively is the challenge.

Thus, one of the software project manager's critical skills is the ability to manage system requirements. Software systems are often intended to support complicated operational needs, such as automating office work, managing mission-critical tasks in an aircraft or weapons system, or supporting and handling complicated financial transactions. These systems are so complicated that any attempt to fully specify their capabilities is bound to fall short. A 1994 IBM study (Gibbs, 1994) found that 88 percent of large distributed systems that met published requirements were not operational. In fact, the most disciplined government programs in terms of requirement specifications have been the most spectacular failures.

The Reconfigurable Cockpit Simulator

Your assignment is to manage the development of the software for a reconfigurable cockpit simulator for a Stealth fighter. The simulator is a mock-up of the Stealth fighter cockpit. The instrumentation is identical to that of the actual fighter. The windshields have been replaced by high-resolution monitors connected to top-of-the-line graphics generators. The flight controls include the same tactile feedback as those in the real cockpit.

This is not a video game, but a serious tool for skill and mission training. It presents to the trainee a faithful representation of all the displays, instruments, and out-the-window visualization of the modeled simulation.

Skill training includes take-off and landing under various conditions (weather, terrain, etc.), formation flying, and engagements. For the simulator to be effective, the simulator must model with high fidelity the actual response of the fighter to the pilot's controls. There cannot be any discernable time lag cause by system overhead. Further, as the Stealth is modified over its lifespan, the simulator must be modifiable to reflect these changes. In fact, it should be capable of being configured quickly to model the characteristics of the different versions in deployment. This flexibility is what is meant by *reconfigurable*.

The trainer (the person who creates the lessons) must be able to program threats (enemy aircraft, missiles, and antiaircraft fire). An important

Inadequate Requirements

Successfully addressing customer satisfaction risk requires you and the customer to agree unequivocally on what makes a system successful. Rarely are you handed a complete set of interface specifications that have to be met to declare victory. The more common, and probably worse, situation is that you are given a detailed set of requirements, which in practice do not really specify the system. Further, you will not be able to address cost and schedule risk unless you have a means for achieving requirement stability.

There are two common causes for insufficient requirement specification. First, the customer often does not fully understand what is required. For example, a cus-

feature is the ability to save a session and play it back for the student as a teaching aid.

Mission training comprises rehearsing a planned mission as preparation. It requires accurate modeling of the real terrain, placement of cultural items (roads, building, airfields), as well as the expected weather. The ability to quickly create the scenarios is essential.

A trainer workstation is attached to the cockpit simulators. The trainer controls and monitors the missions. In addition:

- The hardware interfaces are stable, adequately documented, and readily available.

- The simulator is a standalone system with no need to interface with other systems.

- A software model of the aircraft's response to the controls (thrust, pitch, yawl, and drag) is available as an off-the-shelf product from a third party.

You are given two years to deliver a working system. The delivery date is a hard customer requirement and not negotiable.

As the new project manager, you are faced with planning, staffing, and delivering the software with this system. Your company has some experience in modeling and simulation, but this is your first manned simulator. No one you know has ever flown a Stealth fighter.

> **TIP**
>
> It is wise to assume that you never have a complete specification of the system.

tomer who runs a bank may need to extend his or her checking account management software to include Internet accessibility. The customer understands the need for security and data integrity and may even have some idea of the acceptable response time. On the other hand, the customer may not have thoroughly examined how a user will interact with the system. He or she probably has not considered the user who submits 300 transactions in a day. Therefore, the customer may need you and your team to help him or her think through these issues.

Second, even if the customer is capable of thinking through the details of the complex system required, he or she may not know how to document these requirements effectively. There are two types of requirements:

Static. A quantitative description of the capacity and performance of the system; for example, a database must handle 1,000 transactions a minute.

Dynamic. How the users and others interact with the system so that the task gets accomplished; for example, how the user enters a new record in a database.

Usually, a system is specified in a requirements document that consists of a long list of static requirements and a set of constraints on the dynamic requirements. For example, the document might contain the line "the system must handle 1,000 transactions a minute" (a static requirement). Another line might read "the system is entirely menu-driven from a mouse; there are no keyed-in commands" (a constant on the dynamic requirements). Sometimes, a detailed description of the dynamic requirements, called a *concept of operations document*, is provided along with the static requirements. The statistics show that systems that meet the written requirements are often not operational; the stated static requirements were met, but the unstated dynamic requirements were not.

One of the advantages of object-oriented development is that it includes *use cases*, a method for specifying and managing dynamic requirements. Use cases provide a format for specifying the dynamic requirements. They capture in detail how the system will behave in response to user interaction. When you and your customer share the use cases, a common understanding of the expected behavior of the system can be reached. In addition, use cases form a bridge between the customer's view and the designer's and implementer's view of the system. (Use cases are discussed in more detail in Chapter 2.)

Unstable Requirements

Even after a software project is near completion, requirements continue to be discovered or refined. These changes may be discovered during design reviews, or early testing or through unexpected system component interactions. Unstable requirements will impede your ability to deliver a useful project.

Requirements may become unstable for several reasons:

- Customers develop a clearer understanding of what they need as the program develops.

- Customers come to realize that the original requirements failed to capture their intent.

- Customers may have asked for something that they do not really need and are willing to forgo later in the development.

- The customer's needs change.

- The customer staff or management changes. (Someone arrives with his or her own ideas and an urge to make a difference.)

These unanticipated changes in requirements, if discovered during the later phases of development, could be the cause of a major project setback and, thereafter, for recrimination. In order to be successful, the project manager needs tools to manage requirements that will be changed, refined, and discovered throughout the development cycle. Object-oriented design provides these tools.

One of the more insidious forms of this enemy is sometimes called *function creep*. It is the slow addition of system function throughout the development so that in the end, the customer expects significantly more than you originally signed up for. Throughout the development, your staff or your customer has small suggestions that will lead to a system improvement. Over time, however, suggestions add up until your ability to deliver the system is in jeopardy. Every software project manager has experienced function creep without any concomitant relief on schedule or budget. Use cases, explored in Chapter 2, allow each of the functional enhancement suggestions to be captured and addressed in a disciplined way.

Inadequate Customer Communications

Another project management enemy and one of the potential causes of project failure is poor communication between the customer and the developer. Given the difficulty of specifying the requirements, it is essential that you and the customer maintain open and constructive communications to ensure that you are building what the customer expects. To accomplish this requires ongoing interaction.

In addition, every development project is based on less than perfect information. The development effort begins with a set of assumptions about how the project will go. Almost certainly, these assumptions will have to be adjusted as the project unfolds. There will be trade-offs in budget, schedule, and functional content. You and the customer must share in these trade-offs, so the communications channels must be in place to permit reaching agreement.

An example of a poor customer/developer communication style is an adversarial approach, sometimes called *correct by construction*. The customer requires that reams of requirement and design specifications be created by your team. He or she must review and approve the documents before coding is begun. The premise is

---

Requirements for the Reconfigurable Simulator

As a project manager, you are handed thousands of pages of requirements. As you go through them, you come to realize they consist mainly of the descriptions of the instrumentation given in gory detail. You are left with many questions, which primarily concern how the trainer needs to interact with the system. The authors of the specifications were the aircraft engineers, who do not have full appreciation of the operational considerations of the skill and mission training. What information does the trainer's workstation need to display? How are the scenarios built? Are they stored and retrieved? Does the trainer have a set of scenarios that are used as lesson plans? Does the trainer need to stop the lesson from time to time to make a point? How exactly does a trainer monitor four simulators at once?

You have a fairly good idea of the static requirements. But your understanding of how the system is used, the dynamic requirements, is much less clear.

You have another concern. The requirements in many cases look more like a wish list than a serious attempt to describe a system that can be delivered on time. For example, one requirement is that a checkpoint be made as often as every tenth of a second, and that playback go backward and forward in time. Furthermore, certain of the requirements seem expensive to implement and not as important as the others.

And never forget, the requirements may change. After all, it is not due for two years.

that if the documentation is sufficiently detailed and found to be correct by the customer, then the project is correct by construction. The developers only need build what has been documented.

Certainly, adding formality and discipline to the development process is a good idea, but there are several problems with the adversarial approach. This approach is defocusing; it adds risk and expense to the project. Since the entire success of the project depends on correct documents, the customer and the developer focus their attention on the documentation, not the project. An unreasonable amount of effort may be spent in the attempt to create a correct diagram. In fact, so much of the project's budget can be spent trying to finish the flawless design that the project may be canceled before the software is coded.

This approach also discourages *shared* responsibility. If the document is incorrect, and the project is delivered as specified, then it is the customer's fault if it does not work. If is not delivered as specified, it is the developer's fault. The clear placement of accountability may appear to be an advantage, but in practice, it has been shown to be dysfunctional. It hampers the essential constructive communication between the customer and the developer.

Experience has also shown that no amount of formal process, checkpoints, or design review can completely eliminate the risk of delivering a nonoperational system. While effectively establishing dynamic and static requirements helps, you and your customer need to maintain an ongoing dialog. To ensure this, develop a common vocabulary to discuss the system specifications in a way the customer can understand. Assess whether this project will serve his or her needs. This will drive the design process. As the project proceeds, the customer's understanding of the program will evolve. Only by taking advantage of the increased understanding can you and the customer ensure that what is delivered is acceptable. Communicating in this way provides an ongoing view of what will be delivered and a chance for you to respond to the customer's reaction as the project proceeds. Chapters 4 through 9 discuss how to promote this kind of communication.

Poor Team Communications

A software system of any significant size requires a team of developers. It is not unusual to have 10, 50, 100, or even 1,000 developers on a development team. Each developer is responsible for a piece of code that must work in conjunction with all of the code being generated by all of the other developers. Clearly, communication among team members is imperative.

As the number of developers increases, each developer has that many more people to synchronize. Accordingly, as pointed out in Fred Brooks' *The Mythical*

Man-Month, the amount of communication among developers increases almost quadratically with the size of the project.

Poor communications thus is an enemy with two faces: too little and too much. Too little communication will result in a system that does not come together. Too much communication results in too much time spent coordinating efforts and not enough time spent developing code. Unless you take steps to explicitly manage the communications within your development team, they can get out of hand.

FOR FURTHER READING

Everyone who develops software should read Fredrick P. Brooks and Fredrick P. Brooks Jr., *The Mythical Man-Month* (Addison-Wesley). The anniversary edition was published in 1995.

One approach to managing a program of any significant size is to break down the development team into functional subteams. This divide-and-conquer approach is essential, but it is not without communication problems. If there are communication barriers among the teams, friction is the result. This poor communication across teams will have a negative effect on the project, in particular, each team may meet its own goals to the detriment of the total program.

The standard, adversarial approach to cross-team communication is ineffective. In this approach, each team creates an interface document according to their given specifications. The premise is that if each team meets the interface specifications, then their respective components should integrate and work together. If the integration fails, one of the teams is to blame. This, too, is an example of correct by construction. The problems with this approach are similar to those found in poor customer communications. Teams focus their efforts on creating correct, perfect documents instead of a well-coordinated functional system. While the approach emphasizes teamwork within a subteam, it also promotes finger-pointing between teams. Chapter 4 discusses the integrated program team approach, one method for dealing with this enemy.

Unnecessary Complexity

Unnecessary complexity ties up your resources so that you can never achieve victory. I will discuss complexity in more detail later in this chapter. For this discussion, think of a program with many internal interactions as being complex. Highly complex programs take an unaffordable amount of time and resources to develop, maintain, and extend. If you do not manage the complexity of the program, you will find your team working harder and harder to do less and less.

As programs grow in size and have more interactions, there are more opportunities for something to go wrong. Each of the interactions has the potential to introduce a bug, due to unexpected consequences of interactions. Not only do complex programs tend to have more bugs, but the bugs are difficult to spot during development. This explains why there is so much emphasis on testing and debugging large programs. The more complex the program, the more expensive it is to develop and the more expensive it is to maintain. In fact, if the design is too complex, you may never debug it.

It is important to realize that the same set of requirements can yield designs of varying complexity. Initial designs tend to be more complex than necessary. It takes time and effort to find simpler designs that meet requirements. One of the most important lessons of modern product development is that the effort and expense of improving the design is much less than the expense of detecting and removing the defects in unnecessarily complex designs. This insight leads to the slogan "quality is free." For example, if two printers can do the same job, but one has 5 moving parts and the other 50, the simpler design with fewer moving parts will be a more reliable, more easily manufactured product. Software works in much the same way. Imagine building a database application in which every entry requires that five files be updated, each of which has to consistent with the other. A program that keeps the data in a single file is likely to be more successful.

Complexity also leads to incomprehensibility. Larger programs by definition have more components. As the number of components grows, each component has an opportunity to interact with more components. As the number of interactions increases, it may not be possible to understand what the program is doing, making it impossible for anyone to fix or extend the program.

One of the goals in managing the complexity of the code is to put in place an understandable design. If you are going to develop large programs, you will need a way to explicitly manage the complexity of your system. Object methodology provides some powerful weapons in defeating this enemy.

Ineffective Team Behavior

Stereotypically, programmers do not normally form teams. They take pride in their individual accomplishments and their ability to solve difficult problems, and they are proud that they can bend the complicated computer platforms to their individual will. They tend to view teams as a mechanism that stifles creativity. Their heroes are not great team members or even team leaders but the few individual programmers who are creative and prolific.

Neither are programmers trained to be team members. With a few exceptions, computer science departments do not train their students to participate in the development of large systems. It is frustrating for many young programmers that as team members their communication, coordination, and consensus-building skills may be more valued than their individual programming skills. They generally equate meetings with *not* programming; that is, with *not* working.

Every programmer coming out school knows two things:

- He or she can write 1,500 lines of flawless code over a weekend.
- Most everyone else writes lousy code.

It follows then that if the project is not coming together, it must be the other guy's fault.

Unsurprisingly, programmers have little patience for management attempts to foster teamwork. They find most of the management team discussion (empowerment, quality circles) annoying. The saying, "There is no limit to what a man can do as long as he does not care a straw who gets the credit for it," makes them a bit ill. Probably, you are sympathetic to these views. I know I am. The hyped-up language that team management types tend to use no doubt adds to the skepticism. Some of these people may have good ideas, but for developers, the language gets in the way. The comic strip character Dilbert is so well liked among developers and managers because he captures staff attitudes so well.

This behavior causes poor internal communication. Team members will not have the opportunity to collaborate on a problem, resulting in a less than optimal solution. The team member, by working around a problem rather than working with his or her teammate, will introduce unnecessary complexity (state) into the application. The resulting code will be hard to understand and more likely to have defects. Another problem is an increase in development time, adding cost and schedule risk. The developer will take longer to work around a problem than he or she would to work with the other developer to solve it together.

I really enjoy the process of molding a bunch of high-strung creative individuals into a performing team. It takes leadership, a sense of humor, and patience. Every project leader must be a teacher. It takes a village to raise a programmer. Throughout the text, I discuss working with developers in a team context.

Conquering Enemies with Object Technology

Objects are program components that accomplish a limited task, such as maintaining a list, or drawing a line. Object design and development technology have some features that can aid in defeating the enemies:

Dynamic and static descriptions of requirements. Providing ways of capturing not only what the program is supposed to do, but also how it is supposed to do it.

Dynamic and static descriptions and design. Providing ways of specifying not only how the code is put together, but also how the objects interact.

Encapsulation. Hiding the internal working of the object from the rest of the system, which permits division of state, function, labor.

Inheritance. Allowing for more than one kind of type of object, which enables reuse and a focus on new functionality.

Aggregation. Creating a large object from a small simpler object, allowing for handling of complex states.

Packages. Encapsulating objects into larger components with hidden internal workings, allowing for abstraction (detail hiding) so that complex programs can be managed at different levels of detail.

These features are described in more detail in Chapter 2, The Unified Modeling Language as a Management Tool. It is by taking advantage of these features that you can improve productivity of your team and quality of your product. Simply put, object-oriented software projects achieve the manager's mantra, "faster, cheaper, better," for three reasons:

- *Objects provide the flexibility and control necessary to deal with evolving requirements.* The static and dynamic descriptions of requirements provide an unambiguous description of the system, which both the developer and customer can understand. Encapsulation and the dynamic and static design descriptions help you evaluate and limit the impact of any change well into the development. Inheritance allows for the efficient addition of limited functionality.

- *Object use facilitates collaboration.* Encapsulation and the use of packages allows individuals and teams to work on their components in parallel. They can be assured that the internal workings of the components will not impact the other developers' work. In addition, object design diagrams facilitate the most productive level of interaction among team members.

- *Objects help manage complexity.* The function and workings of a well-written object can be easily understood. Because objects encapsulate their function, their interactions can be understood without worrying about the details—again making the code easier to understand. By focusing on the interactions, the developer has the opportunity to find simpler, more elegant designs.

The rest of the book fills in the detail on how to achieve the benefits of object technology.

Attacking Complexity

Dealing with complexity requires constant vigilance. The systems we build are inherently complex; nevertheless, a set of requirements can be met with programs of more or less complexity. Again, a simpler, less complex design results in fewer bugs and code that are easier to maintain and extend.

Fortunately, complexity has a mathematical nature and so can be understood. There are two important fundamental notions to consider regarding the complexity of a software system: the number of states and state transitions and the number of code paths. Let's explore these in more detail.

States and State Transitions

The notion of the state of a software system goes back to the early analysis of Alan Turing, in his article "On Computable Numbers with an Application to the Entscheidungsproblem," in *Proc. London Math Soc.* 42 (pp. 230–265, 1936). As a software system executes, the values that the system maintains in memory constantly change. The set of values at each step is the *state*. The size of the state is the number of variables maintained by the program. The more variables, the larger the state.

The *state space* is the set of all possible values that the system might take. These variables include the actual data manipulated by the system, as well as internal data such as intermediate values used in algorithms, memory addresses, loop counters, states of logical tests, and so on.

As the program executes, its state goes from one point to another in the state space. These changes of state are called *state transitions*. Thus, a computer program can be thought of as a sequence of state transitions. Code debuggers, then, are the tools that monitor the state transitions of a program. Surprisingly, this abstract view of a computer program is actually useful in that it underlies the nature of software complexity.

Code Paths

A *code path* is a sequence of steps a computer program might take. Each code path is a sequence of state transitions. The number of actual state transitions is proportional to the number and length of the code paths. If, at any time, the program has a wrong value for any of the variables, its state is incorrect. An incorrect state is a program error or bug. Each state transition is an opportunity to introduce an error.

To build error-free programs, the programming team must understand the state transitions as the program executes. That is, they must understand how the state changes and is maintained as the system runs. Sometimes a programmer cannot understand how even a small block of code can get into a buggy state. Fortunately, code debuggers exist. In addition to monitoring the state transitions of a program, debuggers enable the programmer to step through the code and monitor its state and then fix the code that created the problem.

Taming Complexity

One operational definition of complexity is the difficulty of understanding how the program gets into any given state. A program with a large number of state transitions and numerous code paths is complex. Limiting code paths and state transitions is a weapon used to tame this enemy.

Some programs, especially data processing systems that handle millions of the same kind of transactions (updating a bank account for example) have predictable and a reasonably limited number of code paths. Other programs that involve human interactions (usually through graphical user interfaces) are less predictable and have many code paths. One of the frustrations that programmers often face is the first time their creation is put into the hands of the user, who immediately implements the program in some way not anticipated by the developer. The code goes down some untested code path and crashes.

The best solution to this problem is to prevent it. Prevention comes in the form of a set of agreed-to dynamic requirements that in practice capture how the user can be expected to use the system. If direct communication with the customer is not possible (say in shrink-wrapped software), then the requirements must reflect a full understanding of how the majority of customers will use the system. Again, dynamic requirements are generated. Further, the design must protect the user from going down the wrong path by disabling the user through such artifacts as graying-out of buttons.

If you consider the number of state transitions, the problem is even worse. There is a state transition at each execution step. Some state transitions result in bugs; some do not. Recall that every code path then is a sequence of state transitions. Thus a program may have millions of state transitions, each an opportunity to introduce a bug. You cannot expect anyone to keep track of the system state and the possible transitions. Trying to get a team to jointly develop a program of any size without explicitly managing state or how it changes is futile. Successful software development must rely on the code design to have an order and structure that permits the designer to understand and deal with its state transitions.

Measuring Complexity

There have been various proposed approaches to defining and measuring complexity. All are attempts to measure how orderly and limited the state transitions are in a system. What state transitions have in common is the ability to measure how a program's state (the value of its variables) might have come about. Generally, high complexity is caused by the program having numerous variables, variables being accessed by more than one function, and a program flow that is hard to follow.

For example, in 1976, Thamas McCabe wrote an article titled "A Complexity Measure," (*IEEE Transactions of Software Engineering*) that focuses on the structure of the code paths in his cyclomatic complexity metric. His metric measures how difficult it is to determine how a state was achieved by considering how many paths need to be considered in reaching the state.

Divide and Conquer

The way to defeat complexity is through the tried-and-true tactic of divide and conquer. You defeat code complexity by dividing a large system into a set of modules with smaller state spaces and easily understood transitions. This brings you back to encapsulation and modularity. In object-oriented technology, the modules are objects and subsystems. If you strive for and achieve a package design that is modular at the class and package levels, the state transitions can be easily followed. The code's complexity is under control.

Complexity causes all sorts of problems for the project manager. If the code is complex, his or her team simply cannot get a handle on what they are doing. In practice, this results not only in buggy code, but in code that is hard to fix. It should also not be surprising that when complexity is measured in a manner that rewards programs with broken-into-cohesive modules, it is found that less complex programs have fewer defects. In the worst case, the project manager might find that he or she has *brittle* code. Code is brittle if every attempt to repair a bug results in a new one. Brittle code results from not being sufficiently modular. If you find yourself with such code, you should seriously consider throwing it away and starting a redesign.

In my personal experience, if the team is working with well-designed code, the defect work-off rate is very high. When a bug is found, its origin (the cause of the incorrect state) is easily found and the fix does not introduce another bug. Overall, higher quality code is the result.

Further, complex code is harder to test. Modularized code makes it possible to test the modules separately. In this way, the number of code paths is managed and there is greater certainty that the tests cover these paths. If the code is very complex, there may not be enough in the budget (or time on the clock) to adequately test the code. Hence the maxim, "Don't test in quality; design in quality."

Another problem resulting from complexity is that it is very difficult for teams to share the work. When the code is not modular, the programmers continually get in each other's way. A change in one part of the program affects another and so must be negotiated with the responsible programmer. The programmers spend more and more of their time coordinating their efforts and less and less of their time writing code. This leads to low productivity and low morale.

FOR FURTHER READING

Fred Brooks discusses this phenomenon at length in his classic, *The Mythical Man-Month*, cited earlier.

Team productivity depends on taming complexity. Using the concepts of abstraction, hierarchy, encapsulation, and modularity, the project manager can explicitly control the complexity of the system.

Collaboration

Collaboration does not happen by accident. It needs to be explicitly planned and managed. The first step is to understand who is collaborating, and for this, it is useful to consider all of the stakeholders as a part of your team. Some team members are obvious: system architects, domain experts, team leads, and developers; but the system testers are also part of your team even though they must have some autonomy.

Complexity and the Simulator

Managing the complexity of the simulator will be a challenge. The system manages a lot of state space regarding the status of the aircraft: configuration, weaponry, dynamics, fuel, damage, orientation, control settings, instrument readings, the external forces on the aircraft, geographical position, and others. The system must respond to several sources of stimuli, including the pilot, the synthetic weather, the modeled threats, the trainer, the geographical database, as well as the model of the aircraft. All of these variables must be consistent in order to provide an accurate representation. For example, the airspeed of the system and the readings on the instruments must be the same, as well as self-consistent. This system is clearly too complex for any one person to comprehend. A top-level package diagram is a start. Within each package, you need to achieve a modular design.

Your team should also include the customer. Adding the customer to the team has many advantages. Having the customer participate in the development activity is the best way for the customer and the project staff to reach a common understanding of what the final product should be. As the project continues, the customer's participation is crucial in resetting priorities and refining the content. When the customer is involved at every step, he or she will not be surprised with what you deliver. The worst outcome of any project is the successful delivery of an unwanted product. That outcome can be avoided when the customer is on the team. Actual mechanisms for including the customer as a collaborator will be discussed in Chapter 4, *Planning Object-Oriented Projects*.

> **NOTE**
> I use the word customer rather loosely. Who the customer is depends on the kind of software project: research and development demonstrations, internal tool development, contracted custom software, or shrink-wrapped software meant for release to the public. In each case, it is possible to identify one or more persons to represent the customer. For shrink-wrapped software, the customer representative could be someone from marketing, or better yet, a panel of actual end users. For internal tools development, the customer should definitely be represented by the end user. For virtually every project, there is someone who wants delivery and someone who wants to use the product.

Development as Collaborative Problem Solving

It is useful to think of software development as problem solving. The problem may be posed as:

Given the system requirements, design, implement, and deliver the best (or at least workable) program that meets the requirements.

Not only are you asked to solve this difficult problem, you are also asked to lead a team of developers to come to a common solution.

The problem-solving process is well understood. Briefly, problems are solved through three stages:

1. Understanding the problem.
2. Designing the solution.
3. Verifying the solution.

In the first stage, understanding the problem, focus on achieving a complete grasp of the problem. Study the requirements. Determine what constitutes a successful solution. A full understanding is achieved by creating a *mental model*, an internal representation of the problem. This model is refined as you proceed through the problem-solving stages. In the second stage, designing the solution, apply your mental model to determine a solution. You may design a solution based on a similar problem you have solved. Using your model, realize the problem is of a certain kind, that experience has shown can be approached a certain way. For example, a multiuser can be approached as a client/server application. In the third stage, verifying the solution, confirm that your solution does indeed solve the posed problem. I describe the stages in more detail below.

> **NOTE**
>
> These problem-solving principles can be applied to software development. Throughout this book, I focus on two elements: leading your team to reach a common cognitive model of the system and problem solving as a staged activity, as applied to software development.

Developers must work together to create a functional project. There are two approaches to software development, top down and collaborative. The *top down* approach occurs when there is a single developer (or possibly a small team of developers) who is solely responsible for designing the software; one person solves the problem. All of the other staff members are assistants. They are given very detailed tasks with little or no discretion. This approach has several drawbacks and is rarely the best choice. It relies on the capability of a single person to understand the entire problem and its solution in all its detail. As the problem grows, eventually it overwhelms the ability of this key individual, who must communicate all of the details to the assistants. This impossible task will inevitably break down communications between the design team and the programmers.

In the *collaborative* approach, each of the developers participates in the solution. The design is treated as a joint problem-solving activity. This is accomplished by approaching the problem at various levels of detail. The experienced developers are responsible for the broad solution, the system architecture; they partition the problem into a set of smaller problems, which are addressed by less experienced developers. This approach scales with program size. If the problem is very large, it can be partitioned into a set of medium-size programs (develop a server and develop five kinds of clients), which can be partitioned into smaller problems. At the top levels, the problem can be understood by the lead developers who need not be concerned with the details. Communications at each level are manageable because the problem specifications, and not the details of the solution, are communicated ("build a set of object classes that do the following..."). Collaborative software development is much like problem solving. However, it consists of four stages:

1. Developing a common understanding.

2. Collaborative design.

3. Joint implementation.

4. Verifying the solution.

In Chapter 3, *Choosing a Development Lifecycle Model,* I will discuss how to map these steps to the software lifecycle model.

In order to solve the problem, the team must share a common mental model, or a clear depiction of how the elements of the system fit and work together. If the elements of the problem appear as a bunch of disconnected items, the team will be unable to see how to manipulate the components to meet their goal. An internal model, the mental model, is usually simpler than the actual system and contains only the salient elements of the problem, allowing the team to ignore the irrelevant details and focus on the part of the problem that will lead to a solution. The model is developed as the team understands the requirements and the problem domain. The model is continually refined and clarified as the team interacts with the system. Experience allows them to correct any misconceptions, add critical components, and so on.

It is imperative that the team, including the customer, develop a common mental model of the problem and the solution. Differing mental models cause arguments as to how to proceed. But once the team comes to a common understanding of the problem, the project can really take off. Your challenge, then, is to lead the team to the development of a common mental model.

A software system is often so complex that it requires a set of system models, at various levels of detail. Abstraction, as an aspect of object design, aids in the development of the collaborative mental models.

FOR FURTHER READING

Software development as problem solving is developed further in Luke Hohmann's thoughtful text, *Journey of the Software Professional,* published by Prentice-Hall in 1997.

The Role of Abstraction

Abstraction is the act of determining the essential structure of a system, aside from its functional details. The abstract view of a system is of the major functional blocks and their interaction. The blocks are described in terms of the roles they play in the system and which functions they perform. The details of how the blocks work are ignored.

Systems are often approached as a hierarchy of abstractions. The top-level functional blocks describe how the major components of the systems interact without reference to their details. Each of these blocks may be described in terms of smaller functional blocks that describe how it carries out its function. The hierarchy focuses down until the final details are addressed. For example, a high-level block diagram for an in-store sales system may include a point-of-sale device, a networked cash register. The device interacts with the central data server, which handles bookkeeping and inventory control, the credit card validation system, and the check validation system. The top-level diagram includes each of these subsystems of the total system. The point-of-sale device itself may be described in terms of smaller functional blocks, such as the input devices (scanner and keypad), the display, the printer, the network interface, and so on. Each of these blocks may in turn be described by how their functions work and so on. Prior to the development of objects, the abstraction of a software system was approached using structural analysis, functional decomposition, and top-down analysis.

The abstract view is an expression of the common mental model of the system. For a team to collaborate in design, each member must have an understanding of the top-level abstractions and how his or her subsystems fit into the full system. It provides a backdrop for design discussion—trade-off and refinements. Establishing and accepting a common abstract view of the system marks the first stage of collaborative concurrent design.

In object-oriented design, the abstract view of the system is captured in package diagrams. The use of packages (described in Chapter 2) makes it possible to divide the problem into a series of nested problems with increasing levels of detail. They contain the roles and responsibility of the major components or subsystems of the program. Packages can contain more detailed packages or classes. Each level provides a level of abstraction, and the levels form a basis for determining and communicating the common models. The entire team agrees on the top-level model; smaller teams of developers develop and agree on the more detailed models. Once the package diagrams are in place, everyone must have access to them. Object design tools provide a common view of the design, and could or should, for example, be posted in the lab.

> **NOTE**
> If you are using a design tool, the common abstract view is the top-level diagram.

Abstraction is an essential concept for the project manager. It provides a basis for dividing the problem, forming the teams, managing the communications, and conquering the problem. Different project teams can address separate functional blocks. I will expand on project organization and communication throughout Chapter 4, *Planning Object-Oriented Projects*.

An Abstract View of the Simulator

A simplified initial architectural view is given in Figure 1.1 (I have omitted the threat and damage assessment systems). For now, it is more important that you understand what it is rather than whether you agree with the solution. Some means of confirming and refining this view are given in Chapter 2.

- Each box is a functional system that represents a division of the problem.

- The arrows represent associations. In brief, if an arrow goes from block A to block B, then block A can affect (usually indirectly) or query the state of block B. In this case, Block A uses the services of Block B, and Block B can in principle be developed in isolation from Block A.

In practice often there should be concurrent design of both blocks.

Each of the blocks in our scenario has an easily stated role. Working bottom to top:

Geographical Data Server. When queried, returns information about terrain and buildings at specific locations.

Weather Server. When queried, returns wind and precipitation data from weather model.

Checkpoint Manager. Stores and retrieves checkpoints when requested by the trainer system.

Scenario Manager. Provides previously stored scenarios to the training system, as well as scenario creation and editing capabilities.

Trainer System. The trainer control point for the system. It supports the loading of scenarios, interventions, and saving of checkpoints, and provides a user interface into the scenario manager.

World Model. Maintains and identifies where the aircraft (and other entities such as threats) are at each point in time.

Aircraft Model. Encapsulates all of the details describing how the aircraft responds to external stimuli such as pilot controls and atmospheric forces. When queried, provides information on the dynamics and orientation of the aircraft, as well as the internal status of such readings as fuel level.

Event/Time Manager. Maintains the wall-clock time for the system and generates the update events as needed to each of the subsystems. Also handles asynchronous events generated by the trainer system.

Controls. Handles the pilot/trainee interaction with the system (flight yoke, thrusters, etc.) and sends the control settings to the Aircraft Model.

Instrument Display. Provides the visual display of the cockpit's instruments. It does not maintain the state of the aircraft, but receives this data from the aircraft model.

Out the Window. Provides a visualization of what the pilot would see given the aircraft orientation, location, weather, and the position of other aircraft.

This abstraction, while complicated, is manageable. A reasonably technically competent person can follow the diagram, which can be used as a basis for discussion on how to add the missing function. Also, it is not terribly difficult to see how one might drill down into the subsystems to determine how they might be addressed. The system has, in fact, been divided into manageable subsystems. It is also clear that each of the systems needs its own architectural diagrams.

Finally, note that this is a static view of the system. It does not really capture how the system will work. There is sufficient reason to doubt that this design is adequate. We will come back to this in the next chapter.

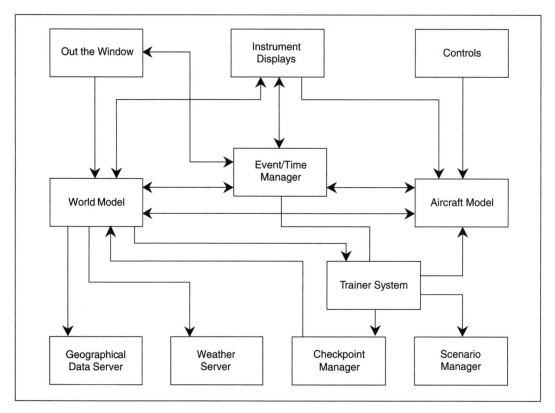

Figure 1.1 *A functional view of the Stealth simulator.*

Team Communications

Team management is a critical component of successful software development. A dysfunctional team will have dismal productivity, make bad decisions (including delivering a product that disappoints the customer), and generally make the lives of everyone involved miserable. To manage teams, you need to be aware of how people communicate effectively. This may seem obvious, but in fact, many projects fail because an inappropriate communication model is set up by management. Objects facilitate the right amount of communication.

Common Vocabulary, Common Language

In order for people to communicate, it is critical that they have a common vocabulary. It never ceases to amaze me how often arguments can arise from different uses of the same words. This is even more important in software production, where it is not always possible to figure out what words mean based on the way they are used. This is probably a reflection of the newness of the discipline. Concepts are still being formulated, and the words chosen to label these concepts are not always adequate nor consistent. An example is the use of the simple verb form *has*, as in "Object A has Object B." Sometimes it means ownership from the point of view of object lifespan management. Other times it means one object is contained in the attribute set of another. This can be confusing to team members.

The project manager, therefore, must establish a framework for precise communication, then insist on its use. The implementation of a standard object modeling language is one component of this communications framework. The Unified Modeling Language (UML) is on its way to being adopted by the industry as the standard modeling language. The UML provides a set of static and dynamic diagrams that specify unambiguously the system and its behavior. Further, UML states a precise, clear way to capture and share requirements. As we shall see in Chapter 2 and throughout this book, the UML, if properly used, provides documentation that facilitates communication with the customer as well as among a project's members.

The initial architecture represented by the package diagram serves two purposes:

- To provide the opportunity to establish a common vocabulary.
- To create a visual representation of the common mental model of the system.

Each package must have a specified function and role, each of their names should be a precise reference to that function; for example, the weather server package in the simulator provides weather data on demand. These names must be written down and adopted and used by the project team when discussing the design, for they form the basis for a common vocabulary that describes the system.

Furthermore, because most software deals with individual fields (banking, business processes, command and control, embedded engine controllers) and therefore have special terminology, such as technical terms, special word usage and abbreviations, it is important that the team have a working familiarity with this vocabulary as well. It is often essential that the team have at least one expert who can define the terms (among other duties).

TIP

I recommend creating individual project glossaries. List the terms that should be used by the team as the project is built and maintained. You will also want to maintain the glossary online as an HTML document for easy accessibility by all team members.

The Right Amount of Communication

In *The Mythical Man-Month*, Fred Brooks points out that individual productivity (lines of code per day) declines with an increase in the number of developers on large software projects. As the program grows, the developers must communicate with more and more of their teammates to come to a common solution. They spend more and more time coordinating their efforts and less time writing code. Clearly, a primary focus of the project manager is to manage team communications.

Software project teams carry out the following functions:

System specification

System design

Implementation

Test

User documentation and training

Maintenance

Configuration management

The project manager needs a way to explicitly manage communications between the people carrying out these functions. One of the challenges is how to partition these functions, create subteams, and manage the communications between the subteams. In this section, I will explore some common approaches. (Specific recommendations are given in Chapter 4, *Planning Object-Oriented Projects*.) There are three communications models a project manager can use: functional communications, unstructured communications, and the product team model.

Functional Communications

Functional communications occur when each of the program functions is assigned to a single team—a design team, an implementation team, and so on. In the functional model, one team completes its work and hands off the project to the next. This sort of organization is common in construction project management, where there are engineers, painters, welders, and so on. When building a bridge, construction does not start until the design is complete; the painting cannot start until the welding is done.

Many try to manage software in a similar manner, with each function handing off their work to the next. It is highly structured and formal, and each team consists of a separate set of functional specialists. The teams communicate by passing formal documents and other artifacts, such as code or test reports, to the team on the next functional level. The work is managed by controlling the document flow. In the case of software, it might work as shown in Figure 1.2.

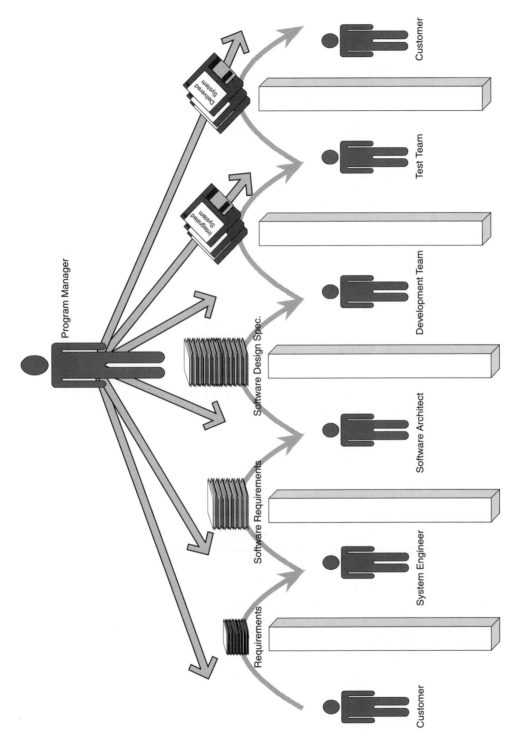

Figure 1.2 The functional communications model.

29

> **FOR FURTHER READING**
>
> The entertaining text, *Managing a Programming Project* by Philip Metzger and John Boddie (Prentice-Hall, 1996), gives an example of a well-articulated view of document-driven functional management.

Unfortunately, the programs managed through a functional communications model rarely succeed. In practice, they seem to be on track until it is time to integrate the pieces: The individual teams finish their code more or less on schedule. The next milestone is to integrate the build and assemble the system from the separate pieces. In theory, since all the pieces meet their interface requirements, and all have passed tests proving they do meet the specifications, it stands to reason that once integrated, the code should work.

I call this approach *big bang integration* because as anyone who has been on a team can tell you, it is at this point that all hell breaks loose. The code does not link. The integration may have failed because of some combination of implementation mistakes and design flaws. Whatever the cause, it must be reworked. However, because the software architect has long ago moved on to another problem, he or she may not be available; the designer may have forgotten his or her own reasoning and require time to get up to speed. Weeks pass and new code is finally built. On the first execution, it crashes immediately, and no one knows why. All of the pieces worked separately. The stress level is now very high because the delivery date is impending, and no one has a clear idea how to proceed. Meetings are held and some approaches are chosen. The team leaders decide to meet daily and report on their experiments. As Gibbs pointed out in 1994, one of two things happen: either the system is never delivered, or it is delivered late, considerably over-budget, and not anything like the original design. In fact, it is likely that the as-built code will have no documented design, leading to maintenance problems.

> **TIP**
>
> The functional method of communications is particularly insidious as it hides the system's deficiencies until it is too late to address them. All of the disciplined effort goes to naught.

In 1994, Don Clausing coined the term *dysfunctional specialization* in his discussion of the functional communications model in *Total Quality Management.*

When it is followed, each specialist works in isolation and focuses on what he or she does best. In industry parlance, each person in the chain is said to "throw" his or her part of the problem "over the wall" to the next person. There are organizations where the software designers and the developers work in different buildings and rarely meet; the lead developer choreographs the entire effort, and it is his or her job to review all documents and keep all of the details straight—which is of course impossible.

FOR FURTHER READING

An excellent view of some of the best thinking on product development is Don Clausing's *Total Quality Development*, published by ASME in 1994.

TIP

Functional communications results in too little communication.

This talk of walls is very telling. The functional communications model results in too little communication. The lack of communication results in:

- Less than optimal solutions.
- No shared responsibility—everyone did his or her job well, yet the result is disappointing.
- The product is less that the sum of the parts.
- Products are not built as designed; the software is hard to maintain or extend. Intellectual property is lost.

Software development is especially prone to the dangers of dysfunctional communication. If a developer discovers that the design specification in some subtle way does not handle a certain timing issue, he or she goes back to the architect, only to discover that he or she has moved on to the next project, having declared victory with the successful review of the design specification. Further, the author of the design specification may not understand the problem, having little interest in this sort of detail. The developer fixes the problem, but gives no mechanism to fix the ossified specification. The code ships, and in the end there is no accurate design document. Maintaining and extending the code is difficult at best.

Alternatively, the architect and developer may solve the problem together, but the change ripples through the project. Other developers' code may need to change. Test plans may need to be updated. Since there is no mechanism for dealing with these changes, suddenly many ad hoc meetings are being called in an attempt to stay coordinated. No one is sure who is responsible and fingers start pointing. In my experience, the developers conclude that the design documents are more suggestion than requirement, and that they are free to implement as they see best. After all, they decide, it is the implementation that counts, and dealing with the architect just is too time-consuming. The walls are reinforced. We have a complete failure to communicate.

Unstructured Communications

Unstructured communications occur when there is no defined team structure. In this model, everyone is supposed to simply work together to get the job done. This form of interaction arises from unmanaged communication. It may develop when a team grows from three or four programmers to a team of eight or more without anyone addressing the alterations necessary to maintain viable communications. It may occur when a manager, who is trying to be enlightened, decides to leave the developers alone to do their work. More projects than you might think fall prey to unstructured communications.

> **TIP**
> Unstructured communication results in too much communication.

Even small teams can benefit from an explicit team communications technique. It is amazing how quickly even a small team will begin to struggle with achieving the right level of communications. The programmers get together and try to work out how their parts coordinate—and since they are programmers, they program; they write their code, occasionally discussing with others what they are doing. They might write a document, but no one is likely to read it. Often the team enters into endless cycles of code-and-fix. Ultimately, the integrations never work as planned. The programmers find they are spending more and more time trying to coordinate and not enough time working. Along the way, communications get out of hand and productivity tumbles. The project manager is then faced with the dilemma described by Brooks: The more people on a project, the less overall productivity. Adding more people later to a project just makes the situation worse. The industry is rife with examples of projects that fall into this mode. Some dig out and some do not. This model results in too much communication, as shown in Figure 1.3.

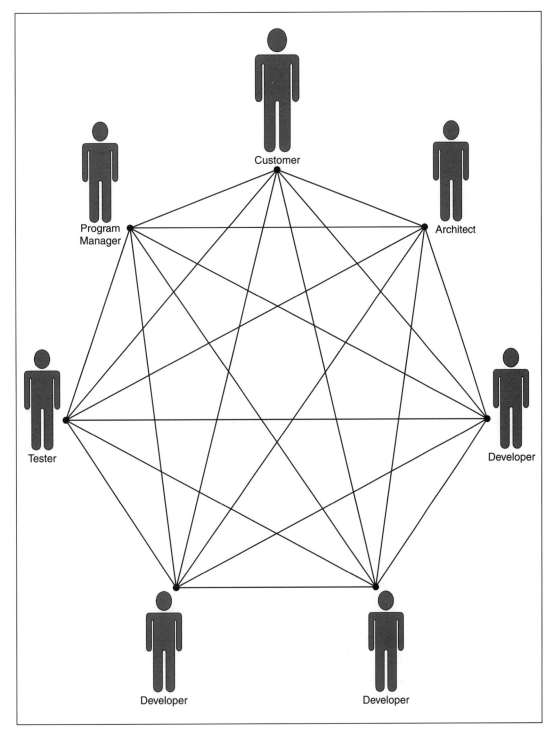

Figure 1.3 *In the unstructured communications model, everyone talks to everyone.*

Obviously, unstructured communication cannot scale to large teams; it fails with as few as four or five programmers. The result:

- Low productivity

- Inability to predict or meet schedules

- Products not designed, resulting in a system that is expensive to maintain or extend

Even when the product does ship, the process is not repeatable. Inexperienced, immature development organizations often adopt an unstructured approach. They feel that development process is unnecessary. They adopt the idealistic view that a bunch of smart developers "don't need no stinkin' management." In previous jobs, they may have been victims of a rigid functional project. In any case, they do not know how else to proceed.

FOR FURTHER READING

For an example of the damage unstructured communications model can do to team members, read Pascal Zachery's *Showstopper,* on the early development of NT, published by The Free Press in 1994.

Product Team Communications Model

The product team model consists of overlapping teams that own the various processes. Each team is responsible for a major activity of the development process. Figure 1.4 gives a simplified example of how this might work It establishes a management structure to facilitate a team approach; in short, it takes down the walls. The product team model has its origins in manufacturing development, particularly the Quality Functional Deployment (QFD) movement, and has been adopted throughout the aerospace industry. It is anticipated that product teams, called Integrated Product Teams or Integrated Process Teams (IPTs),will be implemented in many United States Department of Defense development proposals. Use of IPTs is one aspect of what the government calls Integrated Product Development (IPD). Although this book does not address QFD and IPD per se, it takes what works from these manufacturing approaches and applies it to software.

In a project, one team might be responsible for system design, one for the low-level design and implementation of the each of the subsystems, another for system testing and product delivery. A program team might coordinate all of the project's activities. In addition, ad hoc teams may be organized to focus on special problems that arise during development. These teams will maintain their membership throughout the project.

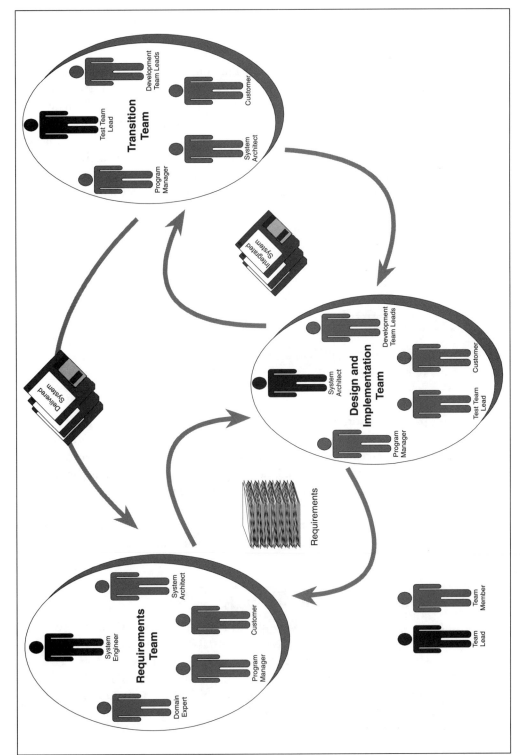

Figure 1.4 A view of the Product Team communications model.

35

Most project members belong to more than one team. For example, the system architect might lead the design, but also be a member of the system test team. And actual membership may vary with the project. A large project may have many such teams; for example, there were more than 200 Integrated Process Teams (IPTs) formed during the Boeing 777 development. The important point here is that the IPTs consist of the stakeholders, those who have an interest in the activity, not just the activity owner. The activity owner leads his or her IPT. I will discuss an organization plan for product team communications in more detail in Chapter 4.

With the adoption of IPTs, the walls come down. How to proceed is decided by those who need to agree. Communication is enhanced by the overlapping membership. In our example, the system architect could speak for the intent of the requirements team to the design team. He or she could also bring the concerns of the implementation team to the attention of the requirements team.

> **TIP**
>
> Understand how people work together effectively and then strive to facilitate that process.

I am particularly drawn to this model for several reasons. The first and most clear-cut is that it works. The second is that it is an application of one of my personal laws of management: Understand how people work together effectively and then strive to facilitate that process. I have found that communications paths on paper are often different from those in practice. Effective projects that may seem to be structured functionally on paper often develop their own communication channels, in which case, the developers rebel against the rigid functional approach and break down the walls. The result is ad hoc meetings in which members of one team ven-

> **The Simulator Team Considerations**
>
> Clearly, it will take many developers to build the cockpit simulator software, maybe more than 50 (I will discuss staffing and sizing in a later chapter). As the work is divided, team communications issues immediately arise. All of the systems must interact, yet few if any of the developers have a clear idea how the system is to behave. The behavior of the subsystems cannot be sufficiently specified to ensure that the delivered system will meet the critical need.

ture into the other's territory to resolve their differences. The leaders of the various teams (say hardware and software) develop a relationship and coordinate their efforts informally. If this works well, products get built with more or less disciplined documentation. Communication, while constructive, is not according to plan and so the results of the coordination are often off the books. Object-oriented development has several mechanisms and concepts for adopting a product team approach which will be explored throughout the book.

Team Dynamics

As a project manager, it is critical that you have an understanding of team dynamics, how people interact and communicate with each other in a team setting. An effective team leader is responsible for forging his or her staff into a functional unit, and its members rely on you to deal with any team interactions. You have no choice but to face this enemy, so this section explores the principles of team formation and gives general advice. In later chapters, I show how object-oriented development provides some tools for addressing teamwork issues as they apply to the development cycle.

FOR FURTHER READING

This book does not address the interpersonal skills associated with creating a team member. Several good texts go down that road, and one of my favorites is Luke Hohmann's *Journey of the Software Professional* (Prentice-Hall, 1997).

Team Formation

In 1965, B. Tuckmann and M. A. C. Jensen wrote an article titled "Development Sequence in Small Groups" (*Psychological Bulletin*, v. LXIII, no. 6, 1965) that introduced a commonly accepted model of how teams form and become productive. Their model is referred to in many articles and texts on team management, and I have found it to be useful. It explains the evolution of team members' behavior as a project progresses. According to this model, teams go through four phases:

1. *Forming.* The initial stage when the individual groups try to determine the purpose of the group and what role they will play.

2. *Storming.* A conflict-filled stage in which the individuals try to form a group by resolving differences in goals and perspectives. The individuals struggle for status and power within the team.

3. *Norming.* Having come to a common understanding of the goals and functioning of the team, the conflict disappears and the members focus on the work at hand.

4. *Performing.* The team has developed a clear identity with loyal team members who have a clear understanding of how the team operates and how they will interact as individuals.

These phases are a natural progression as team members sort out their roles and boundaries. Individuals need to know what they own, what the team expects from them, and who they can count on for what. It is important to programmers that their role on the team be consistent with their self-images. Let's take a look at these stages in more detail.

Forming

The forming stage occurs when the team is first brought together. Some of the members may have worked together, others may have not. In any case, they go into the first team meeting with a preconceived notion as to what role that they would like to play. Usually they are polite and distant as they size up the situation; no one wants to play his or her cards too early. Occasionally, an especially aggressive member will express some criticism, which usually is not constructive. In general though, the team is focused on scoping out the situation: What exactly is required? What are the personal risks and rewards? The various individuals may or may not be excited about the project, but probably there is some buy-in. Most withhold judgment.

As a project manager, you have to accomplish three tasks to move your team through the forming stage. The first is to staff quickly and establish roles early in the project. In this first stage, the team will require less attention than in some of the other stages. At team meetings, you explain the project (including background, customer information, and the like) and set the ground rules for the iteration. You introduce team members and establish roles and expectations. But stay a little distant at this point, to give the members some room to come to terms with their role on the team. Be available, but not obtrusive. Suggested roles are defined in Chapter 4. The artifacts of object-oriented development help. For example, giving a developer ownership of a set of use cases and interaction diagrams is a good way to raise the comfort level of that person early in the program.

Second, share the vision and establish buy-in. Do not just assign staff; enlist them. Every team member needs to feel that he or she is important to you and to the customer. He or she needs to be able to visualize successful completion of the project. It is important that the members believe in the importance of delivering the product. This motivates the team to come together and raises morale. No one wants to just do a job. People want to feel their work (their team's work) is important.

Third, create situations in which the members can interact. Get them moving to the storming stage. For example, assign a short-term deliverable that members have to produce together. Another approach is to divide the requirements and hold a series of meetings in which different members present some aspect of the problem domain. Do not avoid conflict in these meetings; embrace it. Only by successfully managing a team into and through a storming phase, can the team come together as a productive group.

> **TIP**
>
> As manager, you need to set ground rules for team interaction such as requiring prompt attendance at meetings, not condoning personal attacks, and emphasizing the importance of meeting commitments.

If you have a large team, treat it as a team of teams. Designate individual team leads to look after smaller teams. Then form a team of the team leads. But note, in this situation, you have an additional problem: Not only do you have to form a team of your leads, but you also have to teach them to move their teams through the phases—you need to be mentor. I find it useful to meet with the leads both as a team and separately to discuss the status of their teams. If an issue arises in the team meeting that requires attention, I meet with the lead individually and occasionally with his or her team.

Storming

In the storming stage, tendency is for the members to all at once set out to establish their boundaries. Territory is claimed; stands are taken. Though technical on the surface, these interactions are really about establishing dominance or staking out territory. Sometimes the fights become more personal. Members attack each other's competence, sometimes in public, but more often in intensely private conversations in your office. They may also rail against the management for putting them on this team—the project's schedule and budget are impossible, and so on.

> **TIP**
>
> When smart people disagree on a technical matter, take the position that they are probably coming from a different set of assumptions.

This stage naturally requires the most intense focus from the project manager. The first order of business is to be aware of what is happening. During the design meetings, reinforce roles. When technical disagreements erupt, defuse them by focusing on the facts and the logic. I take the position that when smart people disagree on a technical matter, they must be coming from a different set of assumptions, which may arise from a different understanding of the facts or from different life experiences. For example, one developer may be opposed to an approach because it makes memory management harder, and on his last project, memory management was a nightmare. Another may be more sensitive to system performance issues, based on his or her experience. It is important that the project manager set the example of being supportive of different styles of working. Some developers deal in abstractions; others need concrete examples; still others need to build prototype code. You and the team should accept these differences as long as the work moves forward. Everyone must commit to the success of the team and do what it takes to reach that goal. To that end, encourage communication and collaboration. Interestingly, sometimes team members need permission to communicate. Members may have a clear idea of their role and what they own, but they also need to understand they share joint responsibility for the overall product. Encourage them to spend some of their time working with other members on their part of problem if there is a common interest.

Make it clear that programmers are expected to work together. Developers who state that they cannot work with some other developer should be reminded that their job depends on working with everyone on the team.

Obviously, the storming stage requires the most attention of the project manager. You will need very intense and frequent involvement. You must see yourself as a facilitator, reinforcing everyone's role and value to the team.

Norming

In the norming phase, things calm down. Individuals focus on their tasks. The boundaries have been set, and they come to rely on one another. Personal attacks die down and people adjust for individual strengths and weaknesses. Conversely, however, while conflict is at bay, sometimes it is to a point at which issues that should be addressed are avoided. The technical discussions are more likely to be constructive.

Consequently, during this phase, you have to be vigilant that the necessary communications are enforced. When people overlook a good solution to a problem to avoid conflicts, you must reawaken their critical capabilities. (In later chapters, I discuss some specifics that encourage collaboration, such as design and code reviews.)

Performing

In the performing stage, the team members' roles are clear. The boundaries that were set in the norming phase are reinforced. As new tasks arise, each member knows who will complete it. Little time is spent jockeying for position. Usually, if someone does forget his or her place, the team itself will discourage the disruptive behavior. If you have gotten your team to this point, your day-to-day involvement should be minimal. The team will be running itself, and you can focus on process improvement, customer relations (drumming up more business for your team), improved efficiency, and the like.

CAUTION

The performing team may form an us-against-them attitude. This is fine if the "them" is the competition, but if the "them" is the customer or some other technical team (such as the hardware design team), you have more team building to do. You also have to be alert to staleness. Stir things up a bit. Move folks around as a career enhancement. Look for opportunities to promote. Also, move individuals on and off the team. New members bring new ideas. (Of course, this may cause storming to reoccur.)

The Stealth Simulator Team

The customer is a major defense contractor. A managerial contact and a technical contact have been assigned to coordinate efforts. One of your challenges in delivering the Stealth fighter simulator is to build your team. The good news is, you have access to the required skills; but the bad news is, you do not have the luxury of a performing team. Furthermore, no one on the team has built a manned simulator.

When recruiting members, you find some participants who think the project is "cool"; others challenge the two-year requirement and demand to see the budget and the sizing; some think that because they built a video game in college they are ready. You may even have some new hires who have never been on a team before.

Fortunately, you do have some object gurus (object experts are always called gurus) and experienced system engineers. These guys know each other, but have never worked together. In your office, they all express respect for the others and ensure they can work together; after all, they are pros.

Stay tuned . . . .

You will be amazed how useful it is to be aware of these phases. Of all the touchy-feelie material being taught in management classes, these are the ideas I find the most useful, and I refer to them throughout the book.

From Here

This chapter set the framework for the rest of the book. I introduced some common enemies of software development: inadequate and unstable requirements, inadequate customer communications, and poor team communications. In exploring the nature of these enemies, I also introduced some principles that form the basis for the detailed techniques that follow. You may or may not agree that these details apply to your particular situation. That's fine, but make the adjustments, because I believe the principles are fairly universal and should serve as a guide to your application of the methods. As a review, the principles include:

- Plan for your requirements to change throughout the development cycle.
- Facilitate what teams really do.
- Understand and manage team dynamics.
- Use product teams to facilitate the right level of communication.
- Software development is an exercise in collaborative problem solving.

In Chapter 2, I introduce the artifacts of the Unified Modeling Language as tools that may be used to apply these principles. I also include a discussion on ensuring that the design itself facilitates the right level of communication.

2 THE UNIFIED MODELING LANGUAGE AS A MANAGEMENT TOOL

Perhaps believing in good design is like believing in God; it makes you an optimist.

> Sir Terence Conran, British businessman, designer.
> Daily Telegraph (London, June 12, 1989).

Software projects often seem to require extraordinary effort. In his book, *Death March*, Ed Yourdon compares the effort required to bring off many software projects with "climbing Mount Everest barefoot." He also expresses surprise at how willing young programmers are to give it a try. As a project manager, you have the maturity to know better. You are responsible for making the project humanly possible. There are two aspects to accomplishing this task: requirements management and design complexity management.

Most projects begin with more requirements than can be delivered on time and on budget. Though the schedule may be driven by real business needs and is not subject to negotiation, the content may be negotiable. In many cases, you can achieve success by delivering less than the original requirements and still meet the customers' business needs. It is often preferable to deliver fewer of the requirements on time than to be late. In fact, this is likely to be ongoing. Negotiate with the customer. You must have a means of clearly communicating the project's requirements and deciding on those that will be met in a release.

> **TIP**
>
> It is often preferable to deliver less on time than to be late.

It hardly need be said that a complex design is more difficult to implement and even more difficult to debug than a simpler design. One of the fundamental rules of product design is that if two designs can achieve the same purpose, the simpler of the two will lead to a more profitable, higher-quality product. If your design is unnecessarily complex, you and your team will waste a lot of time fixing defects late in the development stage. Hard-won experience has shown that the time invested early in the development cycle clarifying and simplifying the design is recovered in the later stages of the development. Defects introduced in a well-designed code are more easily isolated and removed.

Design management is a matter of faith. You need to believe that the effort expended early on the design will come back in the form of productivity. A project's salvation lies in its design. No amount of code reviews, testing, or debugging can make up for a poor design. When you start losing sleep over a project, your faith in the project design will get you through the night. Thus, this chapter begins with a discussion of abstraction and its importance in software development. It proceeds with an explanation of the features of Unified Modeling Language that you can apply to manage requirements and design complexity. I explain how to use UML to:

- Document and communicate dynamic, operational requirements
- Document and communicate software design
- Evaluate the quality of your good design
- Trace the design back to the requirements
- Represent the code components

Using Abstraction

Abstraction is essential for developing a mental model of a system. Recall from Chapter 1 that an abstract view of a system includes its major functional blocks and their interaction. An abstraction hides a system's details, making it possible to focus on its overall structure. A person can handle only a limited amount of information at one time, so the ability to set aside details and treat large systems in terms of the interaction of a small number of subsystems is crucial. In short, all large systems require the use of abstraction if they are to be manageable. For example, science and mathematics are centered on finding the right abstractions to describe and predict how nature works. Major businesses can be run only by treating the whole as a set of divisions, each of which reports on a set of separate business goals. The general manager does not sweat the details.

There are three aspects of abstraction that you can use to understand and evaluate an object design: hierarchy, encapsulation, and modularity.

Systems are often approached as a hierarchy of abstractions. The functional blocks may be too complicated to approach at a detailed level; they are therefore described in terms of smaller functional blocks and so on until the final details are addressed. A division in a company may be managed as a set of business areas which are in turn managed as a set of departments. At each level, the managers can focus on the goals and measures of their level and not interface with the details as to how the goals are achieved.

From a system view, we use the hierarchy as a first step to state management. The state of each functional block is maintained independently. If another block needs to access the state of another, it queries that block. The partitioning of state into smaller blocks is called modularity. Modularity is critical because it enables people to understand complex system. No one can keep the complex state of a large system in one's head. Fortunately, it is not necessary. Once the abstraction is in place, it opens a series of views of the system that a person can manage: wide views with small numbers of large blocks and little detail, and narrow detailed views. Consider our simulator example: At first approach, it is easy to be overwhelmed by the details. Clearly, to proceed, it is important to first get a sense of the overall system; it is important to plan for and design a system that presents instrument readings, not one that focuses on the details of each instrument.

FOR FURTHER READING

A discussion of abstraction can be found in a number of object-oriented design books. See *Object-Oriented Analysis and Design with Applications*, 2e by Grady Booch published by Addison-Wesley in 1994 and Chapter 4 of *Guidelines for Successful Acquisitions and Management of Software-Intensive Systems, version 2.0* by the Software Technology Support Center (STSC) in 1996.

Encapsulation is the sibling of modularity. Its function is to provide just the right amount of access from the state of the modular units to various parts of the program—enough so that the intended function may be performed, but no more. Explicitly restricting access to variables internal to an algorithm is an example of encapsulation, and explicit management of access to the variables of a system is fundamental for building maintainable, extendible code. Unless access is managed, many of the benefits of encapsulation are lost, resulting again in spaghetti code. In addition, unmanaged code may change a variable, eventually leading to major problems. I will come back to this idea at the end of the chapter.

Object classes provide instances of both modularity and encapsulation. From the outside, the details of how an object accomplishes its tasks are hidden. Once built, they can be treated as *black boxes*; they do things when asked. Once an object is coded and debugged, it can be used with no concern about how the object goes about its task. Its state is self-contained; in fact, many objects have an internal state (intermediate values, counters, and the like) that is entirely hidden from the rest of the system. This facilitates human understanding, and allows the developer to focus attention on how the objects are used.

Unified Modeling Language

The UML is a recent synthesis of earlier object design languages. The Object Management Group (OMG) released version 1.1 in November 1997. It merges Booch notation, Object Modeling Technique (OMT), and Object-Oriented Software Engineering (OOSE), and is likely to be the standard preferred method for specifying object designs for the foreseeable future. There is really no other choice.

The Unified Modeling Language (UML) includes a set of consistent diagrams that may be used to describe and communicate a software system's requirements, design, and code. It can be used to provide views of the system design and requirements at different levels of abstraction, and its artifacts provide the common view that serves as a basis for the collaborative design.

FOR FURTHER READING

To learn more about the UML, I suggest *The UML Toolkit* by Hans-Erik Eriksson and Magnus Penker, published by John Wiley & Sons, Inc., 1998. Also see the UML material published on the OMG web site, www.omg.org. The *UML Primer*, found on that site, is a good place to start.

This chapter does not focus on what the UML is, but how to use it to accomplish the tasks listed, which are the elements of scoping and design activities for object-based software development usually called *object-oriented analysis* and *object-oriented design*. Since there are no standard processes for these, most texts describe a series of techniques from which to choose. Likewise, I present the methods that I use and teach—those I have found to work. They are consistent with the use of standard object practice. At the same time, they mesh well with the management techniques covered in the following chapters.

The UML is primarily focused on specifying and documenting a system's requirements and design. With that in mind, you would expect that the UML is used heavily during the inception and elaboration phases. However, because requirements must be closely tied to test plans, and code should exactly reflect the design, it is important to continue to use the UML throughout the development process. If you use UML only during the early phases and do not tie your project's UML artifacts to your build and test activities, you will lose control of your design. All you will have done is to draw cool pictures.

People who write about software process use the word *artifact* to refer to the tangible output of the process—executable code, source files, documentation, training manuals, test reports, and the like. In short, any output of the development process is an artifact. (The term brings up images of future anthropologists digging up your requirements document.) The term may seem pretentious, but it is useful, and I have not come across a better one.

The UML comprises a collection of artifacts that are used to capture the requirements and design of a software system. The UML artifacts that you should use during the activities are:

Use-case diagrams document the system's dynamic requirements. I will introduce two levels of use-case diagrams: *user level*, which describes how the users interact with the system; and *developer level*, which describes how the system components will interact. The user-level use cases place requirements on the system. The developer-level provide requirements to subsystems.

Class and package diagrams provide a view of the class design of the system. The diagrams contain a representation of the classes and packages (related sets of classes) and how they are associated.

Sequence diagrams tie together the use-case diagrams and the class diagrams. They show how the classes collaborate to carry out a use case.

Component diagrams show how the classes relate to the actual code. In particular, they define the libraries and subsystems that are integrated to make up the system.

These descriptions are, in most cases, incomplete but cover the features you are most likely to use. In fact, unless your team is fairly experienced, I suggest you avoid some of the more advanced UML notions, as they may lead to confusion.

This chapter explores how the UML is used to manage requirements and complexity, and introduces new notions (such as package-level use cases) on how to apply some of the UML artifacts from a manager's point of view. This chapter will not make you an expert on the UML nor on object-oriented analysis and design. My goal is to make you sufficiently aware of the tools and issues to enable you to manage object-oriented development. The project's requirements and design management necessitate oversight. Depending on the size of the project, you either need to look after them yourself or delegate these issues to someone you trust.

Documenting Requirements

Recall from Chapter 1 that the first step in leading the development of a software system is scoping, that is, achieving a common understanding of the problem. This begins with the unambiguous capture and documentation of the static and dynamic requirements of the system. The desired outcome of this analysis is a detailed view of the system shared by you, your team, and your customer. The output of the analysis forms a basis for managing the system's content throughout development. This process begins with the writing of use cases.

Use Cases

Use cases are a narrative operational description of how the system is used. They capture the system's dynamic functional requirements in clear and familiar terms so that both your team and your customer can understand them. Although use cases are not part of UML, the UML developers anticipated that project teams would employ them and thus included use-case diagrams in their specification. A use-case diagram is shown in Figure 2.1 on page 52. Each use case must have a name and number and a description.

The set of use cases is your requirements management tool and is an important program asset. Consequently, they must be maintained in a disciplined manner with unique identifiers that permit traceability; they must also contain rigorous descriptions of build content. I prefer to keep them in a database; but frequently today, teams keep them in HTML files for easy access across the Web. These cases should be backed up; even better, they should be kept under configuration management using a version control tool.

In order to keep use cases focused, their description should adopt the following form:

This use case begins when. . . .

The system responds by. . . .

. . . .sequence of interactions. . . .

This use case ends when. . . .

For example, here is a use case for drawing a line in a drawing program:

D.11 Drawing a line

This use case begins when the user left-clicks on the line icon on the menu bar.

The system responds by changing the cursor to a cross bar.

When the user left-clicks over the drawing, the system draws a cross below the cursor.

This use case ends when the user left-clicks at a second position; the system draws a line from the cross to the second position and then erases the cross.

The associated static requirement for the system might be: "The program will enable the user to draw lines." Note that the use case provides the operational view of the static requirement at a level of detail not found in the static requirements. Also note that the use case describes a rather awkward way of drawing a line. (You might want to check how lines are drawn in your favorite drawing or presentation program.) This use-case specification gives the customer the opportunity to say that this method of drawing a line is not acceptable. It is better to find this out early in the analysis and design process rather than when you try to deliver the system.

System responses are limited to those that the user can see. Behind-the-scenes activities such as system events are not captured at this point. Note that these use cases do not refer to internal program elements. As such, these are more precisely called *user-level use cases*. In the design phase, the user-level use cases are expanded to include program elements. These more detailed use cases are important to developers, not the user; they are logically called *developer-level use cases*. But note: The standalone term *use case* means *user-level use case*. I will explore developer-level use cases in more detail in the next section.

The term *scenario* is sometimes used interchangeably with use case. However, in the UML, a scenario is used to describe a path through a use case. That is, if a use case has branches (when the user is given a choice on how to proceed), a scenario is a path through the use case following one choice at each branch. This way a single use case might generate more than one scenario. Consider the following extract from a Save File use case.

...

The system responds with a dialog box with the text "A file with that name already exists; overwrite or save under different name?" The box includes two buttons, one labeled Overwrite, the other labeled Rename.

If the user left-clicks the Overwrite button, the system saves the current file, overwriting the previously saved file.

If the user left-clicks the Rename button, the systems brings up a dialog box that. . .

...

This use case has two scenarios: one for overwriting and the other for renaming.

It is useful for one use case to refer to another. Consider the simulator example in the sidebar. The Creating a Training Scenario use case will include the Choosing the Terrain and Specifying the Weather use cases. The details of how terrain is chosen and the weather is specified are covered in their own use cases. When one use case refers to another, we say the first use case *uses* the second. In this example, use case T.1 *uses* use cases T.3 and T.4.

If one use case is like another but with an additional set of actions, then the first use case is said to *extend* the other. For example, a use case entitled Drawing a Line with Endtypes (an endtype might be an arrowhead or a cap) might be:

D.12 Drawing a Line with Endtypes

This use case begins when the user left-clicks on the line with an endtype icon on the menu bar.

The system responds by changing the cursor to a cross bar.

When the user left-clicks over the drawing, the system draws a cross below the cursor.

When the user left-clicks at a second position, the system draws a line from that cross to the second position, and the system erases the cross.

The system brings up a Choose Endtype dialog box displaying a choice of possible endtypes.

This use case ends when the user left-clicks on an endtype, and the system redraws the line with the chosen endtype.

Stealth Simulator Use Cases

A use case is the tool you should use to clarify and document the operational requirements of the simulator. In order to understand what the customer really wants, you create an initial set of user-level use cases. The list of use cases for the trainer workstation might include:

T.1 Creating a Training Scenario

T.2 Saving a Training Scenario

T.3 Specify Weather

T.4 Select Terrain

T.5 Saving a Checkpoint

T.6 Initializing a Session

T.7 Intervening

T.8 Reviewing a Session

T.9 Playing Back

T.10 Place Threats

...

The T in the label is used to designate that the requirement relates to the trainer workstation. The list may reach several hundred use cases. Each of these will describe in detail exactly how the trainer (the actor in this case) will interact with the system. Armed with these detailed descriptions, you can go back to the customer and check whether you have a clear view of what he or she expects. It is only by getting down to this level of detail that you have a shot at delivering what the customer needs. You have also expressed the operational requirements in a way that you can use to support the design activity.

Use-Case Diagrams

A *use-case diagram* shows the static relationship among actors and use cases within a system. They provide an early view of the system structure. I find them useful in building and communicating a common view of the system. They provide one starting point for the design, particularly object identification and sequence diagrams.

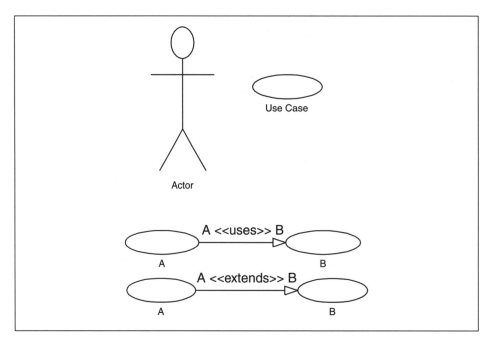

Figure 2.1 *The semantic elements of use-case diagrams.*

The elements of use case diagrams are *use cases, actors, uses,* and *extends.* Actors, represented by stick figures (see Figure 2.1) are anything external to the system, such as a kind of user or an external system, that interacts with the system.

A Stealth Simulator Use Case

The trainer will need to create training scenarios. A simplified use case might be:

T.1 Creating a Training Scenario

This use case begins when the trainer chooses Create Scenario from the Edit menu.

The system brings up the Create Scenario window.

The trainer left-clicks the Specify Weather button, which executes the Specify Weather use case.

The trainer left-clicks the Select Terrain button, which executes the Select Terrain use case.

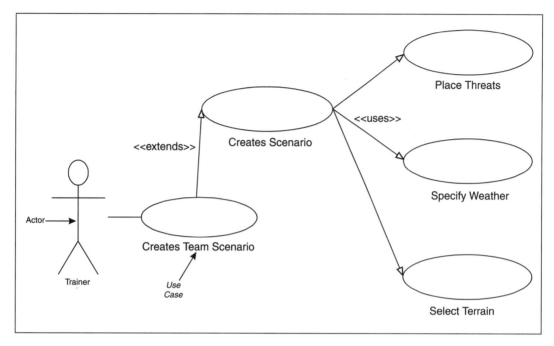

Figure 2.2 A use-case diagram for the simulator.

The trainer left-clicks the Place Threats button, which executes the Place Threats use case.

The trainer selects the initial position of the trainee's aircraft.

This use case ends when the trainer left-clicks the Done button.

This use case uses the *Specify Weather, Select Terrain*, and *Place Threats* use cases.

This use case may be extended to create a new use case, *Create Team Scenario*, by adding the action "The trainer selects the initial position of the second trainee's aircraft" just before the last line.

The use-case diagram for the simulator is shown in Figure 2.2.

Documenting Package Requirements

It is useful to create two types of use cases when designing a system: user level and developer level.

Use cases are typically applied to capture requirements from the users' point of view. All of the actors are external to the system. Their behavior is described by how the system appears to the user; they capture the system's requirements.

Developer-level use cases refine system requirements into subsystem requirements. Actors can include program elements such as a database or a button widget. The descriptions can include interactions between system components. Developer-level use cases also provide a view of the system that is of value to the programmers. The use-case describes scenarios that the developers can use as a source of requirements for package and class design. Each user-level use case is refined to one or more developer-level use cases. The following is an example of the developer-level use case corresponding to the Drawing a Line user-level use case given earlier.

Dev D.11 Drawing a Line

This use case begins when the user left-clicks on the line icon on the menu bar.

The window manager changes the shape of the cursor to a cross.

The window manager passes an event to the line icon widget.

The line icon widget instantiates a new object of the line class with the default values.

The line object registers itself with the window manager.

When the user clicks over the drawing, the window manager sends a mouse event to the line object.

The line object requests the cursor position from the window manager and sets the first endpoint attribute.

The line object requests the window manager to draw across at the location of the endpoint.

When the user clicks over the drawing, the window manager sends a mouse event to the line object.

The line object requests the cursor position from the window manager and sets the second endpoint attribute.

The line object requests the window manager to draw a line between the endpoints.

This use case ends when the line object requests the cursor be reset to the arrow.

Package-Level Use Cases

For large systems, the design problem needs to be partitioned into a set of smaller design problems. The packages provide a basis for the design decomposition. Package design has two areas of focus:

Architectural. Interface to the other packages.

Internal. The class design of the package.

The package-level uses cases are a form of developer-level use cases. They describe the architectural requirements of the package. As such, the actors are primarily other system packages. They might also include other system components such as external processes or hardware subsystems. A useful approach to package design is to treat it as a separate system. Just as the total system's behavior and requirements are best specified by use cases, a package's design should also be driven by use cases. They capture the dynamic view of how the package must behave.

To develop these artifacts, each package team goes through each of the system developer-level use cases in collaboration with the other package teams, keeping the top-level diagram in mind. They develop a set of use cases that begin when the user or another package invokes a service provided by the package. The use case then describes how the package responds to the stimulus. The result is a set of use cases that describe, from a developer point of view, how their subsystem is expected to perform. For example, suppose you are managing a system with a database subsystem. During this phase, the database team would go through every user-level use case and look for references to data being stored, accessed, updated, archived, copied, or deleted by the user. They would develop uses cases around these activities, in which they would treat the user-interface system as an actor. They would assume that requests come from the user-interface packages that their package responds to. Similarly, the user-interface team would generate a use case that would treat the database as an actor that interacts with their package. The package-level use case form is the same as that of the system development-level use cases.

An example of a package-level use case is given in the sidebar. Note that the package-level use case moves the team closer to being able to identify classes and subpackages. The process of moving to class design is described in more detail in Chapter 5.

Stealth Simulator Package-Level Use Cases

Each of the top-level packages of the simulator requires a set of package-level use cases. For example, the World Model package designers develop a set of package-level use cases, which include:

WM 1. Register entity

WM 2. Report entities

WM 3. Store position of entity

WM 4. Report position of entity

WM 5. Detect collision of entities

WM 6. Destroy entity

An entity might be the aircraft, a launched weapon, or a threat. Each of these use cases is written up in detail. For example:

WM1. Register Entity

This use case begins when a Register Entity method is invoked.

The package creates an entity object.

The package creates an entry in the internal entity list.

The package generates a unique identifier for the entity.

This use case ends when it returns the identifier.

Figure 2.3 shows the relationship between the levels of use cases and level of code components. Note that the use cases are also used to generate the system and integration tests. The testing strategy will be discussed in more detail in Chapters 5, 6, and 7.

FOR FURTHER READING

See Putnam Texel and Charles B. Williams book, *Use Cases Combined with Booch/Omt/Uml: Process and Products,* published by Prentice-Hall, 1997.

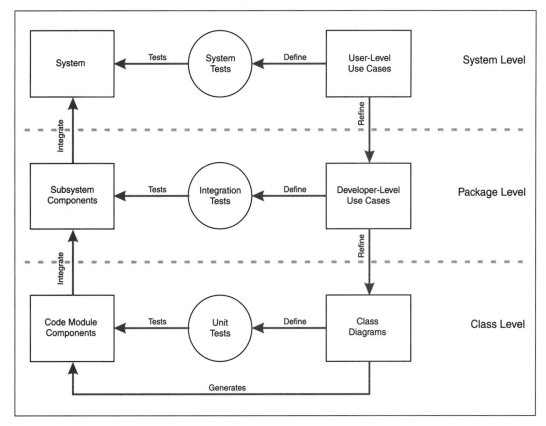

Figure 2.3 *Role of use cases in system development.*

Documenting Software Design

The core idea underlying object-oriented software design is that a software system can be made up of small functional blocks called objects. The software design consists of specifying:

- Objects that make up the system
- Properties (methods and attributes) of the objects
- How the objects are related to each other
- How the objects may be combined into larger functional blocks called packages
- How the objects work together to carry out a use case

This section begins with a discussion of objects, classes, and their specification. After that I introduce the UML-provided artifacts that may be used to capture and communicate design information: class diagrams, package diagrams, and object sequence diagrams.

FOR FURTHER READING

A more complete treatment of the use of UML in software design is Richard C. Lee's and William M. Tepfenhart's *UML and C++: A Practical Guide to Object-Oriented Development,* published by Prentice-Hall in 1997; or Craig Larman's *Applying UML and Patterns: An Introduction to Object-Oriented Analysis and Design,* also published by Prentice-Hall in 1997.

Other object analysis and design books I recommend include:

- *The CRC Card Book* by David Bellin and Susan S. Simone, published by Addison-Wesley, 1997.
- *Object-Oriented Analysis and Design with Applications (2nd edition),* by Grady Booch, published by Addison-Wesley, 1994.
- *Designing Object-Oriented C++ Applications Using the Booch Method,* by R. C. Martin, published by Prentice-Hall, 1995.

Software Objects and Classes

If a software system were a wall, objects would be bricks. Objects are the smallest building blocks of a software program. They are blocks of code that manage their own state and have limited functionality; they are the first level of abstraction in a software program and encapsulate their internal state. They hide how they carry out their function. Each object has three properties:

State. Data structures.

Behavior. Methods that accomplish the intended functionality.

Identity. A unique label.

The variables that comprise the state of the object are called *attributes*. The attributes of a line object are position, color, line style, and so on. The state of the object is determined by the value of the attributes. The fact that objects contain and manage their state is an example of the use of encapsulation, which makes it much easier for project managers to divide the work and manage communications.

Objects also have behaviors; that is, they do something when asked. For example, if the object were a linked list, it would, when asked, add a member to itself or return the value in its nth entry. The behavior of an object of a given class is specified by its methods. There are five types of methods:

- Setting the state of the attributes (sometimes called *sets*)
- Returning the state of the attributes (sometimes called gets)
- Modifying its own state (through some internal algorithm)
- Invoking the methods of other objects or system services (such as drawing themselves)
- Creating and destroying themselves

The scope of the attributes is always within the object. With this discipline, it is relatively easy to track what a method does and how it interacts with the other parts of the program.

Continuing the analogy, if objects were bricks, then classes would be the brick molds. All of the objects in a program that share the same description (attributes and methods) are said to be *instances* of the same *class*; they are made from the same mold. For example, there may be many lines created in the execution of a drawing program, each of which is an instance of the line class. In object-oriented programming, you first define the classes. The program creates instances of the class, the objects, as they are needed.

Objects as instances of classes have unique labels just as instances of variables or structures, which allow you to track the state of each object individually. In the UML, classes are shown in class diagrams. Each class is shown as a box containing three areas: class name, the attributes specification, and the methods specification. The general form and an example for the line class are shown in Figure 2.4.

The methods for creating an object are called *constructors*. The syntax for invoking a constructor and thereby creating the object is often the operator *new*. When new is invoked, the program allocates memory for that object. To destroy the object and free up the memory, a *destructor* method is invoked with the operator *delete*.

Class design is meant to be language-independent. Even old-fashioned Job Control Language modules may be thought of as objects (they use files for message passing). However, at the detailed class specification level, language specifics do show up. At this point, notions of variable type must be specified, understandably since the class specifications are used for code generation.

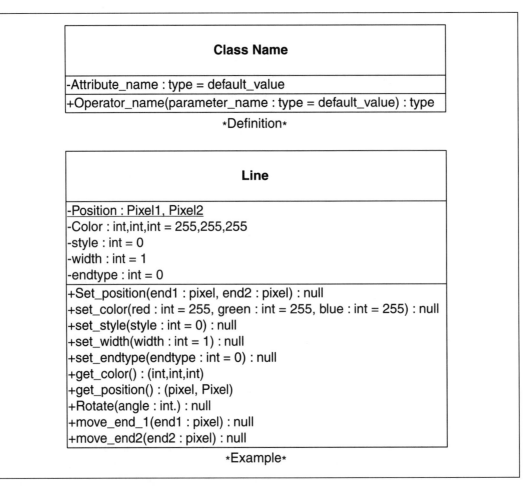

Figure 2.4 UML class specification.

Class Relationships

Classes may be related by *inheritance*. In UML, inheritance is also called *generalization*. Class A inherits from class B if every method and attribute of A is also found in the specification of B. Objects of class A are said to be a kind of object of class B. Let's say Class A specifies objects for a user-interface window. There are several kinds of windows—pop-up dialog, data entry, data visualization, and others—all of which have position and size. The state and methods for moving and sizing windows can be common to each kind of window; on the other hand, each of the kinds of windows has unique states and methods. In object design, one

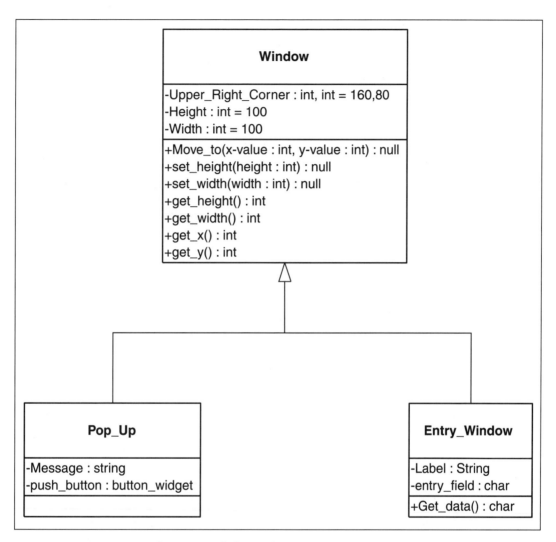

Figure 2.5 UML specifications of class inheritance.

might define a class called *Window* and have each of the kinds of windows inherit from the base class. Each of the derived classes reuses the move and size routines. An example of using the UML to specify inheritance in a class diagram is shown in Figure 2.5.

In the early days, much was made of inheritance. It was promoted in the name of efficiency and reuse. As in our example, the different kinds of windows can reuse the code that places and sizes windows. This reuse leads to more stable code and efficient development. Unquestionably, inheritance is a useful and powerful tool, allowing for the incremental addition of function to an existing class; however, inheritance is often misused. Code using inheritance becomes rigid, and it becomes difficult to predict how changes in the base classes might affect the system. The modern design pattern books should know how to avoid inheritance in order to keep the system more modular.

> **NOTE**
>
> A class can also inherit features from more than one class. This aspect of the UML, called *multiple inheritance,* is much out of favor. Experience has shown that the use of multiple inheritance leads to unforeseen complications, and thus is best avoided.

The point is, just because there is more than one kind of object does not mean you should adopt inheritance. For example, there are solid lines, dashed lines, and dotted lines. Defining each style of line as a class inherited from a general line class would result in an inelegant and unnecessary explosion of code, which would be hard to modify if required.

Objects need to interact in order to be useful. The most fundamental way for objects to interact is for the methods of one object to invoke the methods of another. In particular, if we intend in our design for methods of objects of classes A and B to invoke each other, we say they are *dependent*. The UML notation for dependency is shown in Figure 2.6. It is possible to have bidirectional dependence. By specifying in advance which type of objects can interact with others, you maintain control of your design and your code. As we shall see, specifying helps you manage complexity.

It is often useful to have the attributes of one class contain another class, like a structure made up of other structures. For example, you may find a class is becoming large and awkward to manage; in that case, you might be able to specify the class as being made up of separate subclasses. The state of the subclasses is managed separately, thus reducing overall complexity. When one class is a type in the attributes of another, we say they are related by *aggregation*. In UML, aggregation is one of the ways classes are said to be associated. This is shown in Figure 2.7. In the figure, objects of class A have objects of class B and C as attributes. Note, aggregation is only unidirectional.

There are several circumstances when aggregation helps clarify a design. In their text *UML and* C++, Richard Lee and William Tepfenhart, extending a joint

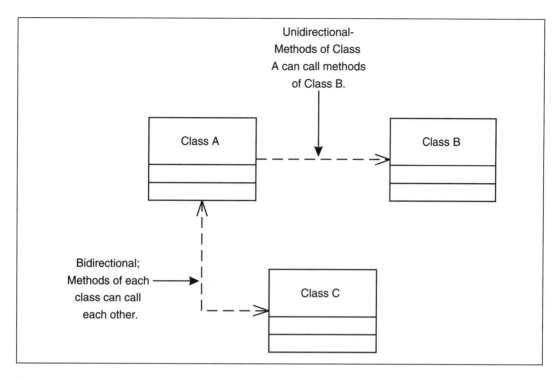

Figure 2.6 UML specification of association.

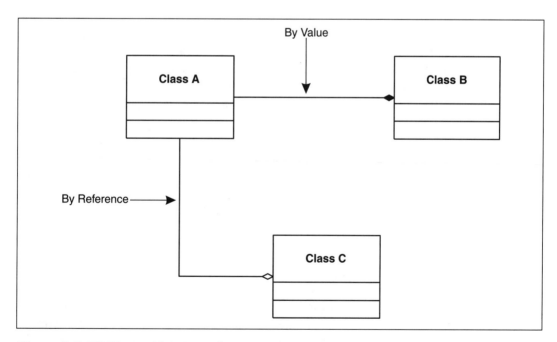

Figure 2.7 UML specification of aggregation.

paper of Morton Winston, Robert Chaffin, and Douglas Herman, identify seven kinds of compositions:

Assembly-parts. A wheel has spokes and a hub.

Material-object. Paint has pigments, solvent, and a fixative.

Portion-object. Days have hours.

Place-area. Massachusetts has Cambridge and Boston.

Collection-members. A phonebook has an alphabetized list of names.

Container-content. A chamber of commerce has member firms.

Member-partnership. The 1997 Boston Celtics had Dana Barros, Chauncey Billups, Bruce Bowen, Dee Brown, Andrew DeClercq, Tyus Edney, Pervis Ellison, Dontaé Jones, Travis Knight, Walter McCarty, Ron Mercer, Greg Minor, Roy Rogers, John Thomas, and Antoine Walker.

Class Packages

Objects provide the lowest level of abstraction. They enable encapsulation by including their own attributes. Modularization is achieved by limiting access from the state to the methods of the class. (In fact, the UML promotes the defeat of modularity by permitting public access to the attributes. I strongly recommend never to use this feature). The collection of objects and their interactions are usually too detailed for individuals and teams to deal with effectively. A mechanism is needed for combining classes to create addition layers of abstraction. Packages provide this solution.

At the lowest level, a package is a collection of classes whose objects collaborate to provide a service. A class can belong to only one package. Further, while not strictly required, every class should belong to a named package. Packages may be combined to form more general packages, and so on; in this manner, a hierarchy of abstraction is formed. The system architecture is captured by the package design.

The *object model* is a hierarchy of class packages. The root of the hierarchy is the top level. The branches are the classes. This is diagrammed is Figure 2.8. In the UML, the packages are dependent if there are some member classes of each package that are dependent. The notation for packages and package dependencies is given in Figure 2.9. Like classes, dependencies may be bidirectional or unidirectional. The dependency is unidirectional when the methods of classes in one package can call methods of classes in the second package, but not the converse. In the figure, objects from classes in package A may call methods from objects from

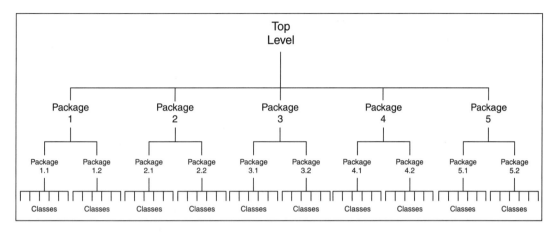

Figure 2.8 *A system object model.*

classes in packages B and C. Objects from B may call into A, but not into C. If the objects of classes of package A call into objects of classes of package C, we say A depends on C. In this case, C can in principle be developed in isolation from package A. None of its classes have any knowledge of package A.

I approach the design of packages as if they were subsystems. Each package should provide a service, much as a code library does. The associations may be thought of as the interface or specification into the library. The methods specified by classes in the package constitute a system interface. In this way, the packages and their association make up the architecture—the high-level design—of the sys-

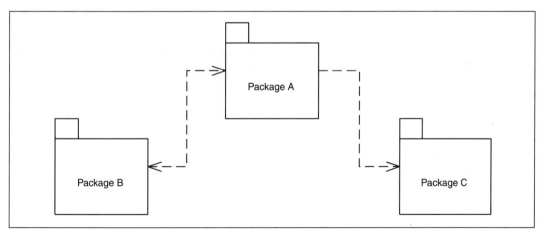

Figure 2.9 *Package association.*

tem. In some package designs, modularity is tightly controlled by only allowing objects from outside to invoke a specified set of methods from objects of a limited set of classes.

TIP

The packages and their association make up the architecture, the high-level design, of the system.

Classes within packages are expected to have many relations; they are likely to be associated, and may be related by inheritance or aggregation. We say that the classes in the package have *cohesion*. Classes between packages should be more loosely coupled. The only permitted relationship is association. The packages provide modularity of the design.

The Top-Level Package Diagram

Large problems need to be broken down into smaller problems. If you have a large system, you will need some techniques for both designing the system as a whole and creating more detailed design of the program's subsystems. One of the strengths of the UML is that it provides for maintaining views of the systems at various levels of detail.

The top-level architecture is the basis for dividing the system into subsystems. The developer-level use cases give a detailed view of how the top-level packages interact. The remaining artifacts make up the subsystem design. The package-level use cases constitute the dynamic view of the package's requirements. (This will be discussed in more detail later.) The class and package diagrams are the static view of the design—how the program elements relate to each other. The object sequence diagram constitutes the dynamic view of how the objects collaborate to carry out a use case. The top-level package diagram takes on a special role. It represents the common view of the overall system. The names of the packages make up the vocabulary that the team uses to discuss design issues. Note that the conceptual system diagram of the simulator (Figure 1.1) maps directly as the top-level package diagram for the simulator example seen in Figure 2.10.

Packages then establish new levels of encapsulation and modularity. For example, the state of all of the cockpit displays in the simulator architecture is contained in the instrument display package. Since none of the other packages has a need to know what the displays read, there are no associations into this package. On the other hand, the controls do need to know the position and state of the aircraft, the threats, and the weapons. They attain this information by calls into objects of

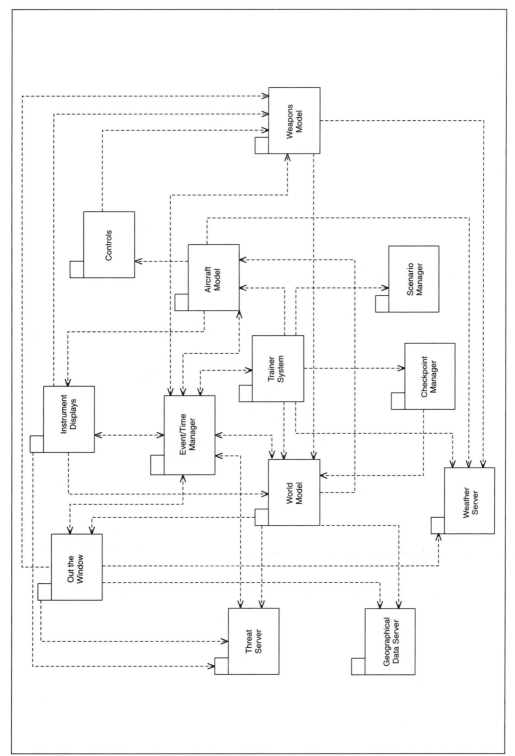

Figure 2.10 The top-level package diagram for the simulator.

classes found in the World Model, Aircraft Model, Weapons Model, and Threat Server packages.

The services that the package provides often are used as a library by the other components. The packages should be built and integrated as *subsystems*. Assigning this effort to a team makes good sense.

TIP

Packages provide a convenient basis for dividing effort among teams.

The Manned Simulator Architecture

You are fortunate to have access to a system architect who can help you get a handle on what is involved in building the manned simulator. He prepares a top-level class diagram (Figure 2.10) that shows the major components and how they are associated. He also describes the role of the package. Starting at the bottom:

Geographical Data Server. When requested, provides elevation and features at a given coordinate system.

Weather Server. Gives simulated wind, temperature, and precipitation data at a given location and altitude from a weather simulation.

Scenario Manager. Maintains the training scenario database; provides the usual database functions: store, retrieve, update, and query.

Checkpoint Manager. Maintains checkpoint database along with playback facilities.

Trainer System. Provides the trainer workstation user interface, including scenario creation, access to the scenario database, checkpoint save and playback, session initiation and intervention; grants access to scenario and checkpoint managers.

World Model. Maintains the geographical position of the aircraft and the threats (missiles), and provides them on request; detects collisions, and informs Aircraft Model and Threat Server.

Threat Server. Supplies data about missiles and other threats, damage potential, radar signature, and visual image.

Packages are also a convenient basis for dividing effort among teams, for these reasons:

- The classes within a package are likely to be tightly associated, and to call one another frequently. The developers of the classes within a package need to collaborate more closely than the developers who are writing classes in different packages.
- The classes within a package often require similar special skills.

By dividing the design into packages and assigning the packages to teams, you have an opportunity to achieve the right level of communication. The teams can focus on

Weapons Model. Provides data about weapons, such as air-to-air missiles, to counter the threats.

Event/Time Manager. Maintains the simulation time and informs other systems when to update their state. Those objects that require the manager's services register themselves on initiation.

Aircraft Model. Maintains the state of the aircraft: altitude, dynamics, damage, and fuel on board.

Controls. Provides an interface to the simulator cockpit controls and sends that information to the aircraft control model. The aircraft model gets the state of the controls at every timestep.

Instrument Display. Provides an interface to the cockpit displays. At every timestep, the instrument objects query the other subsystems and update the displays.

Out the Window. Provides a graphic rendering of what the pilot would see through the windshield.

Your system architect also provides a brief description of each of the associations.

Clearly, this system is involved, but you have some idea how to approach each of the packages. Further, you are more comfortable about how you might organize your project. The design of each of the packages requires different skills. Fortunately, you know where to find them. You have some concern that the associations are not correct, but put them aside for the moment.

the details and make their package services available to others. When someone from a different team needs to use the services provided by the package, the appropriate developers can negotiate the exchange.

In practice, the specifications of a system's packages may be both top-down (starting with an initial top-level package diagram) and bottom-up (deriving classes and packages from the use cases). I have found that you have to use both. In fact, for reasons that will become clear, I believe it is essential to have an initial version of the top-level diagram early in the project. The top-level diagram provides:

- The common view of the system, which enables collaborative design

- The basis for sizing the effort and estimating the required staff and effort

- A basis for program organization: Different development teams work on different sets of top-level diagrams

The second and third bullets will be explained in Chapter 4.

An experienced designer can put together the top-level class diagram of a large system by analogy, realizing that the system is much like one he or she worked on a few years ago, and that the same architectural design should work. He or she will reuse the experience and start to jot down some packages. (All of this will be addressed in more detail in later chapters.) This top-down approach is gaining popularity with the increased use of design patterns.

FOR FURTHER READING

The classic, and still the best, patterns book is *Design Patterns: Elements of Reusable Object-Oriented Software* by Eric Gamma, Richard Helm, Ralph Johnson, and John Vlisside, published by Addison-Wesley in 1995. Also see Thomas Mowbray's and Raphael Malveau's *CORBA Design Patterns*, published by John Wiley & Sons, Inc., 1997; and Martin Fowler's *Analysis Patterns: Reusable Object Models*, published by Addison-Wesley, 1997.

Design patterns are an attempt to create a menagerie of generic package and class specifications that can be used repeatedly. The discipline of design patterns is still in its infancy, and I expect it will gain in importance.

Class and Package Diagrams

Class and package diagrams provide a static view of the classes in the design which illustrate how they relate. They use the notations given in Figures 2.4 to 2.9, and their function is to provide an authoritative, common view of the design. There can be many different class diagrams, which you can use to get as many views of the design as you need. A class may appear in as many diagrams as you like, and a class diagram may be used to express any combination of:

- The class inheritance structure
- The package structure
- The encapsulation of state including aggregation
- The class associations

But note, your design must include the contents of each package so that every class occurs in at least one diagram. The set of diagrams that express the package hierarchy is called the *logical view* of the design.

Classes from different packages also may appear in the same diagram, a convenient capability, as it allows you to create a diagram consisting of all the classes that collaborate to carry out a use case. Members of different teams may share such diagrams.

Sequence Diagrams

It is important to reiterate that class and package diagrams are static. As such, they are not adequate to determine whether the design is adequate to meet requirements. In fact, you cannot determine from the class diagrams whether the system will do anything at all. Sequence diagrams meet this need. The elements of sequence diagrams are objects and method invocations, and are sometimes called messages.

Sequence diagrams are derived from development use cases; they show the objects and messages that carry out the use case. There should be one sequence diagram for each developer-level use case. The objects in sequence diagrams are instances on classes in the object model. The methods in a sequence diagram must be those found in the class specification.

Figure 2.11 shows a sequence diagram for our line drawing example, where the boxes with underlying dashed lines represent objects. Increasing time goes downward; the arrows represent messages, which are executed in top-to-bottom order.

Figure 2.12 is a collaboration diagram. It contains the same information as a sequence diagram. The numbers of the messages in the calls designates the calling sequence. Which one to use is a matter of taste.

Often, inexperienced teams will start their design by creating a class diagram. They will talk through a scenario describing the role the classes play (as if they were objects). At the end of the session, there is a class diagram, the static view. They neglect to capture the dynamic view. After a few days, they forget the motivation for the design, and frequently need to revisit the class diagram to recall what

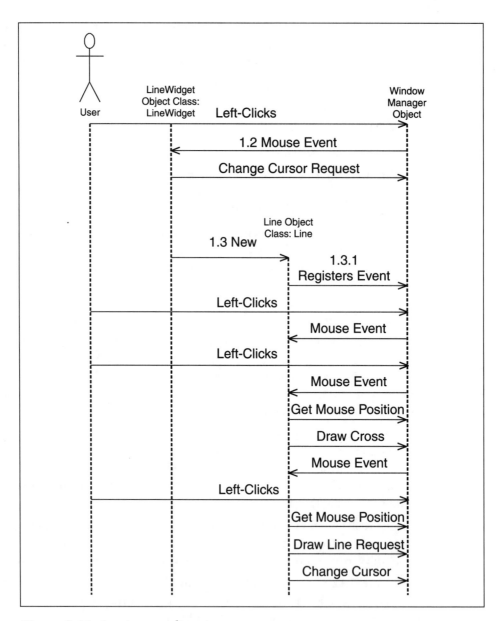

Figure 2.11 *A sequence diagram.*

they had in mind in the first place. The way out of this vicious circle is to be sure that you never create a static class diagram without at least one accompanying sequence diagram.

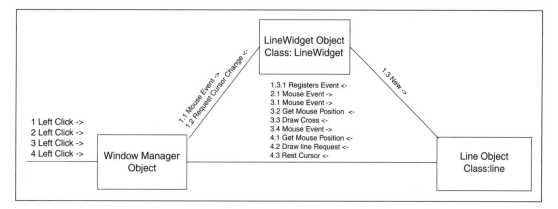

Figure 2.12 *A collaboration diagram.*

> **TIP**
> Never create a static class diagram without at least one accompanying sequence diagram.

Attributes of a Good Design

A good software design must support the "-ilities":

Comprehensibility. The ease of understanding the code design.

Maintainability. The ease of finding and removing defects.

Extensibility. The ease of modifying or adding functionality to the system.

Not only does your team need to be able to work efficiently with the design, it is very likely that developers who are not currently part of the team may need to either maintain or extend the code. As a manager, it is your job to ensure that the code you produce is well designed; that is, that meets the "- ilities", even though you will not have the time to study your project's design in detail. You need to provide some degree of oversight of the design. Here are some rules of thumb that you can apply to determine whether you are to have a design that delivers the potential benefits of object-oriented technology:

- *The packages should support modularity.* The classes *within* a package should be more tightly related than classes from different packages. Otherwise, the packages do not represent a higher level of abstraction that is a hallmark of a comprehensible design; the packages will not have clearly understood interfaces. Impacts of changes will propagate throughout the system, interfering with maintenance and extensibility. Have your lead architect confirm that there is low coupling between packages—only dependencies.

- *You, the manager, should understand the design.* You must know the role of each class and package, and be able to easily explain the abstraction. If you cannot understand the design, it will be difficult for a new team member to understand it.

- *The top-level architecture packages are a reasonable basis for team formation—the class packages should reflect skill areas.* Otherwise, you will have problems efficiently partitioning the effort into development teams.

- *A good design should have clear encapsulation in classes with no public attributes.* Certain of the object programming languages, notably C++, permit direct manipulation of an object's attributes. No matter what anyone tells you, under no circumstances allow this. Using this language feature defeats the advantages of encapsulation. The resulting code will be difficult to debug, extend, and maintain; changes in the attributes of a class at some later date will have unexpected consequences.

- *There is little or no two-way package dependency.* If the dependency is bilateral, it is for an easily explained reason. Objects that play the role of server to other objects should have no special knowledge about their clients. Packages that have two-way dependencies may need to be maintained together. If the packages have only one-way dependency, it is more likely that they can be maintained in isolation.

- *The depth of any inheritance tree is limited to two or at most three.* Multiple inheritances should be minimal, or better yet, avoided altogether. If the inheritance is too deep or too complex, the design will be difficult to modify. A small change in one of the base classes may have major ramifications throughout the design.

Here are some warning signs of a poor design.

- *A class with too many methods.* Having a class with 50 methods and 1,000 lines of code defeats any advantage of object technology. Such classes become complex, buggy, and hard to maintain. Most classes have 50 to 70 lines of code.

- *Many small classes also defeat the purpose of object design.* Such classes are probably being used as glorified global variables, thus defeating modularity and encapsulation.

Programmers who are new to object-oriented design often make these sorts of errors, probably because they are using an object-based language but have not yet learned how to build a good design. When you come across one of these signs, raise questions; be skeptical, but open-minded. There may be good reasons for these choices. However, you or your delegate should require that the design be disciplined and easy to defend.

Components and Subsystems

In a large software development, source files are written. They contain the set of language-specific instructions that implement the design, which are compiled to create *modules* or *object files*. The modules are linked to form subsystems, which can then be linked to form the system. In some cases, certain of the subsystems are delivered as separate files that are linked at runtime. These subsystems are called *dynamic linked libraries* or *DLLs*. As noted previously, the class and package design is called the *logical architecture*, while the hierarchy of modules, subsystems, and systems is called the physical architecture. The term *code* is used loosely to refer to all of these.

As a program manager, you are concerned not only with managing the design, but with managing the actual code. After all, the executable code is the centerpiece of your deliverable. Three issues deserve your attention:

- *Synchronization of the design to the code.* Unless the code exactly implements the design, all of your team's design efforts amounts to little more than drawing pretty pictures. Your design will be of no use as an aid in debugging, maintaining, or extending the code. Object design tools facilitate the sychronization by providing a sophisticated code-generation facility. The tool will generate the skeleton: the headers and the class specification with all the code except the body of the methods.

- *The mapping of modules into subsystems.* Subsystems should be designed to establish well-defined blocks of functionality. They should be set up so they can be developed separately from the other components. Ideally, the subsystems could be reused in other systems. This is especially true of DLLs.

- *Multilevel testing.* Each level of code can and should be tested in isolation. This testing strategy enables you to find errors generated from state interactions in as efficient a manner as possible. There will be module or unit testing, subsystem testing, and system testing. It follows that each subsystem must have a well-defined interface that is executed by the tests.

The UML not only provides artifacts to describe requirements and design, it also enables a way of describing the actual code components. In UML, kinds of code are called *components*. The default mapping of design artifacts into components is that:

- Each class maps to a module
- Each package maps to a subsystem
- The top-level package diagram maps to the system

However, this mapping may not be optimal for all systems and this should be managed explicitly. In many cases, the granularity of the logical and physical need not be the same. For example, you may want a module to contain more than one class if they are tightly related; you may also want a subsystem to include more than one package. The UML allows for this situation with component diagrams. An example is shown in Figure 2.13. In the diagram, the box with the rectangles represents each of the components. The dashed arrows represent dependency. In the figure, the system requires the three DLL files to execute. Subsys1.dll depends on the two module source files. A change in either of those files means that

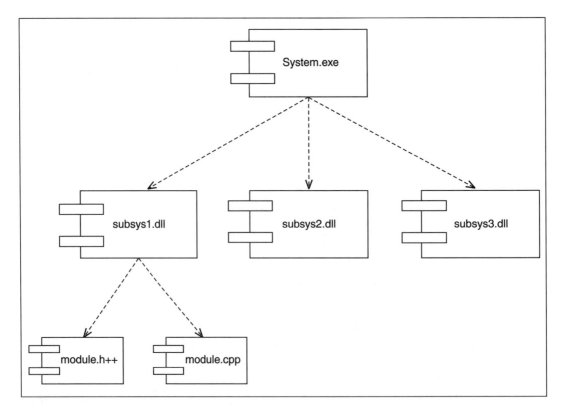

Figure 2.13 A component diagram

subsys1 would have to be relinked. However, a change in the module files leaves subsys2 unaffected.

Levels of Testing

It is useful to think of a computer system as composed of a hierarchy of components. The system is composed of subsystems; the subsystems are made up of modules. Functionality and state are encapsulated at each level of hierarchy. Tests are designed to exercise the external interfaces at each level of hierarchy. With this testing strategy, you can manage the complexity of the system and easily isolate the defects. During the construction phase, discussed in Chapter 4, you will conduct three levels of testing: unit, subsystem, and system.

Unit tests could also be called class tests, for they address individual classes or a small set of classes if they cannot be separated. However, the term *unit test* is more common. A unit test exercises the class methods in isolation from the other classes to determine whether the class works as the developer intended.

Unit tests are written and conducted by the class developers. The state space of each of the classes should be sufficiently small so that is it possible to simply test the external interfaces of the classes directly through a user interface. Each developer of a class should design a small user interface that directly invokes the public methods of the class and displays the outputs. In addition, the developer needs to design a test case that documents which of the methods are invoked with which values, along with the expected output.

Subsystem tests determine whether the subsystem works as the architect expected. They exercise the external subsystem interfaces and display the output. Unlike classes, the state space and set of possible execution paths of the subsystems are too large to exhaustively test the subsystem. Instead, you need to test the expected code paths. This is achieved by developing a set of test cases derived from the subsystem scenarios. Like unit tests, the subsystem test requires that a user interface to the subsystem be developed and a set of test cases be written. In this case, the tests need to be written and conducted by development team test leads. If a system is so complex that it is better comprised as subsubsystems, then the team building the subsystem may choose to develop and conduct subsubsystem tests. This decision should not impact the overall system development.

System tests confirm that the entire system behaves as the user expects. Like subsystem testing, the tests are not written to traverse all the possible code paths. System tests, derived from the user-level use cases, are designed to traverse the code paths the user will execute. The user actions are randomized to add to the realism of the testing. Of course, there is no test fixture required, as the system's own user interface is sufficient to drive the application.

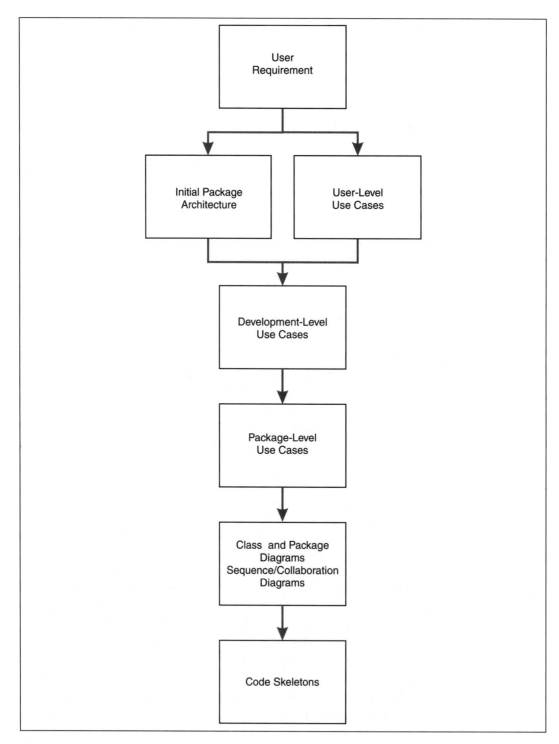

Figure 2.14 *Traceability from use cases to code.*

Traceability

The design should flow from the requirements; the code should flow from the design. The ability to link code to the classes to the requirements is called *traceability*, a hallmark of a well-managed development program. Traceability helps ensure that your team is spending its time meeting requirements. In addition, traceability establishes a mechanism for validating that all of the planned requirements are being met. Traceability should be two-way: from requirements to design and from design to requirements.

Traceability from use cases to code is shown in Figure 2.14. User-level use cases and the initial package diagram are refined to yield developer use cases. These in turn are further developed to sequence diagrams, from which the actual objects and messages are specified. The sequence diagrams link back to the class diagram. The class specifications are used to generate the code skeletons.

Sequence diagrams may be used in two ways during the elaboration. The first is to derive the classes, an approach discussed in later chapters. The second use of sequence diagrams is to verify that the class diagrams can be used to confirm the adequacy of the design, specifically, that the existing classes and their methods are sufficient to carry out the system- and package-level use cases. To do this, the designers walk through each of the use cases and generate a sequence diagram using the existing class design to show how the actions of the use case are carried out. If the designers discover a gap, the static class design needs to be augmented. By going through this process, the team can be assured that the class design is adequate—it supports the required actions as defined by the use cases.

From Here

This chapter completes the discussion of the theoretical and technical underpinnings of the project management techniques that follow. Armed with the techniques and tools of the first two chapters, we are ready to proceed to the practical day-to-day management of the object-oriented project. We start that discussion with an exploration of software development lifecycle models.

3 Choosing a Development Lifecycle Model

[We] are like dwarfs on the shoulders of giants, so that we can see more. . .

Bernard of Chartres, philosopher (c. 1130).

Product development starts with an idea and ends with a fielded product. A product lifecycle model is a delineation of the steps that transform that idea into a finished product. The lifecycle model is the center of the product management process. It contains a unified view of a development project's components:

Phases. The steps in the lifecycle that mark the project's progress. Inception and elaborations are examples of system phases.

Activities. The actions required to create and deliver the project. Examples include requirements analysis, design, code, and test.

Deliverables. Tangible or demonstrable products created during the project. Examples include the product itself, manuals, and documentation.

Milestones. The important project events. Occasionally, milestones serve as decision points. Examples of milestones include completion of critical reviews or of a deliverable.

Different lifecycle models have different lifecycle components, and there is no one correct lifecycle model. As a project manager, it is important for you to understand the underlying concepts and reasoning behind the various models, because some are more suited to object-oriented development than others. Ultimately, you will tailor and/or combine the models and create one that meets your needs. The Controlled Iterative Development Lifecycle Model, described in detail in this book, is the one I have found best suited to object-oriented software development, so it might be a good place for you to start.

Choosing the right model is critical. The lifecycle model you choose becomes your management tool; it is the common view of how the work will be done. A lifecycle provides the means to:

- Establish control points
- Plan and track progress
- Plan and track budget
- Assess status
- Manage risk

Likewise, choosing the wrong lifecycle model can seriously impact your team relationships and add risk to your program. A principal cause of ineffective management of software projects is blind adherence to a lifecycle model that does not meet the program's economics. When your team has made the commitment to deliver a product on a certain date, with the wrong lifecycle model, their time may be misspent. When the model fails to work, the inefficient manager blames his or her team. He or she may insist that they stick to the model. The team responds by questioning management sanity, as well as the entire notion of the software process. In contrast, the efficient manager understands the rationale behind the model, chooses the model deliberately, and is able to explain it to the team.

> **TIP**
>
> You must understand and facilitate how software development teams really work.

To optimize overall team efficiency, you must understand and facilitate how your development teams really work. Armed with this knowledge, you can then adjust the lifecycle model as appropriate. This chapter presents some of the standard models, and recommends one that is well suited to object-oriented development. The goal of this chapter then is to set the groundwork for choosing a lifecycle model for object-oriented development.

Lifecycle Model Principles

The choice of a lifecycle model is driven by the economics of your situation. The fundamental goal of any project manager is to deliver the project in the most economical way possible, minimizing time and effort. Many of the early techniques of software management were developed in the 1970s, a time when coding was inefficient, and economics called for minimizing coding and compilation cycles. In such an environment, refraining from coding until the design was approved, or using your team to discover errors during code walkthroughs, made sense. Today, in a personal computer or workstation environment, the compilation cycles for individual components are essentially free. There are adequate design tools. In most projects, the expense is generated by the requirements analysis and design phases. A major risk is delivering the wrong product. Today, therefore, it often makes more sense to let the compiler discover the coding errors and let your team optimize the design.

As mentioned in Chapter 1, much of the overall project management literature is better suited to construction projects than software. The science of project management was developed as a tool to aid the construction manager to plan and track the required schedule, budget, and resources. At some level, the software project manager is faced with the same issues—schedule, budget, and resource management. But building software is different from building a bridge. The techniques for managing construction projects can be modified to deal with the challenges of requirement specification, system complexity, and communications management inherent in large software programs. Building a bridge is an exercise in dependency management; managing software is primarily an exercise in content management. The requirements of a bridge are well understood and fully specified early in the design process. The activities of building a bridge—excavation, erecting towers, stringing cable—must happen in a fixed order. The scheduling and review of each task is essential to managing the project risks. The focus of the project manager is to ensure that the right tasks happen in the right order and to do what is necessary to mitigate any slips.

Bringing the construction management mentality to software development leads to a waterfall lifecycle: specifying requirements and designing, followed by coding and unit testing. One activity does not start until the other is complete and reviewed. In practice, taking this rigid approach appropriate to construction *adds* risk to the projects. Some of the spectacularly expensive software project failures over the last few years adopted the construction project approach. The activities of system design and implementation should *overlap*, since it is difficult to fully understand the requirements and complexity of the design before beginning the project. Consequently, software project developers need to:

- Respond to changing requirements discovered throughout the development.
- Continually confirm with the customer that the product being developed will in fact serve his or her needs.
- Manage content throughout the development cycle.
- Be more flexible to allow for workarounds to missed dependencies.
- Foster team collaborative problem solving in order to develop an adequate design.
- Establish and maintain major milestones that mark the progress of the software project.

You are much more likely to succeed if your choice of lifecycle accounts for these differences.

FOR FURTHER READING

The Project Management Institute (PMI), the professional organization for project managers, has an Information Technology Special Interest Group concerned with software development. The web site is www.pmi.org.

TIP

Major milestones in development projects mark the transition from one phase to another. This transition has to be done in public with some fanfare in order for the team of developers to believe the program is in fact moving forward. The public nature of the event reinforces the understanding that the project is important and that progress is appreciated. As project manager you should celebrate the completion of milestones (formal design reviews, alpha releases) while not wasting the team's time in unnecessary, elaborate preparations.

Software Development as Team Problem Solving

Several other books have also pointed out that software is not built like a bridge, but is designed as a product. In Chapter 1, we explored software development as a team problem-solving effort. Recall that the term "problem solving" does not mean fixing a flaw or defect, as used by Don Clausing in *Total Quality Development*. Instead, it refers to solving a puzzle or completing a math problem. This insight is central in choosing a lifecycle model, because a lifecycle model built around problem solving is not focused so much on dependency management as on facilitating the problem-solving process. The features of the problem-solving paradigm include:

- More focus on quality by design, not quality by test
- More iterative design and development phases
- Defect prevention rather than defect correction
- Concurrency of design
- Focus on processes and metrics
- Cross-functional teams establishment
- Shared responsibility among team members for ensuring delivery of a successful product

Experience has shown that taking a collaborative problem-solving approach, when applied wisely, leads to development that is more efficient and to improved products.

FOR FURTHER READING

Pick up a copy of Luke Hohmann's *Journey of the Software Professional* (Prentice-Hall, 1997) and Peter Jones' *Handbook of Team Design* (Mc-Graw Hill, 1998) for more extensive discussions of product development as problem solving.

NOTE

Cross-functional design and development teams, sometimes called *joint application design teams, integrated process teams,* or *integrated product teams (IPTs),* often include customers and/or users of the proposed product. Many U.S. government agencies require that suppliers of new systems, including software, adopt the use of IPTs. In the next chapter, I will discuss how to organize your product around the use of IPTs.

When an individual or a team solves a problem, they engage in four activities:

- *Scoping.* Ensuring they fully understand the problem.
- *Designing.* Developing an approach to solving the problem, usually using some sort of sketch or diagram.

- *Implementing.* Carrying out the design.
- *Verifying.* Confirming that the solution actually solves the original problem.

It is important to understand that these are *activities*, not *phases*. An activity is something you do to reach an outcome. Phases are the steps in the lifecycle that mark the project's progress.

> **FOR FURTHER READING**
>
> For more information on how people solve problems, read George Polya's classic, *How to Solve It: A New Aspect of Mathematical Method,* 2nd edition (Princeton University Press, 1957).

Problem solving does not progress in a linear manner from one activity to the next. You do not wait until you have fully scoped the problem before you start a design; nor do you restrict yourself from revisiting the scope once you have started a design. Your understanding of the problem continues to deepen by trying out some design alternatives. Ironically, some lifecycle models impose exactly these rules on a team!

Problem-Solving Phases

Again, software development occurs in phases, the periods of task-related work during which the problem-solving activities occur. Phases are not strictly tied to problem-solving activities since the activities often span the phases—a critical point that may take some getting used to. Time and budget are allocated for each phase of the project, and progress is tracked through the major project milestones that mark the transition between the phases. By tracking progress in this way, you have the correct level of view into the workings of the project to control cost and schedule risk. Problem solving has four phases:

Inception

Elaboration

Construction

Transition

> **TIP**
> Phases should not be strictly tied to activities.

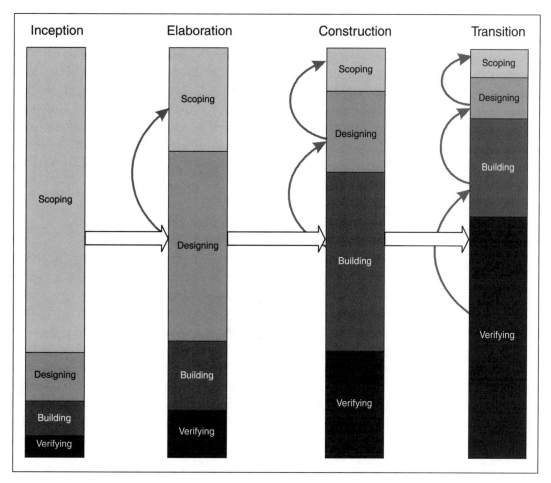

Figure 3.1 *How people solve problems.*

Although the phases are tied to the activities, the mapping is not perfect. The phases are not marked by completion of activities, but by achieving a level of understanding of the problem and the solution. Figure 3.1 illustrates the relationship of the phases to the activities.

The first phase of problem solving is the *inception* phase. During this phase, you begin by scoping the problem to understand its extent and limits. It is more than gathering requirements. You also build your initial mental model of the problem during this phase. For example, if the problem contains a lot of details, you may decide to cast a simpler less-detailed problem. Once you understand how to approach the simpler problem, you can deal with the details later. Alternatively, you may break a complicated problem into a set of simpler problems and decide to

> **NOTE**
>
> The 80–20 rule states that *for any activity, the initial 80 percent of the benefit is achieved with the first 20 percent of the effort.* An important implication of the rule is that the remaining 20 percent of the benefit takes 80 percent of the effort. The general applicability of the rule follows from the difficulty of dealing with the interactions of the parts you generated initially. Polishing off the project means that all the pieces have to work together perfectly. Toward the end of the effort fixing one interaction may affect many others, and so every change requires an increasing amount of effort and time. Every project manager has stood witness while the initial coding goes along well only to discover that productivity comes to a grinding halt as the team struggles to complete the effort.
>
> A good rule of thumb is that for the inception and elaboration phases, declare victory as soon as you sense the 80–20 rule kicking in. It is not wise to spend the effort polishing up the requirement analysis or design when they will only undergo change anyway. Take advantage of your ability to iterate through. I suspect that many of those programs that spend millions of dollars and never get out of the requirements or design phases are victims of this rule. If you have a good design, your constructed code will be well enough encapsulated that you will in fact overcome the 80–20 rule as you go to system test.

attack those one at a time. The bulk of activity during this initial phase *is* scoping, but you may also engage in the other activities. As you gain understanding of the problem, you may engage in design, implementation, and verification to confirm your understanding. Furthermore, you may gain initial understanding of the problem by trying out different designs to determine whether your model is valid.

Once you sufficiently understand the problem, and have a mental model, enter the *elaboration* phase. Here, it is best to apply the 80–20 rule and not wait until you feel you have a perfect mental model. Begin the design of the solution here. You may discover gaps in your understanding; perhaps some word is being used in a precise technical manner and you need to investigate the usage in your problem; perhaps you discover an ambiguity and need to backtrack for clarification. Your understanding of the problem continues to deepen while you design a solution. The designing activity helps you refine your mental model. If you wait to start designing until you fully understand the problem, you might never start the design.

The *construction* phase begins when the design is in place. In this phase, you may fluctuate between design and implementation of activities. At any point during the implementation, you might discover a flaw. To correct it, stop the implementation and go back to the design. You may discover that the flaw was due to a subtle misunderstanding of the problem during scoping, bringing all three activities into this phase.

Once you think you have a solution, you enter the *transition* phase. You start to verify your solution. You will probably discover a flaw, which may be in the implementation or may ripple all the way back to your understanding of the problem. If necessary, adjust your understanding, your design, and your implementation. Even though you have progressed to the point at which you are verifying the solution, you continue all four activities to some degree.

The ability to manage a project through these phases while allowing the various activities to continue at some level has long been recognized as critical to success. A robust lifecycle model should provide explicit techniques to meet this need. With this thought in mind, let us explore some alternate lifecycle models.

Four Lifecycle Models

The software development literature contains a variety of lifecycle models: waterfall, spiral, rapid application development (time-boxes), and controlled iteration. All lifecycles have scoping, design, implementation, and verification activities, but they differ in how they schedule and organize the practice of these activities.

If you are approaching this literature for the first time, you are likely to find it confusing. Many practitioners use these terms loosely. One source of the confusion is that the various models have incremental variants (which will be discussed later in this chapter). In order to understand the various lifecycle models, therefore, it is useful to agree on certain terms:

Release. A complete version of the product, which has been polished, tested, hardened, and prepared for release to the customer.

Build. A coherent version of a system that meets predetermined functionality and has completed a development cycle. Builds are often demonstrable versions of the code.

Phase. The components of a development cycle from inception through transition.

Integration. A version (partially functional) of the total system that is compiled and linked as part of the development process.

Two other words that are often confused when discussing lifecycle models are *iteration* and *incremental*. Iteration refers to repeating an activity (such as requirements analysis or design) throughout the development phases. Incremental refers to the process of adding function through successive implementations. In object-oriented development, both concepts apply.

Waterfall

Barry Boehm introduced the waterfall lifecycle model in the 1970s as a response to the undisciplined code-and-fix mentality of the 1960s. It was the first widely adopted lifecycle model, and was discussed at length in his text, *Software Engineering Economics* (Prentice-Hall, 1987).

As shown in Figure 3.2, this lifecycle consists of eight phases:

Feasibility. Determining the design and development approach.

Software plans and requirements. Development of a complete, validated specification of the products requirements.

Product design. Development of a complete, verified specification of the architecture and high-level design of the product.

Detailed design. Development of a complete specification of the detailed design (control, data structures) of the project's modules.

Coding. Coding and unit testing of each of the modules.

Integration. Compiling and linking of the modules to create a fully functional software product.

Implementation. Installing and integrating the software into the operational environment.

Operations and maintenance. Developing updates.

Unlike problem-solving phases, these eight are defined by their activities. The goal is to complete each activity before moving to the next phase. Most implementations of this model place milestones and formal reviews at the end of each phase.

In *Software Engineering Economics*, Boehm allows for some iteration of a phase's predecessor. In practice, however, most waterfall projects are managed with the assumption that once the phase is completed, the result of that activity is cast in concrete. For example, at the end of the design phase, a design document is delivered. It is expected that this document will not be updated throughout the rest of the development. You cannot climb up a waterfall.

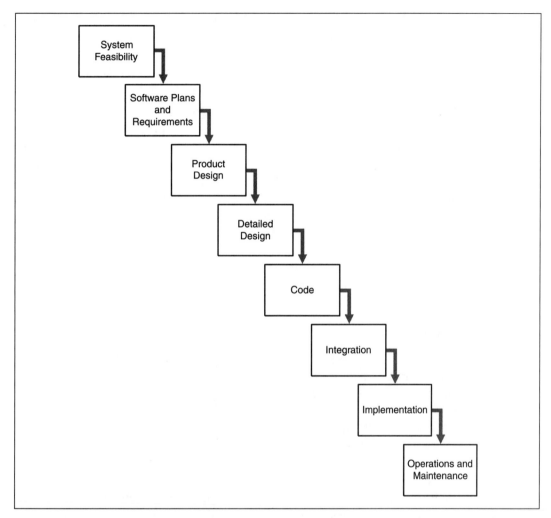

Figure 3.2 *The waterfall model.*

Project Management Aspects of the Waterfall Model

It is easy to understand why managers adopted the waterfall model. Teams complete the required activities in a natural order. By paying attention to the activities, defects are found early, when they are relatively inexpensive to fix. The goal is equally simple: Complete the required activities. The model, too, is easy to plan and staff. You assign requirements analysis to system engineers who hand off requirements documents to the software architects. They in turn hand off specifications to the coders, who hand off code to the testers, and so on. The milestones are easily understood: design complete, code complete, and the like. The staff are assigned from each function to each of the phases, and then are free for the next project. In form, it appears much like a construction project: First you do the architecture, then you create the specs, then you grade the land, and so on. By adopting this model, you can easily use the standard formalism of project management.

Experience has shown, however, that the model does not serve the needs of the software development team. When strictly applied, the model does not reflect the problem-solving nature of software development; rather, it requires the team to do the impossible. It entails that the requirements be fully understood before design, that the design be fully understood before coding, and so on. Tying the phases rigidly to the activities does not reflect how people or teams really work. Teams, like individuals, iterate through the activities. When you try to enforce a waterfall, your people have no way to account for rework and iterations that are going on behind the scenes. Worse still, the term "Design Complete" is inaccurate; it implies that it is somehow shameful to revisit the design during implementation. In turn, unnecessary destructive morale problems arise.

> **NOTE**
> Lifecycle model phases should reflect the problem solving stages and not be so closely tied to the activities. Further, they should allow for increased understanding of the requirements and design throughout the development. The goals of each phase should not be the completion of an activity, but the ability to move on to the next phase of problem solving.

Managing to a waterfall model tends to lead to the poor communications inherent in functional team communications. Software projects from that period bring up nightmare visions of faceless teams of designers passing specifications and flowcharts (remember those?) to teams of anonymous coders, who would blindly implement the design. Such a scheme required flawless execution at each step. No wonder an inordinate amount of time was spent on design reviews, code walkthroughs, and the like. Most often, the integrations failed.

Another flaw with the waterfall model is that it gives a false impression of the project's status and progress. On the surface, assessing the project's status should be a straightforward matter. At the project reviews, you determine how far along in your project is in the given activity; 35 percent done with design, for example. While this looks good in a report, practically, it is meaningless. First, the design is never fully completed until the code is released. Second, project leaders who use this sort of status checking find they spend most of their time with your team reporting over 90 percent complete. In practice, trying to measure software progress against a waterfall model leads to developers keeping two sets of books: one they report, and one they believe.

Yet another flaw in this lifecycle model is that the integration happens in one big bang at the end. In such projects, there is insufficient opportunity for the customer to see what he or she is going to get. This explains how a project can go through a disciplined process, meet written requirements, and still not be operational. Another effect of "big-bang integration" is that previously undetected errors or design deficiencies will emerge, adding risk when there is little time to recover.

Recommendation

The waterfall model is falling out of favor. However, I have included it for a couple of reasons. First, some misguided souls still using the model may need salvation. Second, understanding its flaws will improve your ability to assess other lifecycle models. When is it right to adopt this model? Never!

Spiral Model

The spiral model is an elaborate form of the waterfall model introduced by Barry Boehm in an article published in *IEEE Computer* in May 1988. Boehm points out that the builds may be thought of as iterations through four high-level phases:

Determining objectives. Product definition, determination of business objects, constraints.

Evaluation of alternatives. Risk analysis, prototyping.

Product development. Detailed design, code, unit test, integration.

Planning the next iterations. Customer evaluation, design planning, implementation, and customer delivery.

These are then broken down into more detailed phases. For example, two builds have 40 detailed phases. Figure 3.3 shows a simplified version of the spiral model. In this diagram, the radial distance from the center reflects effort spent.

The premise behind the spiral model is that there will be two or more builds, with each build closing in on meeting the customer's needs. The first build, called *initial operational capability (IOC)* is the customer's first look at the system. After the delivery of IOC, a planning phase begins, during which the program is reset to respond to the customer's reaction to the IOC. The project then reenters the determining objectives phase armed with the experience gained from the delivery of the

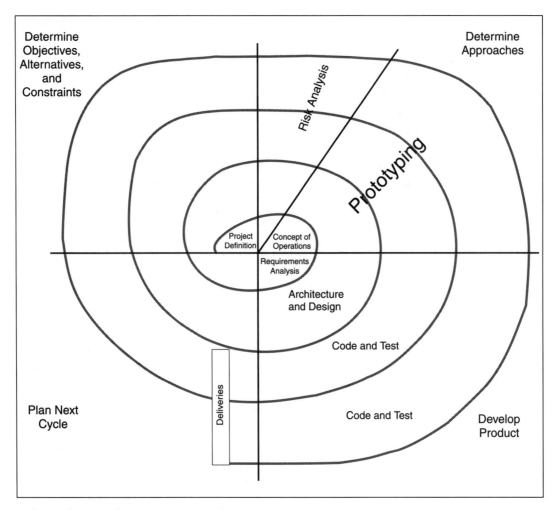

Determine Objectives, Alternatives, and Constraints

Determine Approaches

Risk Analysis

Prototyping

Project Definition

Concept of Operations

Requirements Analysis

Architecture and Design

Code and Test

Deliveries

Plan Next Cycle

Code and Test

Develop Product

Figure 3.3 A simplified spiral lifecycle.

IOC and the subsequent planning. The activities in the second and succeeding builds may be somewhat different from those of the first. The first build may be a prototype and so may not undergo much testing. In the second pass, you build an operational system. This release is called *final operational capability (FOC)*. Although this second release is called *final*, the spiral may continue indefinitely, generated by each of the customer's responses to the build initiating a new cycle. With each build, you and the customer can develop a better idea of what is required. Ideally, the degree of change from one build to another diminishes, and this process will result in an operational system.

Project Management Aspects of the Spiral Model

The spiral model addresses many of the deficiencies of the waterfall model. With its multiple builds, there are several opportunities for customer involvement during which the customer and the development team can jointly move toward the correct solution. Because it does not rely on the impossible task of getting the design perfect and documented, it is definitely an advance over the waterfall model.

That said, there are three concerns with the spiral model: The model is overly elaborate and so is hard and expensive to adopt. The large number of intermediate stages makes documenting the processes and training the staff a challenge. (I am sure someone has succeeded, but I have never seen it done.) The model may also be unaffordable. The time spent in planning, resetting objectives, risk analysis, prototyping, and the like seems excessive. It is also difficult to keep a staff fully occupied during phase 1, 2, and 4. Finally, unless it is carefully managed, the spirals may not converge on a solution. Careful content management is essential or the project will spiral to oblivion.

Recommendation

Organizations can use Spiral Models successfully, but to do so usually requires significant tailoring. The form that Boehm published is probably too detailed to match your project's needs. For example, you may need more integration testing, user-interface reviews, and less constraint analysis. In particular, the detailed activities within the phases would have to be modified in order to take advantage of object technology. Finally, there is little point is going through the effort, because all of the benefits of the spiral model can be found in the controlled iterative model.

FOR FURTHER READING

To learn more about the spiral and waterfall lifecycle models, I suggest you read Barry Boehm's seminal text, *Software Engineering Economics*, published by Prentice-Hall in 1981. His article, "A Spiral Model of Software Development and Enhancement", printed in *IEEE Computer*, May 1988, is also important.

Another useful reference was published by the Software Technology Support Center (STSC) of the United States Air Force. The text, *Guidelines for Successful Acquisition and Management of Software-Intensive Systems, Version 2.0*, was published in 1996, and it is available through the web site http://stsc.hill.af.mil/ (see Chapter 3).

Rapid Application Development: Time Box Model

The rapid application development model emerged in the early 1980s as a response to the overly formal lifecycle or spiral models. I saw it applied at IBM in the mid-1980s. Rapid Application Development (RAD) is not so much a model as an approach. The proponents of RAD development argue that a formal lifecycle model is inherently inefficient, and that much of the documentation and reviews of the lifecycle and spiral methods are a waste of time. The formality interferes with customer communication, they argue, essentially saying, "Forget all that and build something." There is no well-defined lifecycle model. In its place is a sequence of evolutionary system integrations or prototypes that are reviewed with the customer. In this way, the requirements are discovered. The development of each integration is restricted to a well-defined period of time, known as a *time box*. Each iteration is scheduled to be done within its time box. The application of the RAD method can be summarized by the following pseudocode.

```
Analyze Requirements;
Develop Initial Design;
Do until done
{Develop the build within proscribed time;
Release to customer;
Get feedback;
Plan version to respond feedback};
```

Your team simply continues through the loop, delivering releases, taking suggestions for improvements, and rebuilding the code until everyone decides the product is good enough.

The RAD approach has several important features worth noting:

Separation of phases from activities. Each time box includes analysis, design, and implementation.

Constant integrations. Isolate problems and elicit customers feedback.

Moving the focus from documentation to code. It's what on the screen that counts.

Effective use of off-the-shelf tools and frameworks. Permitting quick initial views of the product.

Ongoing customer involvement. Ensuring the operational utility of the product.

All of these are found in the controlled iteration model, discussed next.

Project Management Aspects of RAD

Successful implementation of this approach relies on two assumptions:

1. There is an efficient, accelerated development process for responding to the feedback.

2. You and the customer will eventually agree the project is done.

The first assumption may be reasonable; in fact, if you use object-based techniques with a development environment, including collaborative object design tools supporting code generation and the like, you can go through each loop in a reasonably short time.

The second assumption is more problematic. Since the customer always has feedback, the exit condition may never be reached. The fact that closure is never reached—that there is always more development to do—is considered a strength of this method by some of its advocates. This flies in the face of the need to meet a schedule and a budget.

FOR FURTHER READING

For more information about the assumptions underlying RAD, read the article "Evolutionary Rapid Development," by Richard De Santis at the Software Productivity Consortium Web site, http://www.software.org /pub.darpa/erd/erdpv010004.html.

Also check out Ian Graham's SOMATIK process, which is an object-oriented version of time box development. His book is titled *Migrating to Object Technology*, published by Addison-Wesley, 1995.

Recommendation

The decision to use the RAD approach should be based on your analysis of the project's risks. In theory, RAD minimizes the risk of not achieving customer satisfaction. The use of a time box is supposed to mitigate cost and schedule risk; but beware, the approach, blindly applied, places no bounds on the cost or completion date of the project. Teams developing commercial projects that try RAD can evolve themselves to death, and never ship the product.

If cost and schedule are not a concern, the RAD method might be appropriate. As an example, consider a team that is developing tools for use within their own company. Their budget is constant from year to year, and not directly tied to delivery; further, each of the customer releases is deployed. Such a team should consider an evolutionary variant as a way to reduce the turnaround time to customer feedback. Even so, a configuration management process for prioritizing features and changes is a must.

Generally, I do not recommend this approach. In most instances, the risk of not coming to closure is too great. While it is important to receive and respond to customer feedback, a project manager must work with both the team and the customer to bring the project to a successful conclusion. He or she must employ a lifecycle model that does not result in an infinite loop.

NOTE

In informal conversations, I have found that many people seem to be confused about the terms *spiral* and *evolutionary*. Many use spiral to mean "not waterfall"; that is, some sort of managed iterative process. Others use spiral to mean RAD. While I suppose people can use words however they want, the inconsistent use of words can be confusing. If you are discussing someone's lifecycle model, consider asking a few questions to learn whether he or she is using the words the same way as you are.

Controlled Iteration

The controlled iteration lifecycle model is an emerging model. I first became aware of it from documentation accompanying Rational Software's Rose object design tool. Rational promotes its use in their training course. At this writing, the well-known object technologists Booch, Jacobson, and Rambaugh, have announced their intention to publish a book on what they call the "objectory process," a version of the controlled iteration model. Hans-Erik Eriksson and Marcus Penker mention the objectory process briefly in their recently published book, *UML Toolkit* (John Wiley & Sons, Inc., 1997). The version I discuss here of controlled iteration is an elaboration of the earlier versions.

The controlled iteration model takes advantage of the flexibility and modularity of object development to provide a lifecycle that both matches how people work and allows for sufficient management control. It incorporates some the valuable insights of the RAD movement, while supporting a more predictable development process. The model provides a disciplined management process: The phases are scheduled, budgeted, and tracked; they have defined exit criteria. As I discuss later, progress is defined in terms of tangible artifacts, and project milestones mark the transitions. The outcome of the phases is a product build.

Controlled Iteration Phases

The phases of the controlled iteration model are the same as those in problem solving described earlier in this chapter. When applied to the problem of team software design and development however, they become:

Inception. Achieving initial understanding and agreement of the product definition; that is, what will be delivered.

Elaboration. Achieving initial understanding and agreement of the product's detailed design; that is, how it will be built.

Construction. Creating the initial fully functional product build.

Transition. Delivery of a product that meets the initial goals.

Note that the goals are *not* tied to the completion of the activities, only that the activities are developed well enough so that the necessary level of agreement and understanding is reached to enable progression. As a rule of thumb, if you feel the 80–20 rule has kicked in, then it is probably time to move on to the next phase. This practice helps you maintain momentum. The goals use the word "initial." It is understood that the product content and design may change throughout the development. On the other hand, management practice requires that there be phase exit criteria. (The exit criteria for the phases are discussed in detail in Chapters 5 through 8.)

The four phases of the lifecycle do map to the four phases of problem solving, and thus reflect how teams work together to solve problems. By allowing the various activities to continue from phase to phase, and to permit design and requirements analysis changes during the phases, the right level of communication is encouraged. A product team organization works well with this model.

From the point of view of project planning and management, time and budget can and should be allocated to each of these phases. Major project milestones mark the transition between the phases. By tracking progress in this way, you have a clear view into the workings of the project so that you can control cost and schedule risk. In short, the use of the model allows for disciplined well-managed projects while providing a framework for facilitating the real work of a team. Figure 3.4 provides a view of the model. The shading indicates the intensity of the activity. More effort is expected when the shade is dark.

In the *inception* phase, the team's goal is to gain a common understanding of the product's definition. By including the customer in the team, you, your develop-

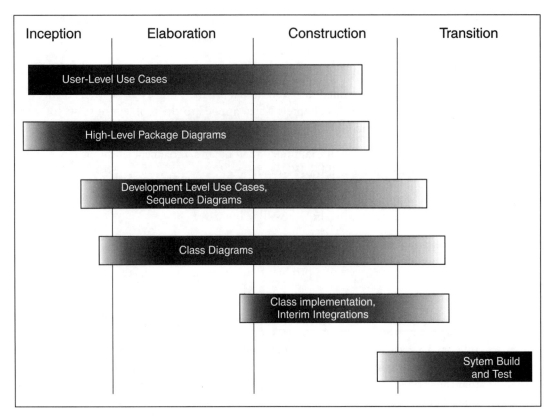

Figure 3.4 The controlled iteration model.

ment team, and your customer complete this phase by agreeing on the product requirements. The content may in fact change, but at least at that point in time, all
are in agreement. The agreement is reached by developing a set of use cases and
other artifacts that specify the behavior of the desired system. Note that to end the
phase, formal proof that you have completed all the requirements is not required.
The phase ends when your team (including the customer) has reached a comfort
level that indicates it is time to move on to the next phase. Also note that during
elaboration, some amount of design and even implementation is appropriate. You
should encourage any affordable activity if it helps add to the conviction that the
use cases are adequate. For example, user-interface layout should start during this
phase.

The goal of the *elaboration* phase is to complete enough of the detailed design
to start building the code. In practice, this means that the object class and package
diagrams are in place and fully populated. Often this phase ends when there is no

way to proceed without going ahead with the building. I try to move the team to the next phase when I suspect the 80–20 rule has kicked in. While the bulk of activity is spent on design, other activities also occur during this phase. In particular, the requirements are refined as new issues arise during the design activity. Note that the end of elaboration phase does not mean that all design activity ceases. In addition, some amount of implementation is often very useful here as a way to gain confidence in the feasibility of the design.

In the *construction* phase, the goal is to build functionally complete, operational code that is ready for system test. This phase differs from the traditional code and unit test phase in at least two respects; inclusion of the other activities, and the use of frequent interim system and subsystem integrations. As discussed in more detail in Chapter 7, *Managing the Construction Phase*, you will integrate the code at various levels as it is built; you will not wait until the end of the phase to see if the code comes together. This incremental integration strategy removes a great deal of the risk from the development. Progress in this phase is marked by how many of the use cases have been implemented in the integrations and how many can be executed. The phase ends when you can show that all of the planned use cases can be executed in the integration.

The *transition* phase looks much like other back-end processes—system tests, alpha, and beta releases. The focus is on the transition of the code from the development organization to the customer, and possibly, the maintenance organization. This phase differs from other back-end processes only in that it will go more smoothly. Unlike the system integration phase of some previous development models, it starts with fully integrated code. In this phase, it is not whether the code will integrate, but whether it functions under operational loads; for example, the Stealth simulator will be tested by student pilots during its transition phase. Second, with the emphasis placed on the design during the elaboration phase, the code will not be brittle—fixing one problem usually will not introduce another. Finally, because there was frequent integration and test during the construction phase, there are no unpleasant surprises during this final phase.

As you move through the phases, the product becomes increasing well defined and concrete. The specification is not assumed to be complete and unchangeable from the beginning, but hardens throughout the development cycle. Change in requirements is allowed and facilitated early in the cycle and becomes more expensive, but not impossible, toward the end of the cycle.

Project Management Aspects of Controlled Iteration

At this point, you may be asking, how can this possibly work? It all seems fuzzy compared to the rigidity of the waterfall model. How can you manage this model?

These questions are answered in detail in the following chapters, but some discussion of the general approach is in order here. The paradox underlying the model is that what you need to make it work is exactly what you need to manage any software project well:

Tight integration of the project's functions. Since requirements analysis, design, implementation, and testing happen in parallel, you need mechanisms for keeping them synchronized.

Control of the design throughout the development process. Given that the design is allowed to change, you need collaborative mechanisms for maintaining design integrity throughout the development.

Well-managed, cross-functional communications. The various functional groups continue to interact throughout the development, and thus need well-defined requirements analysis and design artifacts.

Mechanisms for content management. The use-case database provides an authoritative, definitive specification of the project's (or build's) content. You and the customer use the database as a basis for negotiating content change.

Visibility to the work in progress. In the inception and elaboration phases of the development, user interface prototypes are reviewed with the customer. In the construction phase, there is a sequence of interim integrations that may be shared.

If you have processes that meet these criteria, you can move your team through the stages. Object technology is the key enabler, providing the artifacts and communication mechanisms you need to make it all work. Here are some processes needed to support this model.

Requirements management. Including the ability to trace system requirements to use cases, sequence diagram, classes, integrations, and the system test plan.

Design management. Allowing for shared, synchronized views of the design, maintained under configuration management tools.

Build and integration. Including an ability to define the integration's content in terms of use cases.

Test and quality assurance. Supporting three levels of testing:

- *Unit*. Tests individual classes. The tests are written and conducted by the developer, but documented and audited by your quality assurance staff. Unit tests determine whether the class works as the developer intended.

- *Subsystem.* Tests cohesive code groups (usually packages). They determine whether the package works as the architect intended. The tests are written and conducted by the development team test lead.

- *System.* Tests whether the system works as the customer intended. The tests are written and executed by a test organization.

Recommendation

Controlled iteration is the preferred lifecycle model for object-oriented development. It comes closest to meeting the criteria set at the beginning of the chapter. It differs from the other models by supporting the iteration of the activities throughout the phases. Along with incremental, partial builds (integrations), this model fosters the right amount of communication both within the team and the customer. Try it; you'll like it.

Incremental Builds

One pass through each of the lifecycle models discussed in this chapter produces a system build (well, the spiral produces two). However, in most cases it is a good idea to develop a product to release with *incremental builds*, a sequence of builds where each has greater functionality than the last. Producing two or more builds in the course of the product release helps address these project risks:

- *Customer Satisfaction.* It provides an opportunity to confirm that the design is on track by letting the customer "kick the tires." Based on what he or she sees, the customer may ask to change the product content. Interim builds give you a chance to respond.

- *Schedule.* Delivering intermediate builds gives focus to the team, helps maintain project momentum, and helps to keep the team on schedule.

Your development lifecycle should then consist of a sequence of builds, where the content of each is planned in advance. If you have a multiyear schedule, you may plan for roughly one build a year, each with more functions. These builds may by delivered to the customer for evaluation or merely demonstrated. At the end of each build, you respond to the lessons learned from the build, to customer feedback, and to the changing requirements, then revise the plans for the next build.

Adopting this incremental variation of a lifecycle model has several advantages. First, it reflects the problem-solving nature of software development. People do not solve big problems all at once; they solve them by breaking them into smaller problems. The best way for a team to solve a large design problem is to approach it incrementally. The greater the amount of design, the more difficult it is to get it right. Trying to do too much design without an implementation results in low productivity, thereby adding to cost and schedule risks. Some of the more spectacular software project failures have been caused by teams trying to design too large a system at once. The projects end with nothing but volumes of useless design.

Incremental builds give you greater control over your costs and schedule risks. If you give the team a year to deliver a partial build, which the customer and management will see, they are likely to come through. With the build complete, cost and schedule risks are decreased. At the end of the build, you and the customer are certain that the allocated function is in place.

Development teams can handle only so much requirement analysis and design activity before they run out of speed. They function best with partial builds on a yearly cycle. Adopting a development plan with construction starting more than six or seven months after the onset slows a team's momentum. The team begins to feel and act as if they are bogged down; productivity sinks. Using an incremental approach addresses these risk areas. Incremental builds also curtail staff instability. Maintaining the same staff through a multiyear development lifecycle is highly improbable. By the time you start implementation, some of the designers may be gone. It is easier to change staff between builds than during a build.

Providing partial builds to the customer is also a great way to reduce customer satisfaction risk. Putting a working version in the customer's hands gives him or her a way to evaluate whether you are on track to an operational product. In a commercial setting, you can use the build to support market research: bring in potential customers and have them evaluate usability.

One of the variables in planning an incremental version of a lifecycle is the extent of overlap between builds. It is preferable to start the next build during the current build. This approach is illustrated in Figure 3.5. For example, you can start the inception phase of the second build during the transition phase of the first. Taking this approach helps smooth staffing exchanges: The development staff can turn their attention to a review of requirements while the customer and system test staff are evaluating the build.

Every lifecycle model can benefit from including incremental builds. If your project schedule is longer than a year, I strongly recommend you include incremental builds in your plans. For example, if you insist on using a waterfall model, it is essential you apply it in incremental builds. Some, but not all, of the drawbacks of the waterfall lifecycle model are addressed (see Figure 3.6.).

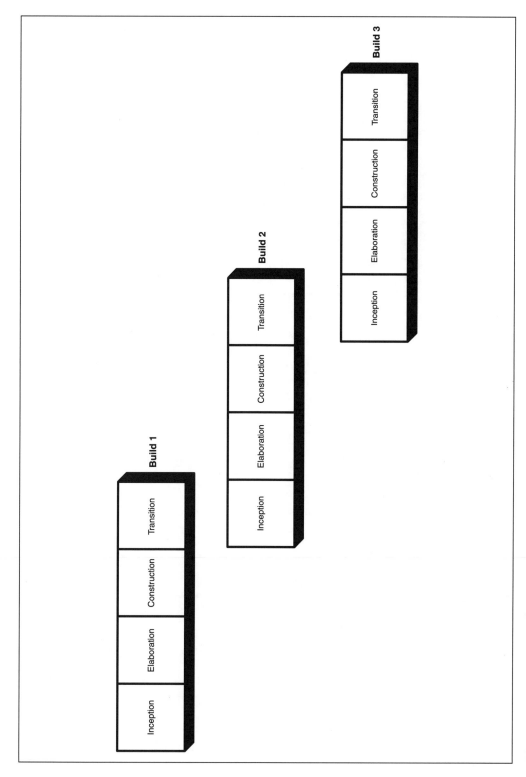

Figure 3.5 Incremental controlled iteration.

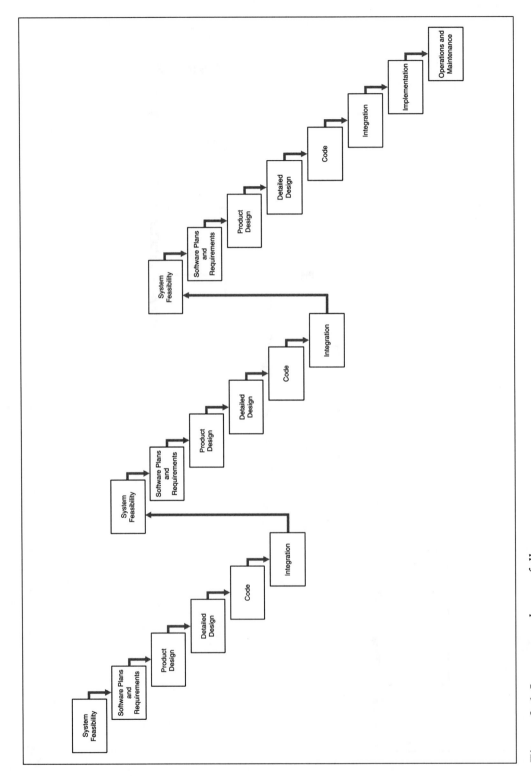

Figure 3.6 Incremental waterfall.

> **Simulator Development Lifecycle Model**
>
> Your organization is already familiar with the controlled iteration model; you choose it without a lot of thought. Given the two-year schedule, you decide to adopt an incremental approach with two builds.

Recommendation

In most situations, an incremental controlled iteration lifecycle is the model of choice. I prefer to have the builds last about a year. In addition, I usually plan for the elaboration and transition phases to overlap. I suggest you consider these choices as a starting point in your planning although you may find the number of builds and the degree of overlap may need to be adjusted to meet your situation.

From Here

In the next chapter, I begin to tie the material from the first three chapters together. Chapter 4 details how to organize a software project using an incremental controlled lifecycle model. The budget is tied to the lifecycle phases, and the staffing plan is organized around the use of the UML.

4 PLANNING OBJECT-ORIENTED PROJECTS

"Manage the process, don't let the process manage you."

Khoa Nguyen, CEO Videoserver, Private Communication (1990)

This chapter marks a departure from the previous two in that we turn from the conceptual to the pragmatic. From now on, I will focus on the practical, day-to-day activities and issues of managing your project. It all begins with the Software Development Plan (SDP), which documents exactly how you intend to manage your program. It includes your:

Program deliverables, including all of the code, documentation, reports, and training you expect to deliver.

Choice of development lifecycle, including whatever tailoring of the cycle you plan. Document how you will apply the model to your particular development. For example, there may be special activities to support scoping and testing activities. This can include any special system testing.

Program staff organization, consisting of staff size and program roles, team structure and the allocation of responsibilities.

Required resources, including, but not limited to, equipment, software tools, and libraries.

Schedule, including planned dates for the delivery of code and documentation, and the major program milestones.

Work breakdown structure, comprising the tasks required to meet the schedule.

Program time-phased budget, which permits the tracking of progress and estimation of the final program costs.

Risk planning, identifying risks you expect and how to address them.

This chapter details not only how to organize a software development plan, but also how to determine its contents.

NOTE

The concepts discussed to this point can be applied to every software development project, not only object-oriented ones.

The industry has come to recognize the importance of SDPs. For example, the Software Engineering Institute (SEI), an organization that defines and measures software development, uses the Capability Maturity Model (CMM) to assess a software organization's ability to manage software development. It considers the consistent preparation of SDPs by all of the organization projects one of its primary requirements. The federal government requires SDPs as a part of its process for awarding government contracts; in fact, there are some standard military SDP formats. Other government entities and nongovernment clients also often require an SDP as part of an organization's bid. For these reasons, unfortunately, SDPs are often written just to pass a CMM evaluation or to meet a proposal requirement. In my view, this is wrong. You should write the SDP because it is the right thing to do. It should not be treated as an item to check off some list.

The SDP document itself is not as important as the act of preparing it. The preparation gives you the opportunity and forum in which to think through all of the issues listed. As the project manager, the SDP is your document, so prepare it with that in mind. It should describe your understanding of what needs to be done and how you intend to go about it. In effect, it defines the project. Use the SDP to communicate your intentions to your management and customer. If they accept the document, you can be assured that they concur with your approach to the program's management. Thus, preparing the SDP is the first step in taking charge of your project.

It is often said that you can't fight reality. So while preparing the SDP, address the reality of your project: the actual schedule and budget. Too many development plans rely on divine intervention and not solid management. If you have been handed an impossible schedule and budget, don't try to step up to do the impossible. Instead, prepare a plan and look for an opportunity to negotiate a reasonable schedule and budget. Without such a plan, you have no basis for negotiating a

Planning the Simulator

You have started planning to develop the simulator. From the description of the project, you understand that the two-year deadline is reasonably firm. You are concerned that this is not enough time and so have decided to look into the matter. You discover that it has been determined that the new aircraft is needed for a strategic mission. Based on this, a multibillion investment has been made in the aircraft, which will have little value unless pilots can be trained. The aircraft program manager has convinced the Pentagon that there is no need to build a trainer aircraft—that the simulators will suffice. The aircraft is in production and will be available for deployment in the two-year window. Unless you have a simulator available for training, the planes will sit idle, drawing a great deal of attention to your sponsor, your company, and yourself. In short, there is no relief. You have two years.

compromise or for convincing management that the task is impossible. Face it: You cannot build, for example, a manned simulator in three months, no matter how much it is needed. It is your job then to impose the discipline and focus that your management may be lacking.

So, write the plan not only because it is required by some process, but because you *need* to do the planning. The document is one of the tools you will use to communicate the plan and to reach a common understanding of the project with your team, your customer, and your management.

This chapter contains a summary of the components of an SDP and some practical advice on tailoring the content to object-oriented projects. We will explore each of the elements briefly, and then explore how to approach them in the object-oriented project.

Developing the SDP

The content of the Software Development Plan is more important than its form. This seemingly obvious fact is often overlooked when the focus is on adhering to process. If you have the content, you can deal with any SDP outline easily. However, creating a truly useful SDP is not easy. For mathematical types, it is a constrained optimization problem with incomplete data. If you put together your project's SDPs simply by assembling corporate boilerplates, you are doing you and your project a disservice. You will miss an opportunity to release a useful document.

To make the most of the SDP preparation, approach it as a problem-solving exercise. Recall that problem solving goes through these four phases: scoping, designing, implementing, and verifying. The early phases in particular apply to writing the SDP. As you will see, a successful plan implements each of the essential elements discussed earlier in this chapter into these phases.

Recognize that you will need help. First, assemble your planning team. The size of the team depends on the size of the project. At the very least, you need to have a development manager and an experienced architect. In many instances, you need an expert user or a domain expert. Each of the members of the team will focus on different aspects of the plan and the planning process. The development manager will look after the project organization, the work breakdown structure (WBS), and the time-phased budget. Ideally, the manager will take the lead development role once the project gets underway. The architect will provide the top-level diagram and the project sizing. The user/domain expert will help the team understand the requirements.

> **NOTE**
>
> Is the project planning activity part of the inception phase? There is room for debate on this point. True, preparation of the SDP involves the requirements analysis and design activities of the inception phase, but the desired outcomes of the SDP preparation and the inception phase are different. The outcome of the SDP planning activity is the *decision to proceed.* Ideally, an SDP supports a go/no-go decision. The completion of the SDP marks the point in time at which you have a clear view of how you will carry out the project. In some settings, such as competitive government procurements, the planning is a part of the more elaborate proposal preparation phase. The go/no-go decision is determined by whether your team wins the bid. The inception phase has a very different outcome: the development team's common understanding of what will be developed.
>
> Another difference between the two phases is the amount of committed investment. During the planning phase, a minimal amount of resources are committed, just enough to determine whether the project makes sense. A rule of thumb is that the planning should take between 5 percent and 10 percent of the expected labor cost of the development. Inception occurs after (more likely during) staffing ramp-up and may take as much as 25 percent of the labor expense.

Scoping the Plan

Before writing the SDP, ensure that you and your planning team have a clear understanding of the development problem. As for the project itself, develop a mental model of the problem. To achieve this level of understanding, assemble all of the available data related to the project. Then analyze the data to a point at which you can write a plan you can stand behind. During plan scoping, conduct the following activities:

- Define the problem

- Analyze the requirements

- Prepare a top-level package diagram

- Estimate the time and effort needed to deliver the product

Let us look at each of the activities.

Defining the Problem

In creating your SDP, you need to first figure which problem you are solving. Ask: What are the constraints and what are you optimizing? Here are some examples of development problems:

- Deliver the requirements (whatever they are) at minimal expense

- Deliver the requirements at a certain date no matter what the expense

- Given a fixed time and budget, deliver as many of the requirements as possible

- Optimize profit, taking into consideration the trade-offs between development expense, product features, service expense, and the market opportunity window

- Deliver all the requirements on a given time and budget

Each would lead to a different plan.

In practice, you may not be given such a clearly defined problem, and you may need to meet with the customer and management to pin down their expectations. You and they need to reach a clear agreement of exactly what constitutes success in your project—again, which problem you are solving. This understanding should be stated up front in the initial section of your planning document.

Posing the correct problem is not always easy. It is a fact of life that often the time-value of a product and the total development expense are out of balance. Your customer and/or manager knows the business worth of the project—what they are willing to pay for its development. They are less sure of what it will cost. Often the business value of the initially specified product does not support the budget. (A

> **NOTE**
>
> Often, you *are* expected to do the impossible: deliver all the require-
> ments with an inadequate schedule and/or budget. In that case, either
> have the problem reset to one that is more reasonable or simply bail out
> early. You are not doing you, your management, or your customer any
> favors by wasting resources on a guaranteed failure. In most instances,
> there is room for negotiation and the problem can be recast.

good rule of thumb is that for a commercial product, the development costs should
be from 14 percent to 18 percent of the anticipated revenue.) This explains the adversarial relationship than can develop between the executives of the company and
the development organization. The executives know what the business can bear
and are frustrated that the actual costs are higher. The development managers feel
they are constantly asked to do the impossible.

The program manager must bridge that gap and ensure that the development
plan is both executable and serves the business need. There is often room for discussion. For example, the executives or customers might be willing to forgo some
feature once they understand the cost and risk it brings to the project. It is your
job to resolve these issues. To do this, you must understand both the business context of the project and the development realities for your plan to achieve the right
balance.

> **TIP**
>
> Understand the customer's bottom line and plan accordingly.

In a commercial setting, the business context is driven by the *business case* for a
product. The business case is a spreadsheet that contains both marketing assumptions and development and service expenses. It includes the anticipated sales (depending on when the product hits the market); its price; and the expected
production, warranty, and service costs. From this data and your company's business model, you can determine the limits on your cost and schedule in order to
make your development a sound business investment.

If you are working as a contractor, other considerations come into play. If your
contract is to develop a high-tech prototype, there may be a fixed budget but a flexible schedule. On the other hand, if your contract is to deliver your software as part

of a large expensive program—say supporting a major war game—you may have no flexibility on the schedule. Perhaps your sponsor is counting on you to provide your product at a conference that has a fixed date. If you miss that date, your project is a failure. There are many other such development situations: internal tools development, a subsystem in a larger product release (such as an operating system or as embedded software in a manufactured product). You may have contracted to deliver software to another business, such as a bank that has a critical need for your work—and which may well sue your company if you fail. In each of these cases, you need to balance budget, schedule, and content. The bottom line is that you need to understand the customer's bottom line and plan accordingly.

FOR FURTHER READING

For another view on the different kinds of object projects, see Alistar Cockburn's *Surviving Object-Oriented Projects, A Manager's Guide*, published by Addison-Wesley in 1997.

Requirements Analysis

The customers' description of what they want—their requirements—is the second source of input to your plan. Of course, you start with the requirements document the customer supplies. As we have discussed before, however, customers rarely provide enough detail to specify an acceptable product. Thus, you need to expand and analyze those requirements to the point at which they can serve as the basis for a sizing estimate. This is easier said than done. Sometimes you can meet with your customer, sometimes you cannot. You might find that the customer is impatient with your tedious questions. Perhaps your customer is the marketing organization that can give only a conceptual definition of the product, such as, "The word processor will be responsive and productive, yet fun, and appeal to a younger user." In that case, your domain expert can serve as a surrogate customer, helping you refine the requirements to the point at which the project can be sized.

You may find that at this stage you simply do not have the budget to explore the requirements further and therefore must make intelligent guesses. Your objective then is to develop the best plan you can within this limited planning budget. I suggest you focus on creating some very high-level use cases (much like the description of the simulator found in Chapter 1). By working through the simulator example, you can understand the problem as a high-level of abstraction and establish a means for developing a cognitive model. Discuss your high-level use cases with your domain expert and, if possible, your customer.

Top-Level Package Diagram

Once your planning team has an initial understanding of the system's requirements, it's time to assemble a top-level package diagram. Your lead architect will create the diagram based on his or her best understanding of the requirements and his or her experience with building a similar system. The role of the diagrams in an object-oriented design, as discussed in Chapter 2, is to provide an object-oriented version of the system architecture by replacing the functional block diagrams found in earlier design methods.

The top-level diagram is the center of the entire planning process. It provides an early view of the overall system that will be built that all can share. As explained in the following section, it also provides input to the estimation process. The sizing of the total effort is reached by sizing each of the packages. The WBS consists of tasks that implement the packages. The staff will be organized around meeting these tasks. For example, consider the overly simple check verification system shown in Figure 4.1. The system consists of a data entry application in which the store owner enters the check data. The application then dials a server that downloads the data and checks its database to see if the check is valid, and returns an acceptance code and a server application. The top-level diagram consists of the entry application that receives the dial, checks its format, and dials the server, the server application, the database, and the dial-up services. Both the client and server application rely on the dial-up services. As a manager, you will plan around building (or buying) the code that implements each of these packages.

Estimating Your Project's Size and Effort

Armed with your understanding of the problem and the top-level diagram, you are ready to estimate how much effort (person months) it will take to deliver the system and, in turn, to determine a realistic budget and schedule. The estimates round out your understanding of the program. Once they are in place, you have a view of what is required, what you will build (the package diagram), and the effort required.

There is an inverse relationship between the amount of money invested in the program and the quality of the estimate. Estimates made during the planning stage, before there has been much investment, are most useful, but they are not very accurate. Of course, your ability to estimate program size, duration, and expense improves as you proceed into the development cycle. The more you know about the effort, the better you can estimate. By the end of the project, you are able to be 100 percent accurate in your estimates. So, there is a balancing act between the quality of the estimate and project investment. You should strive to have sufficiently accurate estimates to support a go/no-go decision before 5 percent of the initial budget

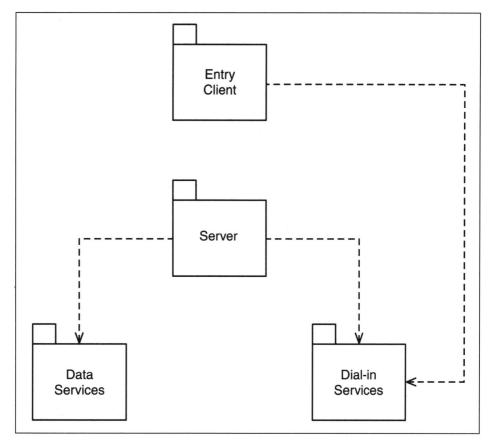

Figure 4.1 *Top-level package diagram for the check verification system.*

is spent. If you spend 30 percent of the budget and discover the original budget is only a quarter of what you need, your managers will be justifiably upset.

In practice, you should do the initial estimate once you have the package diagram and before you have the detailed estimate use cases. Barry Boehm shows that error bounds for effort estimates are commonly from .5 times to 2 times the actual effort at the onset of requirements analysis. With the package diagram in hand, you should get within 25 percent of the actual value. This is why these estimates are sometimes called *rough order of magnitude (ROM)*.

Even with an expected error bound of up to 25 percent, the schedule and budget estimates have several uses. First, you can use the estimates to determine feasibility of the project—whether you can deliver the system within the available budget and schedule. If your estimates show that the effort is out of line with the schedule and budget, you are ready to go back to the management with a no-go decision, and you have the data and analysis you need to back up the bad news.

Second, the cost and schedule estimates are needed to create the budget and staffing plan. Even if you have a fixed schedule and/or budget, the estimates will help to determine what can reasonably be expected to be delivered during the fixed duration or for the fixed budget. In addition, the practice of carrying out the estimate is useful in finding opportunities to improve productivity.

Third, the estimation process itself will teach you much about the management of your project. It forces you to assess the opportunity for reuse, the experience of the staff, the modularity of the design, team cohesion, process maturity, and so on.

Finally, making estimates and tracking them throughout the project is a step in organization process maturity. Over time, you can use the estimates to calibrate your organization. It forces you to look at productivity as measured by klocs/programmer-year (klocs = thousand lines of code). This measure of productivity has been maintained throughout the software industry for many years. Purchasers of software services often use it as a determination of the competitiveness of your organization.

In practice, you need to develop five estimates:

Size. Lines of code, function points, number of modules, number of classes.

Effort. The product of the number of persons and the duration in months.

Duration. Number of months it will take to deliver the product.

Productivity. Size divided by effort.

Development Cost. The labor cost of the effort.

The estimation procedure starts with a rough sizing. As discussed in more detail in the following section, size estimates are derived from your understanding of the requirements and the top-level diagram.

Once sizing is in place, proceed to the other variables. Unfortunately, they cannot be approached one at a time because they all depend on each other. For example, the effort depends on the sizing, the complexity of the code, the productivity, and the number of programmers you plan to assign (which determines the cost). This is due to the fact that productivity declines with the number of programmers. Similarly, the duration depends on the number of programmers. Presumably, more programmers can get the work done faster. The reality is that accelerating the schedule by adding more programmers will lower productivity and raises cost.

Measuring Productivity by Lines of Code

We need some measure of the size of the project and of productivity. To date, the only universally recognized measure is number of lines of code. But even this needs to be qualified in terms of which language and whether it is ported, reused, generated, or entirely new. So, though everyone seems to count lines of code, no one is happy about it. The assumption that the amount of time it takes to write a line of code is a useful number seems ludicrous. It supports the "Dilbertian" mode of thought that lines of code are like lightbulbs falling (gently, I hope) off the end of an assembly line.

All estimates of size have problems. The main advantage of lines of code is that unlike function points, they can be counted automatically. Classes, while more meaningful than lines of code, can vary in size and effort. The advocates of function points probably have the best case. However, function points are more useful for estimating the size of data processing applications than scientific computing or highly interactive programs, such as our simulator. One of the strengths of this approach is that it provides a language-independent view of productivity. Function points per person-months is more meaningful than lines of code per person-month. However, function points are not universally accepted. In particular, their applicability to scientific programming, embedded systems, and the like has been questioned.

It is important that your organization choose *some* consistent measure of size; but be prepared to report on productivity in terms of lines of code. This may be the only way executives or contracting agencies have of comparing the relative productivity of organizations.

I recommend that once your team is sufficiently competent at object-oriented designs, and when classes have adequate modularity, you adopt classes rather than lines of code as a measure of size. A good rule of thumb for making the transition is that, in a good design, the average class has about 60 lines of code. Incidentally, defects-per-class is a more meaningful measure of quality than defects-per-kloc. More on that later.

Here is one way through this maze. Start by making your best guess of productivity. This guess should be based on your previous experience and your consideration of a number of other factors:

- Program size
- Amount of reuse
- Experience of the staff
- Your ability to staff
- Modularity of the design
- Code complexity
- Team cohesion
- Process maturity
- Choice of language
- Nature of the application
- Efficiency of the programming environment
- Requirements stability

A single programmer using Visual Basic to build a back-office application will experience much higher productivity than a programmer using C++ as a part of a team that is building an operating system. He or she need not spend time dealing with team members. In addition, he or she has a less complex program and a more efficient programming language. (Note however: My teams using Java programming environments in the right context have exhibited unprecedented productivity. The data is not yet in, but the rules may have changed.)

Once you have guessed your team productivity, use the allocated schedule to assume the duration. With these values of productivity and effort in place, the effort is the quotient of size and productivity. To complete your development cost, you will also need your *labor mix*—the cost per hour for each category of labor used in your project. A labor mix example is given in Table 4.1. Your organization will most likely have a larger number of categories. As a project manager, you need to be familiar with them. From this, you can derive an average cost per hour and an estimated cost by multiplying the effort by the average labor cost.

FOR FURTHER READING

To learn more about function points, see Capers Jones *Applied Software Measurement,* second edition, published by McGraw-Hill in 1996.

Table 4.1 Labor Mix

LABOR CATEGORY	$/HR
Senior Manager	100
Manager	75
Senior Developer	75
Developer	60
Junior Developer	50
Technical Writer	35
Administrator	25

Parkinson's Law

In 1957, C. Northcote Parkinson, an English economist, published a series of essays entitled *Parkinson's Law.* These humorous essays addressed different aspects of organizational efficiency. In passing, he observed that work expands to fill a vacuum: That is, if, for example, you have allocated six hours to accomplish a job that could be done in six minutes, you will take six hours. (This by the way is not Parkinson's Law. The law refers to the rate of growth of bureaucratic organizations. He observed that the growth is independent of the workload).

His observation was so compelling that it has become known as the *Parkinson effect* (some texts refer to it as the Parkinson estimation). The generalized form of the Parkinson effect is that a development job will take exactly as much time as allotted: That is, if you tell me I have two years, then the job will take two years.

The effect is real. Teams do seem to pace themselves in order to meet a deadline. I am amazed at how often a 12-month program is delivered with minutes to spare. If a team feels there is plenty of time, they will not finish early. Instead, the team will add content to fill in the extra time. Without explicit management of this effect, the team will add content right up to the deadline—adding risk and creating an unnecessary crisis situation. Watch out.

Estimation Methods

Of all the estimation methods, I have found three to be useful in sizing object-oriented projects. Each calls for input from an expert or, better yet, experts for each package.

- System analogy
- Package-level analogy
- Parametric models

I will address each of them in turn.

FOR FURTHER READING

See William Roetzheim's and Reyna A. Beasley's *Software Project Cost & Schedule Estimating Best Practice,* published by Prentice-Hall in 1997.

System Analogy

The system analogy method consists of estimating the effort, productivity, and cost of a system development by assuming these values are similar to those of a similar system. If your organization has already built a system with the same requirements, you have a baseline of experience to use. In this case, have a few of your software engineers read over the requirements, look over the familiar package diagram, and come up with an estimate. Keep in mind that the consensus of three or more experts is likely to be more accurate. Statistics teach us that the average of a large number of estimates of a value is likely to be more accurate than any one estimate. Averaging the estimates of several experts is sometimes called the *Delphi* technique, named for the home of the famous Oracle of Apollo who was believed to be able to predict the future. Note, this technique only works if your organization has enough relevant experience.

Package-Level Analogy

The package-level analogy technique entails applying expert opinion at the package level rather than at the system level. Even if you have never built a similar system, presumably you have access to expertise in the component technology. The technique consists of estimating the time and effort for each of the packages individually, taking into account the extent to which they interact with the other packages and the total integration. Also do code estimates for each package.

To apply this approach, an expert estimates each of the packages separately in the implementation of that package. If you have a technical lead in mind for a package, have him or her do the estimate. The estimates should include both size and effort. This way you can and should compare the productivity assumption behind each of the estimates. If one package estimate comes in at ten times the productivity of another, a mental alarm should sound. Ask questions to identify the differences and make the required adjustments. Once you have the component size and effort estimates, sum them and put in the additional effort for the system: integration and system test, program managers, program technical leadership, customer delivery, documentation, and the other collateral efforts to reach the total effort and size. These values, along with the planned development duration and labor mix, provide what you need to complete the budget estimates.

The package analogy method works for several reasons. First, it takes advantage of the internalized mental model of the package experts. These people are so close to the issues that their intuitions are surprisingly reliable. Each of the package estimates then has some reasonable probability of being correct. Second, it is a well-known statistical principle that combining several independent estimates yields a better estimate than separate estimates. In practice, this means the errors are randomly distributed about the correct value. It is likely there are as many overestimates as underestimates. The errors balance so that the combined estimates are useful. When this is applied, to say, six or more estimates, you have a fighting chance to deliver the program with the combined budget—with one caveat: You must closely watch the budget for each of the packages with the expectation that budget allocations will have to be adjusted. How to do this will be addressed in Chapter 9 on tracking and oversight.

One more warning. Estimates resulting from this method are often proportional to the programmers' motivation to work on the project. If the team wants to do the work, the estimates will be low. If they would rather be working on something else, the estimates will be high. You can spot this phenomenon by comparing the implied productivity against historical experience. Programmers generally are an optimistic, motivated lot, so estimates are usually low. The wise manager will raise the estimates as a part of the planning. If you think the estimates are high, proceed to lower them with caution. Work with the team to determine whether there are reasons for expected low productivity. If the problem is one of motivation, address the issue head on and achieve buy-in. Starting a project with an unresolved difference in estimates will only motivate your team to prove they are right.

Pert Estimation   Pert estimation provides a refinement of the package-level analogy and system analogy techniques. It uses nonparametric statistical estimators to refine the initial expert opinion. To apply Pert estimation, each of your experts must not only estimate the expected size, as in the package analogy method, but also the smallest possible size (the *optimistic* estimate) and the largest possible size (the *pessimistic* estimate.)

Using the Package-Level Analogy Method to Size the Simulator Project

As you approach the simulator project, you assess your overall situation. Fortunately, you work for a mature development organization, and your processes, procedures, and development and design tools are in place. You access the staff you need in-house, and so can depend on a level of competence, not only in software design and implementation, but also in the use of the tools. There is no need to train new employees.

You will do your development in a combination of C++ and Java. Your architect has decided to use CORBAservices to link the Java and C++ components. You have staff who are experienced with both languages. And though you do not have an expert in pilot training, you can make arrangements to hire a consultant. You have been assigned a lead architect who has never built a manned flight simulator. However, she is very talented and has analogous experience building shipboard weapons control simulators.

Your team does not know how to build the interfaces to the flight controls and so you need to hire an outside firm. This adds risk, but what can you do? Fortunately, a qualified firm has been identified and is onboard. During the planning phase, you were able to construct Table 4.2.

As you can see in the table, you will need about 1,200 person-months of effort over two years. This comes to about 50 developers. This estimate is incomplete, as it does not include the test and integration team, quality assurance, tool support, the technical writers, and the technical and managerial leadership.

Also, any one of the package estimates is suspect, but your working assumption, based on previous experience, is that the combined estimate is within 25 percent of the actual effort.

Your labor mix is like those in Table 4.1. Your next step is to put together your schedule, staffing plan, and time-phased budget.

Table 4.2 Package-Level Estimate of the Simulator Project

Package	New Lines of Code	Person-Months	Productivity Loc/PM	Comments
Geographical Data Server	1,000	4	250.00	A mature, well-designed server exists and needs only to be integrated in the product.
Weather Server	10,000	36	277.78	A weather server exists, but will require some rework to integrate into the project. The original design team is available.
Trainer System	10,000	18	555.56	This will be built in Java using a toolkit. The line-of-code estimate is not as important as the number of windows, screens, and so on.
Checkpoint Manager	5,000	24	208.33	The Checkpoint Manager is entirely new code. The decision has been made to use an object database. Staff who understand the use of the object database are available, but generally are clueless as to what data needs to be stored. This code is thought to be harder and more risky than the Scenario Manager.
Scenario Manager	7,500	48	156.25	The Scenario Manager is entirely new code. The decision has been made to use an object database. Staff who understand the use of the object database are available, but generally are clueless as to what data needs to be stored.
Threat Server	1,000	12	83.33	You have access to a Threat Server that you plan to reuse. The server's development team is intact and onboard. However, you are not sure that the current Threat Manager really meets all of the requirements.
Weapons Model	30,000	240	125.00	The weapons for this system are still under development. You have little basis for estimate here. You are very concerned about requirements stability.

(continues)

Table 4.2 Package-Level Estimate of the Simulator Project (*Continued*)

PACKAGE	NEW LINES OF CODE	PERSON-MONTHS	PRODUCTIVITY LOC/PM	COMMENTS
Event/Time Manager	7,500	24	312.50	Your team has built numerous Event Managers. This one seems to be business as usual.
World Model	5,000	24	208.33	You do not have access to a working World Model that is suitable for the project. However, the weapon systems simulator has a similar functionality and so you expect to reuse some of that design. Unfortunately the designers of that code have all left to form their own firm.
Aircraft Model	0	24	0.00	You have been assured that a complete, verified, dynamics model of the aircraft is available. That said, reuse is not ever free.
Controls	15,000	240	62.50	A subcontractor will provide this code. However, you have not worked with this firm before and are not sure what it is providing. Its representative will work on-site. Fortunately, they will provide the actual cockpit simulator.
Instrument Display	30,000	260	115.38	There are 150 instruments with various level of sophistication, all needing input. Again, the contractor is supplying the hardware interfaces, causing the same uncertainty as for the controls.
Out the Window	25,000	240	104.17	Graphical real-time display is not one of your areas of expertise. However, there is a team within the company that has the tools, know-how, and experience.
TOTAL	147,000	1,194	123.12	The estimate of 120 lines of code per person-month is not great productivity, but not out of line for a project of this complexity.

The Pert equations for the expected value, E, and the standard deviation, SD, are:

$$E = (a + 4b + c)/6$$

$$SD = (c-a)/6$$

where

a = the optimistic estimate

b = the expected value

c = the pessimistic estimate

According to this technique, the actual size will fall between E–SD and E+SD 68 percent of the time. The value of SD gives you a view of the schedule and budget risk associated with the estimate. The larger the SD, the greater the uncertainty.

To apply the Pert technique to the system analogy technique, simply average the individual estimates of a, b, c, and apply the equations to the averages. In the case of the package-level analogy, sum the a, b, and c estimates over the packages, then apply the equations to the sums. The result in both cases is an estimate and standard deviation for the entire system. You should apply Pert to project size and effort separately. This gives you a view of both schedule and budget risk.

Parametric Models

A parametric model lets you estimate effort from an explicit set of variables: program size, function points, program capability, facilities, modularity, and so on. The parametric model is based on a set of statistical assumptions and mathematical equations that express how the effort estimate depends on the parameters. It is calibrated by fitting the model to the measured productivity of a set of real projects.

Applying the parametric model takes the package-level analogy to another level of detail. The technical expert, rather than relying on gut feeling and experience to estimate the effort, uses his or her insight to assign values to the parameters. All parametric models consist of numerous variables each of which must involve some subjective judgments. Each of the parameter values is tantamount to an informed guess. A parametric model essentially replaces several informed guesses with one informed guess.

There are several parametric estimation tools available. Some of the commercially available tools use proprietary algorithms, while others require an element of faith. Certain of these claim to be tailored to object-oriented projects. But the ones I have seen do not consider use cases as a measure of requirements, but rather seem

Pert Estimation of the Stealth Simulator

You have some doubts about the accuracy of the estimates, but you decide to go ahead and apply the Pert method at the package level to get a better understanding of the estimate. Table 4.3 contains the Pert size estimates for the simulator and Table 4.4 contains the Pert effort estimates for the simulator.

Note the general trend that the expected values are closer to the optimistic values than to the pessimistic values. Overall, you have an optimistic bias, reflected by the calculation of E and SD:

$$E = \frac{109{,}000 + 4 \times 147{,}000 + 198{,}000}{6} = 149{,}167$$

$$SD = \frac{198{,}000 - 109{,}000}{6} = 14{,}833$$

The expected value E=149,167 is more than 2,000 lines of code over your initial estimate. Your SD is almost 15,000. Thus, a more reasonable code estimate is between 135,000 and 164,000 lines of code. As a prudent manager, you communicate your initial estimate at 150 klocs, plus or minus 15 klocs. The round numbers reinforce the approximate nature of the numbers.

It follows that

$$E = 1215$$

$$SD = 61$$

This estimate is 20 person-months higher than the original. Not too bad; that is one person over the two years. However, the SD is 2.5 persons over two years. You decide you are more confident in reporting the required development effort at 1,250 person months. The implied productivity is about 1,500 lines of code/py (person-year) overall. Using the rule of 75 lines of code per class, this is 20 classes per person-year, the equivalent of about 6,000 lines of code per person-year of C, and so is plenty aggressive.

Table 4.3 Pert Data Simulator Project Size

PACKAGE	NEW LINES OF CODE		
	A	B	C
Geographical Data Server	750	1,000	2,000
Weather Server	8,000	10,000	15,000
Trainer System	8,500	10,000	15,000
Checkpoint Manager	4,000	5,000	6,500
Scenario Manager	6,000	7,500	9,000
Threat Server	750	1,000	2,000
Weapons Model	20,000	30,000	40,000
Event/Time Manager	6,500	7,500	9,000
World Model	4,500	5,000	6,000
Aircraft Model	0	0	1,000
Controls	10,000	15,000	17,500
Instrument Display	20,000	30,000	35,000
Out the Window	20,000	25,000	40,000
TOTAL	109,000	147,000	198,000

Table 4.4 Pert Data for Simulator Effort

PACKAGE	PERSON MONTHS		
	A	B	C
Geographical Data Server	3.00	4.00	8.00
Weather Server	30.00	36.00	42.00
Trainer System	14.00	18.00	20.00
Checkpoint Manager	18.00	24.00	30.00
Scenario Manager	42.00	48.00	54.00
Threat Server	12.00	12.00	24.00
Weapons Model	240.00	240.00	300.00
Event/Time Manager	12.00	24.00	28.00
World Model	12.00	24.00	28.00
Aircraft Model	12.00	24.00	24.00
Controls	240.00	240.00	300.00
Instrument Display	220.00	260.00	320.00
Out the Window	220.00	240.00	260.00
TOTAL	1,075.00	1,194.00	1,438.00

mainly concerned with measures of object complexity (such as depth of inheritance). Certainly, it is true you can add effort by making your designs unnecessarily complex, but that insight does not help in planning. The literature on sizing object-oriented projects is remarkably sparse. Therefore, I recommend considering Barry Boehm's Constructive Cost Model (COCOMO) family of models.

COCOMO   The original COCOMO models were released in 1981, and are now the most widely accepted models. For instance, the Air Force, Navy, and NASA all use tailored versions of COCOMO in evaluating proposals. The most recent version, COCOMO 2.0, was released in 1995. The models are freely available from the COCOMO Web site (sunset.usc.edu/COCOMO/) and the algorithms are published. Furthermore, the COCOMO parameters are customizable to your circumstances. Commercial implementations of the model are also available.

COCOMO 2 consists of three models:

Application. Used for applications comprising user interfaces, a database, and a report generator. Many office applications, such as personnel systems, patient tracking systems, and the like, are examples. The model assumes that the developer will use productivity tools such as Java Workshop or Visual Basic, along with a database or spreadsheet application. The input to this model consists of object points—screens, reports, and data files. According to Boehm, most development falls under this model. If you have a large back-office application, you may well find yourself in charge of a team of developers where this model may be appropriate.

Early design. A limited version of the full model, this is intended to be used prior to any architecture analysis and so is requirements-driven. While it accepts line-of-code estimates, it is targeted to those that use function points as a measure of size. (Recall that function points are a way of translating requirements into program size.) If your organization already uses function points, then you might find this model of use. Otherwise, I suggest using the post-architecture model.

Post-architecture. Used to get a view of the project's cost once an initial architecture is in place, but prior to detailed design. This model assumes a lifecycle has been chosen. This is probably the most useful model for the readers of this book because the initial package-level design provides sufficient detail to apply this model. Another advantage is that it bridges most cleanly to the previous COCOMO models. Its includes six overall project scale parameters such as requirements volatility and phasing of activities. Also, for each component (package), the model includes not only size of new and adapted code for each component, but also 17 parameters that affect the productivity of each component.

FOR FURTHER READING

To learn more about the COCOMO model, read the article "Cost Models for Future Software Lifecycle Processes: COCOMO 2.0," by Barry Boehm, Bradford Clark, Ellis Horowitz, and Chris Westland in *Annals of Software Engineering* (v. 1, pp. 57–94,1995). Also check out NASA's *Parametric Cost-Estimating Handbook*, available online at www.jsc.nasa.gov /bu2/pcehg.html. Softstar Systems, too, provides a commercial implementation of the COCOMO model. Its Web site, http://www.softstarsystems .com/, contains both useful information and a set of links.

Practical Advice

It is essential that you make estimates. It is also essential that you enlist the input of the technical experts to do so. This gives you and them the opportunity to discuss assumptions and the development approach. Their buy-in is essential. If you can agree at this stage, they are more likely to be supportive when the project starts. Working together on the sizing is a first step toward you and the leads coming to a common view on solving the problem. It is a step towards team formation.

Use the system's top-level package diagram as component input to the package analogy or the parametric model. Note that both of these methods require expert input. In fact, the parametric model can be thought of as a more detailed method of capturing the expert input. Estimating from the package level has several advantages:

- It encourages consideration of how the development of each package will be approached.
- Aggregate estimates are superior to single estimates.
- The packages will drive staffing and budgeting; thus there will be continuity and traceability from the initial estimates to the actual expenses. This in turn, will help drive process improvement.

I strongly recommend that you use the Pert estimators, which involves only marginal additional effort, and you will be rewarded with somewhat better estimates. More important, the standard deviation computation gives you a way of more accurately communicating the nature of your estimate. Remember, management and customers will hold you to your estimates; over time, they will forget their tentative nature. Discussing the standard deviations from the beginning is a way of reinforcing the risk associated with the use of estimates. Further, the practice of considering and collecting the optimistic and pessimistic estimates gains you some insight on the biases of your team.

I also recommend learning to use the appropriate COCOMO models. Though, the learning curve in adopting the model is not worth the effort for a single project, the adoption of a parametric model such as COCOMO plays a major role in organization maturity. If your entire organization adopts the model, you will have a consistent, repeatable estimation process. Further, as you gain experience with the model, and have the opportunity to compare actuals against the estimates, you can calibrate the model to your organization, which will lead to better estimates. The model parameters also identify focus areas for productivity improvement. The models account for the loss of productivity with size, and reward object-oriented design principles such as modularity and managed complexity. Finally, if you do contract work, a COCOMO estimate can help you determine the bid price. Many government agencies require a version of a COCOMO estimate in software proposals.

Designing the SDP

With the completion of the estimates, scoping is complete, and you have enough information in hand to design the SDP. In this context, designing means creating all of the material that comprises an SDP. The actual building—in this case, writing—of the SDP is the document creation. This section helps you to determine the content.

Develop the SDP elements in the following order:

1. Deliverables.
2. Development environment.
3. Size and effort estimates.
4. Risk planning.
5. Choice of lifecycle model.
6. Work breakdown structure (WBS).
7. Schedules.
8. Staffing and organization.
9. Time-phased budget.
10. Program metrics identification and collection strategy.

This reflects a logical order. First you determine what you must deliver, then you identify the best tools to build the deliverables. These decisions impact the sizing and so on. (Note, however, the actual SDP document may have a different outline.)

Deliverables

Deliverables are the items your team must prepare and hand over to someone; they are the tangible output of the program. Each item must be planned, budgeted, and managed. The types of items your plan should consider are:

- Customer products
- Process artifacts
- Internal deliverables
- Services

A project's products are the items a customer needs to have a fully usable system. The product deliverables include not only the executable code, but also the user manuals, help files, installation scripts, and installation manuals. Depending on the nature of the project, your delivery might also include tutorials, examples, templates, developer manuals, license managers, and interface documents. You must assign resources to the development of these products and establish a method for coordinating their content. But keep in mind that the content of these products may change throughout the development cycle.

Process artifacts consist of those items that your team develops in the course of the development effort. Examples might include use-case databases, object model design files, design documents, or even source code. Sometimes, your customers will expect delivery of these items; sometimes they will not. If when they do, the artifacts require more polish and preparation, your plan must account for this effort.

Internal deliverables are those items that have value to your organization *beyond* the product delivery. They include development artifacts that capture the intellectual content created during the project, such as requirements documents and test plans. In addition, there may be artifacts required to support product maintenance. Among the items you need to plan for are source code libraries, test libraries (including regression tests), make files, problem report database, and requirements and design documentation.

Services are the efforts your organization may be expected be deliver *in addition* to the development of the product and the other deliverables. These may be offered in association with your product. Examples include training, consulting, installation, on-site support, or customization. You may or may not be directly involved in the service offerings, but in either case, the service delivery will affect your staffing and team organization, and so must be accounted for in the plan.

Development Environment

The development environment consists of all the hardware and software required to develop the product efficiently. It includes choice of workstations, design tools, editors, compilers, and the like. Putting the development environment in place takes time: The adoption of tools is often expensive and risky; the team may need training. For these reasons, you must plan your development environment with care. Addressing the construction of a complete development environment with all its choices and considerations is beyond the scope of this section, so here I discuss how to choose design tools and adopt them in an orderly manner. Later in this chapter, I discuss the issues and trade-offs.

Object technology promises increased productivity, but it comes at a price. In order for the team to be fully efficient, you need a well-integrated development environment. In particular, your team will need an object design tool that enables them to take full advantage of the techniques discussed in the book. However, as explained shortly, software tools are expensive and their adoption is not without risk. The costs include not only the per-seat licenses, but also the less obvious support and training costs. The learning curve, too, can impact the schedule. Many organizations cannot take the time to train staff in the use of a new tool set, so they learn on the job—that is, on your project.

There is another more subtle and insidious risk in the adoption of tools. Many immature development organizations adopt tools in lieu of adopting process, believing that using the tools will itself establish a process and enforce a discipline. In fact, exactly the reverse occurs. Adding tools to a chaotic situation will only amplify the chaos.

One of the difficulties of adopting design tools is caused by the state of the design tool industry, which is providing complicated software to a small and fragmented market. For example, code generation needs to support ANSI C++, ADA 95, and whatever version of Java is out this week. Design language standards are still emerging, so it is hardly surprising that the tools are not mature. And it gets worse. A lot of other tools should be integrated with the design tools, such as user-interface builders, requirements trackers, automated test generators, and code analysis tools. To my knowledge, no effort is underway to integrate these tools easily. Further, no one seems to be working on common data formats. Frankly, there are too many possible choices. Fortunately, though, there is light on the horizon: Tool providers are being shaken out; others are being consolidated. Hopefully, we will be seeing fewer, but more robust choices soon. For now, remember: Tools are effective only if they make well-understood processes more efficient. The rule is, first understand your processes, then choose your tools.

> **TIP**
>
> Tools are effective only if they make well-understood processes more efficient.

Adopting Design Tools

For the purpose of this section, I assume that your organization has a code development environment in place, consisting of editors, compilers, linkers, and debuggers. I also assume that you are familiar with configuration management and version control tools, and that you will follow some variant of the controlled iterative lifecycle model. Further, though I don't endorse a particular design tool, there are some clear leaders. You should evaluate design tools from two perspectives:

- Support of the lifecycle
- Risk of adoption to both cost and schedule

Lifecycle Support   The purpose of adopting software design tools is to facilitate the processes and activities of managing an object-oriented project. Armed with the knowledge you gain from this book, keep the following question in mind: Does the tool define my processes or make my processes more efficient? Here are some of the features I consider crucial in a tool:

UML support. Does the tool support all of the UML artifacts you plan to use? In particular, does it support both static and dynamic diagrams? Are use cases supported? Is there a way to trace classes back to sequence diagrams and use cases? Are the sequence diagrams and class diagrams always in synch? Will the same model file work if you migrate from C++ to Java? Is the Common Object Request Broker Architecture (CORBA) Interface Description Language supported?

Management oversight and control. Does the tool report on model consistency, modularity measures (methods per class), or other complexity measures (depth of inheritance)? Is there a way to track stability in terms of number of use cases and classes entered and implemented? Can you assign classes to individuals?

Architectural control. Does the tool support package diagrams? Does it prevent entering associations that are not specified in the higher-level diagrams?

Does the tool enforce the directionality of associations specified in the higher-level diagrams?

Collaboration support. Does the tool support collaboration by allowing the model file to be broken up into separate files with separate read/write permissions? Does the tool link to your current configuration manager? Is the granularity flexible enough to allow for assignment of classes? Does the tool support branching and merging of model files in the same manner as code version controls?

Developer efficiency. Is a code generator available that does not overwrite the body code? Is there a way to tailor the code-generation properties at the package or class level? How many mouse clicks does it take to do code generation? Is there a way to create a development environment in which the developer maintains an active design view, a source code view, and debugger view of the same code simultaneously? How difficult is it to capture any design changes entered into the source code using the tool's reverse engineering features?

Library integration. Is there a mechanism for including class diagrams for existing packages in the design files? Is it possible to include only facade classes, or is it necessary to include the entire library? How do you include classes generated by development toolkits or user-interface builders? Is there a way to integrate object-oriented databases?

Hard copy, documentation support. Does the package support publication of the artifacts in word processing tools or in HTML?

Rest assured, there are tools for which the answer is yes in most categories. If the tool you are considering does not meet this standard, move on and find one that does.

Cost and Scheduling Risks   In choosing a design tool, be aware of the risks and costs associated with the decision. Here is my short list of concerns:

External costs. These are the standard costs: licenses, maintenance, and training. I have found that some vendors expect that you will buy training and consulting materials along with the licenses. If you do not purchase them, many companies are not forthcoming with support and answers to questions. In short, you have a choice, buy the support or assume the risk.

Internal costs. These include the labor or consulting costs associated with installing the tools and integrating them into your environment. The other tools may need to be tailored as well. Once the tool is installed, the work of setting up the property files, the code-generation target directories, and the like begins. Plan to devote about a half a person for the duration of the project to custom-tailor the tool. Some tool vendors advertise their flexibility as a virtue. They provide a macro language, which means their product can meet any process as long as you write and maintain the macros. Don't be fooled: This product strategy only moves the development effort from their shoulders to yours. They have added a lot of cost to the tool. I don't know about you, but I have no in-terest in devoting valuable developer time to maintaining macros in a develop-ment environment. I prefer to buy a more expensive tool that actually meets the majority of my needs.

Time loss. Your team will at first lose time learning to use the tool, so it is best if you can plan and conduct the training, which must include how the tool fits into your development process. This can add a couple of weeks to the program. If your environment does not provide 100 percent access to the tool (due to network instability or problems with the license server), your productivity can drop to zero. If you do not buy enough licenses, and programmers lose time waiting for license availability, you get what you deserve.

Product instability. You are betting your project and maybe your career on the tool. If it has the latest features but regularly trashes the data files, it probably was a bad choice. This is not a time to be a pioneer. Choose a tool others with similar projects have used successfully. Do not rely on new features for any-thing critical. Finally, assess the quality of the product support.

Investment protection. As mentioned, the software development tool industry is not yet mature or stable. Choosing a tool, therefore, requires an investment in time and money. It would be unfortunate if you get up to speed on a tool and then have it disappear; so pick one from a vendor that will be around for a while.

Recommendation

In the face of all these concerns and risks, I still strongly recommend that you adopt a design tool. There *are* tools mature enough to warrant adoption. In fact, I do not know how you will succeed without one. That said, be conservative in your choice. Choose a widely adopted tool from a secure company. Some of the leading tools are Rose by Rational Software, Software through Pictures by Aonix, and ObjectTeam by Cayenne Software. And of course, focus on process facilitation, not the latest bells and whistles.

If at all possible, you train your staff. If that is not possible, add time to your schedules to account for the ramp-up time.

One complication of using design tools is that the configuration management task is more complex. A code release consists of both source files and design files. The same discipline and coordination issues that arise in team source code development apply to the team development of design files. Therefore, integrate the tool with a configuration management system. The developers should be able to check out and check in the design from within the tool.

Finally, you will need one or more tool champions, usually team members who learn the tool and can serve as consultants to the rest of the team. Even if your team is trained, a developer may get stuck on some simple point. Surprisingly, some developers are not particularly good at learning new tools. Having internal experts to get them over the hurdles is very helpful.

Size and Effort Estimates

I have already discussed estimating the project's size and effort requirements. You would be wise to revisit the estimates again in this phase. You may have forgotten something; perhaps you did not include preparation of all the deliverables.

Risk Planning

Your plan needs to identify those risks your particular project is facing and how you plan to meet them. The SDP often contains a section capturing thoughts on this matter. Your plan should contain a risk identification, mitigation table in which you identify the features of the program that may add risk, along with how your plan addresses the risk. Table 4.5 is an example.

Other so-called risk items such as staffing (the inability to staff) or technical (uncertainty about how to design the code) put the project in jeopardy only to the extent that they affect schedule, cost, or customer satisfaction. The risks should be captured under one of the categories. For example, the inability to staff can be considered as a schedule risk—although it may cause budget risk as well since you may have to use expensive contract programmers. I have found that some of the process weenies (process experts are "weenies" just as design experts are "gurus," go figure) go overboard with extensive risk tables. In my experience, being forced to fill out these tables reduces risk analysis to a fill-in-the-blanks activity.

Lifecycle Model

This section of the SDP delineates the lifecycle model you choose to follow and whatever modification or tailoring you have planned. You should briefly discuss

Table 4.5 A Risk Identification/Mitigation Table

CATEGORY	RISK ITEM	PLANNED MITIGATION
Cost	Uncertainty in sizing.	Revisit at phase transitions.
	Open ended requirements in some areas.	Develop use-case database.
	Staff at several sites may need extensive travel; temporary relocations.	Use intranet and collaboration tools to avoid travel and relocation.
Schedule	Dependency on contractor.	Assign liaison, contractor, IPT participation.
	Lack of adequate staff.	Hire contractor labor.
	Staff unfamiliar with some tools.	Training program planned and budgeted.
Customer Satisfaction	Lack of explicit operational requirements.	Develop use cases, requirements review, multiple build.
	Long development period; needs may change.	Prioritize requirements to build most important features in early builds. Revisit requirements yearly.

each of the phases, activities, and milestones at this point. In addition, identify and address any special circumstances. For example, this section might contain how you intend to handle the transition phases: where the system tests will take place, and the level of customer involvement. Another example is whether you plan customer site visits as an inception activity.

Work Breakdown Structure (WBS)

In Chapter 1, I pointed out that when faced with any large, complex system you should break it into manageable pieces. The Work Breakdown Structure (WBS) consists of the complete list of tasks and subtasks required to complete the program. The elements of a WBS are discrete tasks or work packages that can be separately planned and budgeted. Examples of WBS items might include "writing the test plan" or "user interface development."

The structure of the WBS should support both budget tracking and status reporting. Project management tools are designed to produce both items, along with a time-phased budget. Both budgets and schedules consist of WBS tasks: The schedule tracks the amount of time allocated to tasks; the budget tracks the cost. Consider the following criteria when developing your WBS:

Simulator Project Risks

The schedule is the obvious problem. Fortunately, management has given you access to the required staff—either internal or expert contractors. Even so, a two-year program seems challenging.

Initially, however, your budget of $25M seems adequate, but you will have a better idea of this after you develop the time-phased budget. Of course, the budget needs constant attention.

After discussion with management and a meeting with the customer, you conclude that it is critical to put a working simulator in place at the end of the two years. The customer wants six months to shake out the simulator after it is delivered. You realize that the number of threats and weapons really needed at the initial delivery is up in the air. You decide to focus on completing a working simulator as soon as possible. Without any explicit discussion, you decide to reduce the risk by managing content by setting the following priorities:

- Flyable simulator

- Single threat and a simple weapon system

- Advanced weapons

- Number of threats

You realize you will have to prioritize other features, too, such as number of functional instruments.

Easily planned. Each task has a well-defined start and end.

Trackable. The tasks are useful as communications tools in reporting status, that is, accomplishment against expectation. It should be obvious to any interested party whether a task is in progress. Your staff members should be aware of which task they are on working on.

Specify a budget. Each task should have an associated cost.

Have the right level of granularity. If you have too many small tasks of short duration and small budgets, they become impossible to track. If your items are too large, they do not serve a basis for controlling costs and measuring progress.

To support your schedule and budget, maintain the WBS items in a hierarchical structure. The easiest way to display a WBS is as a tree, shown in Figure 4.2. The root of the tree represents the entire product or project. The next level might consist of major functions such as program management, development, maintenance, training, packaging, and shipping. Another approach is to have the second level consist of the product releases. In either case, the tasks are broken into smaller tasks to the level of granularity that works best for your organization.

> **TIP**
>
> Develop a WBS where most of the tasks are of three-months duration. Three months gives you adequate control yet the tasks are not so short as to be annoying.

The hierarchies should reflect your organization's budget-tracking method. Some organizations are concerned with what a release costs; others are concerned with how much an organization spends on the various functions. I prefer the product approach. If you build the WBS development tasks around this hierarchy:

Product releases

    Builds

        Phases

            Packages

then the tasks roll up meaningfully in your schedule and your budget. The schedule consists of the time spent on meaningful blocks of work: releases, builds, and lifecycle phases. This hierarchy is also valid in a budget since it rolls up the cost of each build and product release. It lets you track what a product costs to develop.

> **FOR FURTHER READING**
>
> A more detailed account of the theory and practice of work breakdown structures can be found in Harold Kerzner's excellent textbook *Project Management*, published by Van Nostrand Reinhold in 1998.

Table 4.6 shows how a WBS might be organized. The numbers represent the task's position in the hierarchy. The first decimal point represents the breakdown of the entire program into major subtasks. The second decimal point is the breakdown of the second level, into third-level subtasks, and so on. Figure 4.3 gives the tree diagram for the WBS given in Table 4.6 on page 144.

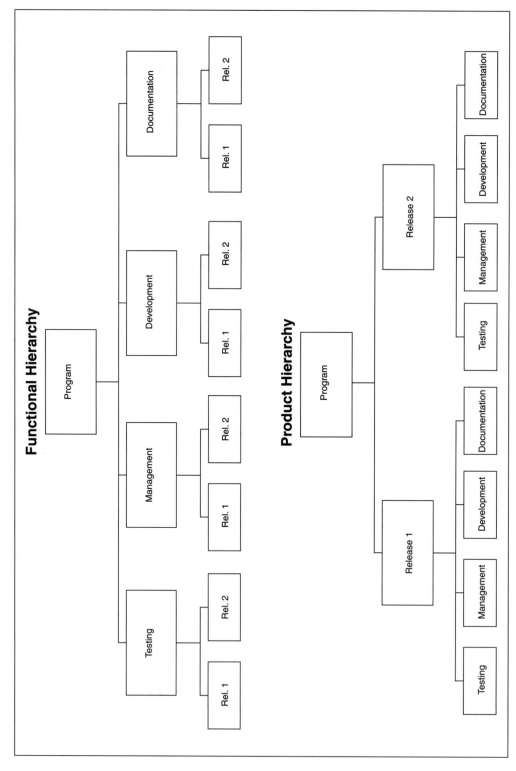

Figure 4.2 WBS *hierarchies.*

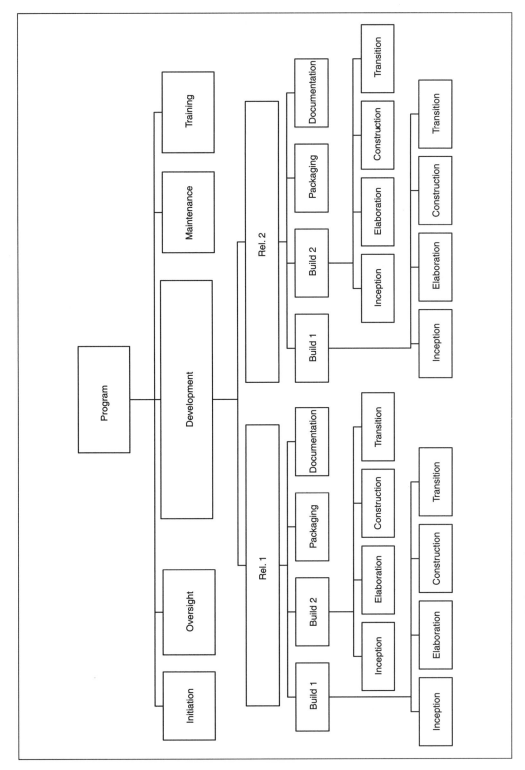

Figure 4.3 Recommended WBS hierarchy.

143

Table 4.6 A High-Level WBS

WBS #	TASK
1	Program (Product)
1.1	Initiation
1.2	Oversight
1.3	Development
1.3.1	Release 1.0
1.3.1.1	Build 1
1.3.1.1.1	Inception
1.3.1.1.2	Elaboration
1.3.1.1.3	Construction
1.3.1.1.4	Transition
1.3.1.2	Build 2
1.3.1.2.1	Inception
1.3.1.2.2	Elaboration
1.3.1.2.3	Construction
1.3.1.2.4	Transition
1.3.1.3	Documentation
1.3.1.4	Packaging and Release
1.3.2	Release 2.0
1.3.2.1	Build 1
1.3.2.1.1	Inception
1.3.2.1.2	Elaboration
1.3.2.1.3	Construction
1.3.2.1.4	Transition
1.3.2.2	Build 2
1.3.2.2.1	Inception
1.3.2.2.2	Elaboration
1.3.2.2.3	Construction
1.3.2.2.4	Transition
1.3.2.3	Documentation
1.3.2.4	Packaging and Release
1.4	Maintenance
1.5	Training

The Simulator WBS

You decide to construct the simulator in two builds. Build 1 will focus on the development and integration of the core packages. Your intent is to deliver a simulator that can be flown. The weapons and threats will be left to the second build. The first build will include the trainer workstation with the capability to create and save scenarios and initialize the system. Given the lack of threats and weapons, the scenario creation will be limited to these functions.

Following the decision to deliver the simulator in two builds, you adopt a version of the WBS shown in Table 4.6 with only one release. If at some later time, the customer asks for and funds a second release, the WBS will be modified. Also, there are no packaging and release tasks as such, and you have not been asked to do system maintenance. Table 4.7 shows the simulator WBS.

Table 4.7 The Simulator Top-Level WBS

WBS #	TASK
1	Program (Product)
1.1	Initiation
1.2	Oversight
1.3	Development
1.3.1	Release 1.0
1.3.1.1	Build 1
1.3.1.1.1	Inception
1.3.1.1.2	Elaboration
1.3.1.1.3	Construction
1.3.1.1.4	Transition
1.3.1.2	Build 2
1.3.1.2.1	Inception
1.3.1.2.2	Elaboration
1.3.1.2.3	Construction
1.3.1.2.4	Transition
1.3.1.3	Documentation
1.4	Training

Schedules

Project schedules itemize when the work on various WBS items begins and ends. For object-oriented projects, you will need to keep and communicate schedules at different levels of detail. One of the themes of this book is that people need to maintain views of complicated systems at different levels of detail: the high-level/low-detail view is used to communicate information to the outside world (senior managers, customers); the detailed view is for your team's use. Since many people are affected by the top level, you have low flexibility. At the low level of schedule detail, fewer people are affected, so you have greater flexibility. Experience has shown that development projects are more productive and less risky when the project manager has some flexibility in meeting internal milestones.

You will need to maintain three levels of schedule, with increasing detail and flexibility:

Master schedule

Macroschedule

Microschedule

The master schedule provides an overall program view. It contains your external commitments and major dependencies. Use it to communicate with your management and customer the common view of what is expected to happen. During program reviews, you use the master schedule to present status reports and your prospects of meeting the schedule.

The master schedule content includes just enough information to succinctly communicate your status: major milestones, demonstrated system builds, formal project reviews, and rolled-up tasks. This master schedule is very rigid; if it is not met, often there are costly consequences. If you are managing a contracted project, this schedule may be a contract exhibit, and not meeting the schedule may be treated as a breach of contract. In any case, a major slip in the master schedule will probably mean you get to spend low-quality time with your management.

The macroschedule gives a project-level view. It is used for day-to-day management of the current build. Reviewed and updated at least monthly, it contains all of the content of the master schedule, plus the development phases, internal milestones, delivery of internal documents, test-planning activities, and infrastructure management. If the milestones from the master schedule are set in stone, the macroschedule's content is fixed in heavy mud. Of course, there are practical limits. A major slip in the macroschedule is probably unrecoverable and will result in a change to the master schedule. On the other hand, delaying a design review two weeks while most of the team continues to move forward is just the sort of flexibility you will need.

The microschedule coordinates subsystem teams and manages internal dependencies. Microschedules are *not* created during the planning process; they are created during the execution of the development phases. For example, the microschedule includes the use cases that will be contained in integration. Microschedules are highly flexible, highly detailed, and usually not shared with anyone outside the project. They are set and reviewed at build meetings and are updated at least weekly. Individual team leaders may maintain their own microschedules.

Gantt Charts

Schedules are usually maintained in a Gantt chart, as shown in Figure 4.4. The chart is a visual representation of the planned tasks and events. The column on the left lists the WBS according to key events such as formal review meetings or artifact delivery. Such events are called milestones. Milestones do not have preset durations and do not have budgets associated with them. The chart shows the placement of the tasks and events in time, which is depicted from left to right. Logically, each task bar starts at the beginning of the task and ends at the conclusion of the task. There are no standard symbols in Gantt charts, although a common choice is to have *leaf tasks* (those at the bottom of the WBS hierarchy) depicted with wider bars of light colors and the higher-level roll-up tasks depicted with dark-colored, narrower bars. In this manner, the chart reflects the WBS hierarchy. For example, a phase might be a leaf task with a wide bar and the build a roll-up task with a dark bar. Milestones often are given as diamonds or triangles. Dependencies between tasks (which task should be completed before the next starts) may be shown as lines linking the bars. Gantt charts also may be used to show additional information, such as work completed and assigned resources.

> **NOTE**
> If you list the tasks in order of their planned completion, a Gantt chart tends to resemble a staircase or a waterfall, which should not be interpreted to mean that a waterfall lifecycle model has been adopted.

As a project manager, you need to become familiar with Gantt charts. Software tools, such as Microsoft's Project or Primavera's SureTrak, are available for building and maintaining Gantt charts. Most likely, your organization has adopted one

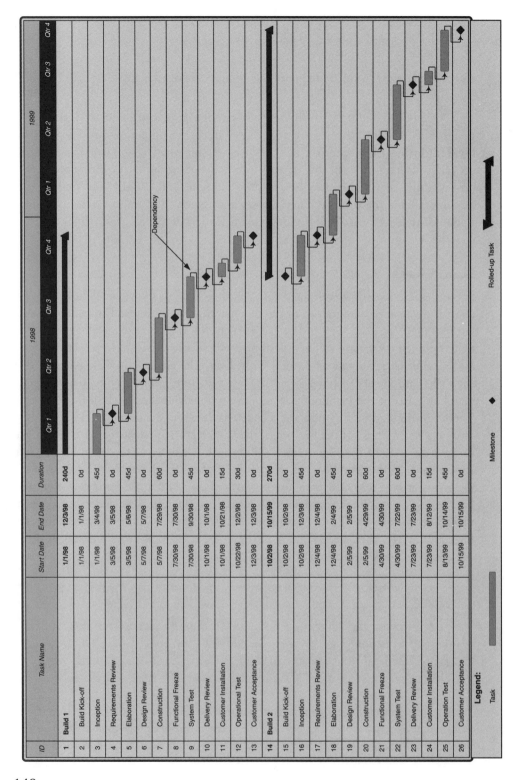

Figure 4.4 An example of a Gantt chart.

148

already. If not, I suggest that you choose one and become familiar with its use. You will constantly be adjusting the schedule in small ways, so it is essential to have a convenient tool at hand. Gantt charts have other useful features, such as resource leveling and critical path analysis. (Sample schedule .mpx files are available at the book's companion Web site. These can be imported into packages.)

Schedule Planning

Both the master schedule and the macroschedule should be maintained in a project management tool as a single project file, which is created by entering the WBS into the tool and assigning start and end dates, or durations and dependencies. If you choose the latter, the tool will compute the dates for you. Next, add the program milestones; then identify which items are part of the master schedule and which belong to the more detailed macroschedule. Tools such as Microsoft Project let you identify the master schedule items in a text field so that the master schedule can be viewed by filtering on that field. In addition, you can enter master schedule milestone dates as *fixed*, so that the tool can highlight the impact of macroschedule slips.

If delivery is years away, it is essential that your master schedule include several builds with incremental functionality. As a rule of thumb, the builds should be completed once a year. The delivery or demonstration of each build not only gives you and your management an unequivocal view of the project's progress, it also sets a milestone that serves to focus the team. This then enables you to use the aforementioned Parkinson effect to your advantage. Further, the builds are one more opportunity for you and your customer to develop a common view on what is needed and what will actually be delivered. The beginning of a build is a good opportunity to reset requirements.

To set the master schedule, assign the content of each of the incremental builds. Ideally, describe the build content by which use cases will be included. It is fair to limit the content to specified scenarios within the use case. Your SDP needs to describe the content *of each* of the builds. A narrative description of what the user can expect the system to do at each build is essential.

There are four principles to consider as you create a master schedule. All address some aspect of risk management:

Visible content. Prioritize the content that the customer must have, as well as that which you feel needs customer review and concurrence. The sooner you discover that the customer has a problem, the better.

Technical uncertainty. If you are not sure how long it will take to develop a certain component, it makes sense to start it as early as possible. In particular,

ID	Task Name	Duration
1	Stealth Simulator Program	871 days
2	Program Start	1 day
3	Initiation	20 days
11	Program Reviews	
53	Development	585 days
54	Release 1.0	585 days
55	Build 1	320 days
56	Inception	70 days
78	Requirements Review	4/10
79	Elaboration	89 days
109	Design Review	8/11
110	Contruction	122 days
137	Readiness Review	1/27
138	Transition	45 days
142	Customer Acceptance	3/31
143	Training	165 days
146	Documentation	240 days
149	Build 2	310 days
240	Fixed Costs	606 days
244	Maintenance	281 days

Figure 4.5 The simulator master schedule.

The Simulator Master Schedule

The master schedule is shown in Figure 4.5. Certain features of the schedule are worth noting. Though you succeed in delivering the simulator in two years, acceptance testing extends the project into year three. This gives you more time not to add functionality, but to harden the implementation. Both the customer and your management agree this is a good plan. Also, the inception phase of Build 2 overlaps the transition phase of Build 1. The overlap anticipates the discovery of new requirements during the Build 1 system test. This positioning helps level the effort, and keeps the development staff productive. It also shaves 12 weeks off the schedule.

you may want to include it in the first build. An alternative is to start the effort during the first build, but not commit it until the second.

Critical functionality. Any core functionality required to deliver a working system should be in the first build. Your goal in the first build should be to deliver a (partially) working system. A working system allows for customer feedback, which in turn allows for adjustments in the second build. This helps minimize customer satisfaction risk.

Resource leveling. Schedule functionality to reduce the chance of having to change staffing needs from build to build. It is often difficult to bring staff in and then take them off a project. Less than optimal use of staff adds to schedule and budget risk. You cannot have staff idle for any period, or assume that 20 people will magically appear during some four-week period. Strive to allocate functionality so as to fully utilize onboard staff; this may require moving them from one component to another within their competency.

I will come back to the macroschedule and microschedule in following chapters.

Staffing and Organization

After you have set up your schedules, you need to create a program organization chart that will help give you a sense of how to set up your staff. Draw this chart in four steps:

1. Develop the hierarchical program organization.

2. Identify project roles and responsibilities.

3. Plan for number of staff in each of the roles.

4. Establish product teams.

Let's look at each of the steps.

Program Organization

We can draw interesting and useful parallels between code organization and development team organization:

- Modularity of design helps limit component interaction and complexity in code.

- Modularity of team organization limits developer communication and complexity of interactions.

- Programmers, like objects, work best when they have a clearly defined responsibility.

- Teams, like packages, work best when their need for internal communication is greater than their need for cross-communication.

In addition to communication management, a staffing plan should invest each team and individual with a clear sense of ownership. If you assign a team the responsibility of delivering a set of packages, your expectations are clear. Everyone knows their role in the effort. They can set their own activities with the understanding that they must deliver their packages and fully participate in the program processes. Team function is enhanced. Any other organization approach is less than optimal, leading to lower morale and greater management stress. The last thing you want is for the team to rely on you setting day-to-day activities.

The implication of these concepts is that project teams should be organized around package ownership:

- Teams should be formed so that they own the design and implementation of one or more related packages.

- Classes, once identified, should be assigned to individuals for design and implementation.

- Owners for each abstraction level should be identified—package leads and system leads.

Create a program organization chart that helps you determine how to set up your staff. These charts come in various forms. The traditional charts are hierarchical, showing who reports to whom. Some managers have tried other approaches, whereby teams seem to float in space; other organization charts look like class diagrams. I prefer a hierarchical view that conveys scope of ownership and responsibil-

> **NOTE**
>
> There are two kinds of teams: subsystem teams, which own the development of packages and their integration into subsystem; and product teams which own development processes such as design and quality assurance.

ity over a formal reporting structure. Figure 4.6 shows a typical organizational structure of a development program. Although it appears to be hierarchical in design, depicting who reports to whom, it is better viewed as illustrating how program responsibilities are allocated. The point is, however you do it, define the key personnel, the leadership roles, and the development teams.

In object-oriented development, the distinction between design and implementation is not very clear. Design produces class specifications. Formerly, writing the headers and class skeletons were development tasks. Today, object design tools generate the code bodies directly from the class specification, the class design. All that remains is to fill in the methods. There is no need to define a point at which the designer hands over the code to the developer.

Another advantage of the organization approach is that it facilitates exactly the right level of communication. Team communications accurately reflect the class and package communications. Interteam communication consists mainly of negotiating the messages that pass among the (loosely coupled) packages and coordinating content of integrations. Each team manages its own internal designs and negotiates interfaces among classes within their packages.

> **TIP**
>
> The team's organizational model should reflect the system's high-level architecture.

You may be asking, "If every developer is a designer, how do you handle the difference between inexperienced and experienced developers?" Simply, make young developers responsible for small elements, usually individual classes. Give more experienced developers the responsibility for the design of larger elements, entire packages, and systems; they can also provide technical oversight and mentor the younger developers. Career growth is associated with the scope of technical responsibility.

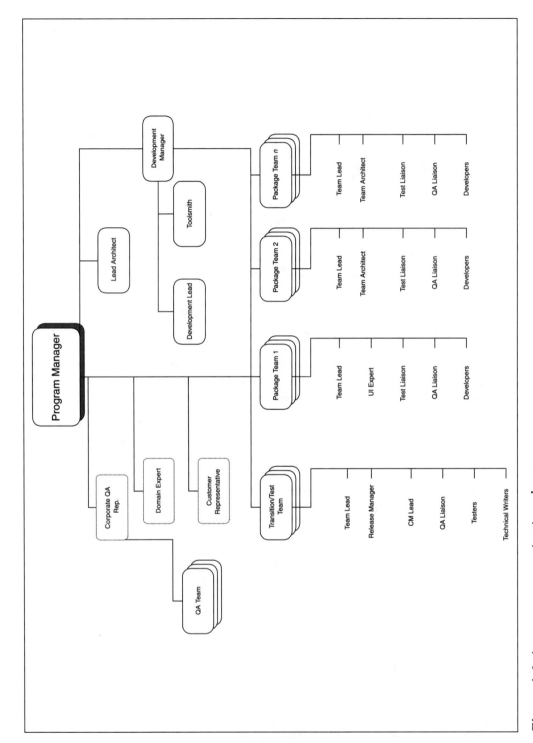

Figure 4.6 A program organization chart.

154

As you know, achieving the right level of communication between teams is key to successful staffing and organization plans. Limiting communication to only what's necessary improves productivity as the program grows. Modularity and encapsulation are the tools that can help you manage team communications effectively.

A subsystem team should be no more than ten persons. If the team needs to be much larger, break it into subsubsystem teams, each of which will integrate its classes into subsubsystems that will be integrated into a subsystem for subsequent integration into the system.

Program Roles

The program member roles and responsibilities are summarized in Table 4.8. It is important to fill each of these roles. And depending on the size of the program, a single staff member may fill more than one role. For example, it is likely that package test and quality assurance liaisons will also be developers; the lead architect and lead developer may be the same person; and so on.

Product Teams

The hierarchical view does not, however, reflect all of the communication paths required for effective teamwork. These paths represent the dysfunctional discipline-based communications discussed in Chapter 1. To solve this problem, you need to define product teams. Product teams are organized so that staff from different disciplines can come together to coordinate efforts on some aspect of the project. These teams *do not* appear in the organization chart.

Product teams are essential for coordinating activities, exposing issues, and communicating activities. Establish product teams as they are needed. Use Table 4.9 for examples of product teams that you should consider.

Note there are no design teams: more to the point, each development team is a design team. In fact, every developer is a designer. This approach rejects the discredited notion that design teams hand over work to development teams. One of the noisiest communication channels in software development is that between the designer and the developer. This is also one of the most critical channels. In practice, the inevitable breakdown of communication between the designers and the developers leads to code that was not built as designed. The best way to solve this problem is to simply eliminate the need for the channel. If the designer and the developer are the same person, presumably communications will be perfect. The developer will build the code exactly how the designer intended.

Table 4.8 Program Roles

ROLE	PRIMARY RESPONSIBILITY
Program/Product Manager	Deliver entire program, including formation of product teams, setting master schedules, allocating budgets, staffing, and process setting and adherence.
Development Manager	Develop the software.
Lead Architect	Specify product functionality, overall architecture package design; allocate function between packages, internal and external interfaces.
Lead Developer	Overall code quality, coding standards, code reviews.
Domain Expert	User-level use cases; consultant on operational use of the code.
Customer Representative	Customer advocate throughout all processes.
Corporate Quality Assurance Liaison	Adherence to corporate processes and standards required for SEI certification.
Subsystem Teams Leads	Develop package classes; team management; set microschedule.
Package Architects	Overall class design within the packages.
User-Interface Expert	Develop the UI specification.
Subsystem Teams Test Liaisons	Represent subsystem teams at build meetings; review and audit unit and integration testing.
Developers	Class design and implementation.
Quality Assurance Team Members	Represent quality assurance function throughout development; audit and document process adherence.
Transition/Team Lead	Manage the system test and product configuration management; transition to the customer.
Release Manager	Build and package release; run build meetings.
CM Lead	Manage configuration management processes.
Testers	Test planning and implementation.
Subsystem Teams Quality Assurance Liaisons	Coordinate quality assurance activities with QA staff.
Toolsmith	Install, customize tools and libraries.

Table 4.9 Product Teams

TEAM	RESPONSIBILITY	ACTIVITIES	MEMBERSHIP
Program	Overall Program Management	Set/Review program priorities Establish master schedule Conduct program reviews Handle program risk management Reviews program metrics	Program Manager (Leader) Development Lead Lead Architect Customer Representative Domain Expert QA Lead Transition Team Lead
Design	Product Architecture and Design	Create and revise package diagrams Arbitrate technical issues	Lead Architect (Leader) Lead Developer Subsystem Teams Leads Domain Expert
Schedule Coordination	Internal Dependencies Coordination	Review detail status Set content of integrations Coordinate content of microschedules	Development Manager (Leader) Package Leads Lead Developer
Testing	Integration and Systems Test	Coordinate, plan, and test environment Test plan establishment and reviews Review test results	Transition/Test Team Lead (Leader) Package test liaisons
Delivery	Product Delivery Activities	Establish release content Plan packaging Coordinate collateral material	Release Manager (Leader) Lead Architect Subsystem Teams Leads
Configuration Management	Change request/ Configuration Management Process	Review and dispose of change requests and problem reports	CM Lead (Leader) Lead Architect CM Liaisons

(*continues*)

Table 4.9 Product Teams (*Continued*)

TEAM	RESPONSIBILITY	ACTIVITIES	MEMBERSHIP
Process	Process Improvement	Review, revise processes and procedures Review metrics for opportunity for improvement	Program Manager (Leader) Lead Developer Lead Architect Team Leaders Anyone Else

---

Simulator Program Staffing

Taking into account the size and effort estimates from Tables 4.3 and 4.4 (on page 129), the allocation of content between the builds, and the master schedule, you come up with the following subsystem teams allocations, shown in Table 4.10. Note that the actual number of person-months exceeds the estimate found in Table 4.4. This is to be expected. The difference arises from the *smoothing* effect, the fact that staff cannot appear and disappear immediately as needed. The ramp-up and ramp-off of staffing is generally smoother, leading to the necessity of carrying staff even when they are not fully occupied. On the other hand, it is remarkably close to your conservative, reported estimate of 1,250, and so you are comfortable in reporting this staffing plan.

Of course, you need more than developers to complete this project. By summing the numbers in Table 4.10, you arrive at the entire staffing plan found in Table 4.11. The transition team includes, in this case, the staff to handle the installation and integration of the simulation hardware. You realize that the plan might be unrealistic, that you probably will not find all 71 people in one day. With the WBS and the staffing plan completed, you have all the data you need to determine your time-phased budget.

Table 4.10 Simulator Subsystem Teams

Team	Packages	Estimated Person Months	People: Build 1	People: Build 2	Planned Person-Months
Trainer Team	Trainer System	18	1.5		
	Checkpoint Manager	24	2		
	Scenario Manager	48	4		
Totals		90	7.5	2	114
Core Services	Threat Server	12	1		
	Event/Time Manager	24	2		
	World Model	24	2		
	Aircraft Model	24	2		
	Weather Server	36	3		
	Geographical Data Server	4	0.3		
Totals		124	10	4	172
Weapons Model	Weapons Model	240	10	10	240
Controls	Controls	240	10	10	240
Instrument Display	Instrument Display	260	11	10	250
Out the Window	Out the Window	240	10	10	240
Total		1,194	59	46	1,256

Table 4.11 Simulator Staffing Plan

Staff	People: Build 1	People: Build 2	Planned Person-Months
Development Staff	59	46	1,260
Transition/Test Team	4	6	120
Technical Writers	2	2	48
Program Manager	1	1	24
Development Manager	1	1	24
Lead Architect/Developer	1	1	24
Toolsmith	0.5	0.5	12
Domain Expert	0.25	0.25	6
QA Staff	3	3	72
Totals	71.75	60.75	1,590

Time-Phased Budget

Once you have a WBS and a schedule, you can go to the next step and develop a time-phased budget which details when you plan to spend the project's budget and what you expect to have accomplished at each level of expenditure. A time-phased budget is sometimes called an *earned value plan*.

At this juncture, you have all the data you need to create your initial budget. You set a project budget by assigning cost to each WBS item. Using your staffing plan and schedule, assign the human resources to each of the tasks. Using a spreadsheet or, better yet, a project management tool, you can calculate the labor expense. Given the labor rates for each job category, multiply the number of hours assigned to each of the resources by the rate. Add your estimates for the other costs—travel, software licenses, hardware, and whatever else you need.

Simulator Budget

From your staffing plan, you assign developers to the WBS tasks, listed in Table 4.12. The percentages refer to how many full-time staff you have assigned—a 200 percent entry is two full-time staff.

Your project management tool computes the number of staff hours for each labor category from your assignments and task durations. The data are given in Table 4.13. (More detailed views of this are available on the book's companion Web site.)

Along with the development staff and technical writers, the plan includes two administrative staff, who will provide secretarial services and assist in schedule and budget tracking.

Table 4.14 shows your rolled-up budget, also a result from your project management tool. The budget includes rough estimates for travel, software licenses, and hardware expenses for the project. The hardware simulator is not included in the budget, as this will be provided by the customer.

Note that your planned budget is $22M. This is less than the allocated $25M, but not by much. This gives you 12 percent management reserve. You'll need it.

Table 4.12 Simulator Labor Assignments

TASK	RESOURCE ASSIGNMENT
Program (Product)	Senior Manager, Administrator (200%)
Initiation	Manager (300%), Senior Developer (200%), Developer (500%)
Build 1	Senior Developer (600%), Developer (4,000%), Junior Developer (1,500%),Technical Writer (300%), Manager (700%)
Build 2	Senior Developer (600%), Developer (3,600%), Junior Developer (1,000%), Technical Writer (300%), Manager (700%)
Maintenance	Developer (200%), Junior Developer (200%)
Documentation	Junior Developer, Technical Writer (200%)

By comparing the planned and actual money spent against the planned and actual completion of the WBS items, you have a measure of how well you are tracking the budget. If the entire budget for a set of WBS items has been spent and the items are not complete, clearly you have a problem staying on budget. A variety of differences and ratios are available for determining budget health of a project once you have a time-phased budget. These ratios can and should be tracked on a monthly basis. (A further discussion of these ratios is in Chapter 9, *Tracking and Oversight*.)

Table 4.13 Planned Simulator Hours

POSITION	PLANNED HOURS
Senior Manager	4,688
Manager	32,336
Senior Developer	27,648
Developer	178,824
Junior Developer	64,024
Technical Writer	18,200
Administrator	9,376

Table 4.14 Initial Simulator Budget

TASK	BUDGET
Program (Product)	**$22,149,520.00**
Initiation	$81,000.00
Development	$17,934,720.00
Build 1	$9,639,600.00
Build 2	$8,295,120.00
Maintenance	$472,080.00
Documentation	$258,520.00
Other Costs	**$2,700,000.00**
Travel	$400,000.00
Hardware	$1,800,000.00
Software	$500,000.00

It is unlikely that you will think of every expense, so reserve some funds for the unexpected expenses. Only a fool would plan to spend every dollar allocated. Put aside between 10 to 15 percent as management reserve to cover the unplanned expenses.

Metrics Plan

The SDP should also contain a brief section identifying which development metrics you plan to collect. In addition, you should discuss how you plan to collect the data to support the metric. Include a description of the procedures and tools you intend to use. Chapter 9, *Tracking and Oversight*, contains a discussion of the recommended metrics for the controlled iteration lifecycle model.

From Here

Now that you have everything you need to write the software development plan, go ahead and write it according to the outline presented in this chapter; or tailor the format to suit what your customer or management expects. In either case, you are ready to start executing your project. The next chapters explore how to achieve successful delivery. Onward!

Part two

MANAGING THROUGH THE LIFECYCLE

5 MANAGING THE INCEPTION PHASE

"If a man will begin with certainties, he shall end in doubts, but if he will be content to begin with doubts, he shall end in certainties."

Francis Bacon (1561–1626), philosopher, essayist, statesman.

Chapter 4 explains the details of developing a software development plan (SDP). This chapter continues by detailing how to put that plan into action. Here, I assume that you have adopted the controlled iteration lifecycle model introduced in Chapter 3, because in this chapter, I will show you how to apply this model to object-oriented projects. The strength of this model is that it more closely reflects how teams actually develop software. The challenge the model presents is that it requires more oversight from the manager. To have a successful project, it is no longer sufficient to assign product-focused activities, such as completing the design document and tracking its progress. The manager needs to monitor and lead the team's overall progress in coming to a joint solution to the problem, which is delivering the right product to the customer on time.

Before we can begin to consider the application of the controlled iteration lifecycle model, however, we must address an apparent contradiction:

- The phases are marked by progress toward understanding and solving the development problem, not by the completion of the development activities.

- A disciplined management process requires that the completion of the phases be determined by the achievement of objective, demonstrable goals.

If the completion of the inception phase is not marked by the completion of a specific step, then how does one determine the phase is complete? We need a straightforward answer to this question, so read on.

165

The *phase exit criterion* is the required level of development of the artifacts for the purposes of completing each phase of the lifecycle model; that is, the artifacts are far enough along to meet the goal of the phase. But note, this does not mean the artifacts are complete in the sense of being locked down with no anticipated further development. For example, completion of the inception phase requires that the use-case database be complete; nevertheless, you should expect that it will be revised throughout the succeeding phases.

> **TIP**
>
> The completion of a phase does not the mark the conclusion of the final draft of an artifact.

Whether the development activities are sufficiently complete to move to the next phase depends on the good judgment of the program manager. In each phase of the lifecycle model, you need to ensure the accomplishment of certain outcomes. For the successful completion of the inception phase these are:

Scoping the project. Reach initial agreement between the team and the customer as to exactly what will be delivered.

Preparation. Establish the basis for the elaboration phase.

The first outcome, scoping the project, reflects the customer focus of this phase. During the inception phase, the project is handed off from the customer to the team. However, the conventional wisdom, based on many years of experience, is that it is impossible for the customer to truly capture his or her requirements in a document. Therefore, a goal of the inception phase is to capture or restate the customer's requirements in a form that serves as a basis for further development. In practice, this means the development of a database of user-level use cases, a prototype user interface, and other design documents. At the completion of the phase, the artifacts are in place, and the team and customer can focus with confidence on development of the product. Further, the artifacts that authoritatively define what was agreed to by both sides are in place.

The second goal, getting the stuff and tools in place, reflects real-world constraints. It is possible and occasionally essential that you start the inception phase without your full staff and without all the software tools and libraries you will need. Similarly, you may not have the development environment in place. This is acceptable to a point, but by the end of this phase, you should be fully staffed and have all the tools and libraries you plan to use.

In this chapter, I analyze the specific activities, artifacts, and deliverables that are required to achieve these outcomes; coordination of the phase activities; and how to manage issues such as team communication and team formation. I also discuss how to know when you are done, and then how to mark the transition to the elaboration phase. The chapter ends with a discussion of customer communications issues.

Management Overview

In the controlled iteration lifecycle model, inception is the first development phase. It starts after the software development plan (or at least its content) has been written and approved. Management is fully committed to the program and you have permission to proceed. In most cases, the program is not entirely staffed, but key members, such as the following, are onboard:

- Lead architect
- Lead developer
- Domain expert
- Leads for each package
- User-interface designer
- Quality assurance lead
- Test and transition lead
- Toolsmith

In addition, you should identify your administrative support staff, such as secretaries and contract administrators.

At this stage, too, you have chosen and installed your object design tool, and have entered your budget into your tracking system. Further, it stands to reason that the customer has provided you with sufficient requirement documentation to enable you to create the project planning artifacts. In particular, you have completed an initial top-level package diagram. The customer requirements document and package diagram serve as the input to the development processes.

Team Issues

The inception phase for many projects is the team forming stage. One of your goals as a manager is to get your team functioning as smoothly as possible. Recall that during team formation, you should be concerned with two issues: The assignment of well-defined and appropriate roles, and your team's willingness to commit to the project. Address these concerns in a forthright manner during this phase.

The organization approach presented in Chapter 4—forming subsystem teams and roles around ownership—is a good way to start. Everyone should know which team they are on and what part of the development processes they own. Define ownership down into the teams; for example, if someone is assigned to the user-interface team, he or she should know exactly which part of the user interface he or she is responsible for. If other team members challenge the assignments, the manager or team lead should determine whether these are legitimate concerns, but be slow to make adjustments. It is better for the team to learn to adjust to each other; after all, it is very unlikely that just the right person will be found for every role.

The second task, achieving buy-in, is at the core of this phase. It is during this phase that the content is specified, the scope is limited, the infrastructure is put in place, and the communications channels are established. By the end of this phase, the team members will have a clear vision of the project, the available resources, and the customer's expectations. Success is defined and can be seen as attainable, so the team members are ready to commit to each other and to the project.

Entering the Simulator Development Inception Phase

You enter the inception phase with your core team in place: lead architect, development manager, domain expert, toolsmith, and test lead. The core services team lead is only available part-time. The out-the-window team is coming off a previous project intact. They are a mature group, completely familiar with the tools and the development process. A new hire with, supposedly, relevant experience has been brought in to lead the training team.

The outside contractor who is installing the simulator hardware and supplying the instruments and control interfaces tells you that they cannot fully staff the program for 30 days, but not to worry as they are sure this is a straightforward effort.

You have allotted 90 days to complete the inception phase, but already you realize you have several schedule risks. By the end of the inception phase, not only do you have to meet the phase exit criteria for the development activities, but you also have to:

- Install the simulators

- Fold a subcontractor into the process

One of your challenges as a manager is to assign the work so that the desired outcome is reached. Depending on the maturity of your team, many members feel most comfortable when given clear, finite assignments; for example, write this plan, do that use case. Provide this guidance when appropriate. It is also important that you share with your team the overall goal of this phase so that they understand what you are trying to achieve and thus can direct their efforts accordingly. This will enable them to more fully accept ownership and responsibility for the project.

Development Activities

In traditional development lifecycle models, the phases are focused on the creation of documents: the first phase on the requirements document, the second on the design document, and so on. In contrast, the controlled iteration lifecycle model recognizes the need to capture requirements and design *together*. Object-oriented design involves progressing from the dynamic view of the system to the static view

---

- Staff the core services and the transition/test teams

- Familiarize the new team leads with the methodology

After a discussion with the domain expert and the lead architect you come to the following decisions:

- For design and implementation purposes, you decide to treat the simulator as a very elaborate black box input/output device. This takes the contractor out of the design process. The contractor must provide a robust, well-documented set of interfaces to the simulator hardware.

- You choose to add a system engineer to the staff to serve as a liaison to the contractor. The system engineer will be a member of the program team and attend the weekly team meetings. Her first assignment is to review all the interface documents to be sure they are adequate. Admittedly, this should have happened prior to hiring the contractor.

- You task the core development and transition/test team leads to come up with a plan that will bring them up to full staff in 45 days. You ask the lead architect to kickoff the use-case analysis. You arrange for the new team lead to have corporate process and tools training.

of the design. The dynamic view captures the system's expected behavior; the static view generates the code. In the inception phase, you focus on capturing the dynamic view.

This lifecycle model also accounts for the fact that it is dysfunctional to generate static documents intended to be finalized at the end of each phase. Rather than generating documents, the activities of the inception phase are devoted to creating so-called soft copy artifacts, primarily databases, that can be updated as needed throughout the next phases. Therefore, you should maintain management artifacts such as resource plans as documents. But be aware that even these might change and so should be kept as soft copy under some sort of version control.

> **TIP**
> Focus development activities on creating databases, not documents.

The development activities in this phase are focused on a common view of the system scope and behavior. From the perspective of problem solving, the inception phase is devoted to scoping: determining and specifying what will be built. It follows that there must be strong attention paid to the customer's needs and expectations. The customer communicates to you what he or she needs to accomplish. Your team communicates how the system will behave. Together, you reach a view of a system that can be successfully deployed. Naturally then, during the phase your team will focus primarily on requirements capture. In addition, you will carry out any design activities that support the phase outcomes.

As pointed out in Chapter 1, there is often a difference between what a customer needs and what a customer wants. The conflict occurs when customers do not realize that what they want, what they have specified, will not meet their needs. What they *need* is a system that meets their business and operational requirements. In the end, you and your customers are better served if you deliver an operational system. If you do, then you and they are heroes. If you do not, an opportunity is lost. Your challenge in this situation, therefore, is to build the customer's trust and confidence, so that you and your team have the freedom to meet his or her needs.

This is done in stages, briefly described here:

1. Clarify with the customer the operational and business needs. Build his or her confidence that you understand the context of the project.

2. Gently suggest alternative approaches, pointing out the benefits.

3. If your suggestions are well received, suggest that your team be allowed to do a full use-case analysis. (You may need to educate your customer about the effectiveness of use cases.)

In general, customers will appreciate this level of technical responsibility and leadership. If you go through this process and the project is a success, you have built a partnership with the customer that should result in repeat business. If you are an internal developer, you will have built a level of confidence with your management that should lead to enhanced opportunities. Looking ahead to the elaboration phase, which focuses on communicating with and among the developers, you will reset the requirements in a form that communicates to them exactly what they need to build in the detailed static design.

The Use-Case Database

The primary requirements-capture activity for this phase is the development of the database of user-level use cases. Each release is specified by which use cases can be executed by a user. The use-case database serves several crucial functions:

> **TIP**
>
> Even if you are familiar with use cases, review the descriptions in Chapter 2 to recall the terms I'll be using here.

Content management. Serves as a means of specifying to your customer and your team exactly what functionality the system will provide.

System and acceptance testing. Serves as input for the system test plan.

Traceability. Serves as input to the design process.

At the end of this phase, conduct a customer design review, at which point you and the customer will have entered into a sort of contract:

- The customer will accept and be happy with exactly what is specified in the use-case database.

- You will be committed to delivering the functionality specified by the use cases.

Negotiate changes in requirements by specifying and accepting alterations to the use cases allocated to the release. It is important that the use cases be maintained in a form that can be shared with the customer and the team. The database should be

Table 5.1 Use-Case Database Structure

FIELD	USE CASE 1	USE CASE 2	USE CASE 3	...
Unique Name				
Unique Identifier (A Serial Number or Label)				
Use-Case Text				
Use-Case Owner				
Revision History				
Allocated Build or Release				

simple, composed of the essential fields shown in Table 5.1. You, of course, are free to add other fields such as date entered, date complete, allocated integration, assigned developer, related system test, assigned developer, and the like.

The database should be network-browsable by the entire development team and, in some cases, your customer. It should have a search capability and a mechanism for generating printouts and reports. Further, it should also allow the developers to add and update the text descriptions. Like any other database, data integrity is critical. You need to develop procedures for locking down baselines and maintaining versions. (Baselines are the versions of the database that reflect an agreed-upon status of the requirements for a given build.)

The use cases should also be maintained in some sort of database tool. Depending on the size of your project, they can be maintained either in an HTML table format or in a personal database tool that permits Web access and sharing within a workgroup. (I always use Microsoft's Access.) By maintaining your database in a desktop tool, you can easily customize the fields you need. For larger projects, you may choose a more elaborate multiuser database. Each use case is a record, and these databases allow different developers to update different use cases. Note, I do not recommend elaborate requirements management tools, as they seem to add expense and effort beyond their usefulness.

Assigning Responsibility

Use cases do not respect package boundaries. In fact, a user-level use case should not refer to program elements, but restrict its content to what is visible to the user.

Mapping the use cases to the system view occurs in the elaboration phase. It follows that you should not assign use cases to the package teams. The use-case database is owned by the design team, made up of the package leads and directed by the system architect. The design team will:

1. *Create the list of use cases.* Initialize each of the records.

2. *Update the microschedule.* Schedule the completion of the use cases on a weekly basis.

3. *Coordinate the efforts.* Assign the completion of the use cases among themselves and other developers.

Recall that staffing may continue into this phase. As developers are brought onboard, every effort should be made to include them in the use-case activity. Their efforts can be coordinated by their package leader. You may also need a database administrator who maintains versions, creates report formats, and adds fields when necessary.

Assigning ownership of the use cases to the design team is an example of the cross-functional management style discussed in Chapter 1. The team collectively develops a view of the total system that can be shared with the package teams, which are responsible for the coherency of the system. Further, the package team representatives can reflect the common view back to their team. With this approach, the fact that use cases cannot be assigned to package teams is not a drawback, but an advantage. Team communication and coordination is enhanced.

Phase Exit Criteria

For the purposes of this phase, the use-case database is complete when:

- All of the use cases planned for the current build are complete.

- The completed use cases have been reviewed by the system architect and the domain expert.

- The customer agrees that the functionality captured in the use cases is sufficient.

Use-Case Diagrams

A database of use cases, while essential for precisely capturing the scope, does not provide an adequate mechanism for communicating the overall system. A list of several hundred use cases does not comprise the structure and abstractions (*uses* and *extends*) to support a person's or a group's ability to comprehend the system. It is a poor mechanism for developing a common model of what will be built. Collaboration requires a mechanism that enables visualization of how the use cases fit together. The use case diagram meets this need.

Like all diagrams, use-case diagrams serve as means of communicating structure. Recall from Chapter 2 that use-case diagrams contain icons for each use case, and show the static relationships between them. Without the diagrams, the use cases become an incomprehensible jumble of disconnected requirements. For the reader, it becomes an exercise, trying to figure out what the system is supposed to do. The diagrams place each of the use cases in context with the others. The diagrams can provide a number of views of the system and serve a variety of purposes. They can be created in such a way as to:

- Provide a structure for discussing the behavior of the system among teams
- Facilitate the assignment among the staff of the detail write-ups
- Support the requirements review with the customer

Use case diagrams serve another essential role: to capture the scope of a project in such a way that supports system design. Preparation for the elaboration phase includes the capture of the use cases in your object design tool, which should, of course, support use-case diagrams. Use the tool as the mechanism for bridging from the development of use cases to the next step in the design process—the development of sequence diagrams.

Remember, use cases and use-case diagrams must be consistent. For example, if the text of one use case invokes another, the diagrams should show a *uses* relationship. Similarly, if one use case contains the text of another, the diagram should reflect the *extends* relationship.

Assigning Responsibility

Like the use-case database, use-case diagrams are owned and managed by the design team. The diagrams are likely to be handled by a smaller group than for the use cases—possibly just the lead architect.

Phase Exit Criteria

For the purposes of this phase, the use-case diagrams are complete when:

- Every use-case diagram is entered into the design tool.
- All of the relationships between use cases are contained in at least one diagram.
- The use cases and diagrams have been reviewed for consistency.
- The use-case diagrams have been reviewed by the lead architect and the domain expert.

The Simulator Use-Case Analysis

Your lead architect divides the use cases into three categories: air flight, weapons systems, and trainer. The pilot is the actor for the first two. The trainer is the actor in the third. Of the three, the third is more challenging for the inception phase. The first two uses-case categories are fully understood by the customer. The simulator is supposed to act exactly like the planned aircraft. The third is less well-defined. Nevertheless, use cases need to be defined in all three categories to drive the design process.

The customer has come up with a training curriculum that contains a set of simulated missions that will be used to train the pilots. The architect realizes that these missions form a great resource for generating the use cases, as they fully characterize the operational requirements for the simulator. The missions are mapped to use-case diagrams.

The design team has created three teams to start the use-case analysis, one for each category. Members from the core services team and the out the window team are assigned to the first team. As the project manager, you are asked to facilitate the availability of a domain expert from the contractor to participate in the air flight and weapons systems use-case teams. The trainer team leader will head the trainer use-case team. Your customer agrees to provide an expert to participate on that team. Each team will expand the mission use-case diagrams to sufficient detail to supply the input to the class design activity. Also, the use cases are distributed among the teams for textual input.

Prototyped User Interface

One of the best ways to capture a common view of the system is to start building and showing it to the customer to see if he or she likes it. Such a strategy makes sense if it is affordable. One of the triumphs of modern object technology is that tools are available that enable you to build prototype user interfaces efficiently. The prototype illustrates the look and the feel of the application for carrying out use cases. It contains the graphical elements of the application, such as the menus, frames, and adornments. The prototype is often executable in the sense that it responds to user interactions: menu bars drop, windows open and close, radio buttons click, and messages appear as appropriate. But no function underlies the interfaces;

if the user invokes a menu item, nothing happens. However, enough of the interface exists to give the customer and the domain expert the sense of how the user will interact with the application, and thus gives them the opportunity to refine the operational requirements and to clarify the joint understanding of the functionality.

Building the prototype user interface during the inception phase enhances project efficiency in two ways:

- The environments provide graphical tools that allow a developer to design a user interface using point-and-click interfaces.

- The prototype builder generates code that can be incorporated in the actual design and implementation.

Start building the user interface directly from the requirements and the use cases as soon as possible. These efforts will not be wasted. Early, when it is not costly to make changes, you can use the initial prototype to confirm your approach with the customer. The prototype serves as a basis of the actual development, and can be extended and refined to become the user-interface component of the delivered system. There are three benefits to building the initial user interface during the inception phase:

- You have a start in building the application, which lowers cost and schedule risk.

- You can provide the customer an opportunity to test the requirements, which lowers customer satisfaction risk.

- The prototype makes the project real to the team, which facilitates their understanding of the use cases and creates the momentum to continue.

Prototyping should be done in a modern interface language and application builder such as the various Java toolkits. There are also interface builders that generate C++ code. Avoid any of those old-fashioned prototyping tools that just mimic user interfaces.

Assigning Responsibility

The prototype user interface is developed by the UI designers. If you have more than one package team with UI responsibilities, then form a product team consisting of the lead designer from each of the teams. The lead architect and domain expert should also be on the team. This group will ensure that the user interfaces are consistent in style, look, and feel across the application. Nothing annoys a user more than an application whose mouse clicks and the like are not consistent. Only a general product team can ensure that the application appears and behaves as a single environment to the customer.

> **Simulator Prototype User Interface**
>
> There is no point in prototyping the pilot's user interface—the cockpit. The contractor will deliver it. The user interface expert focuses on prototyping the trainer workstation.

Phase Exit Criteria

For the purposes of this phase, the prototype user interface is complete when it reflects all the use cases. It should be sufficiently functional to allow the user to execute the user interface components of the system. The goal is for the customer, lead architect, and domain expert to be able to execute the user interface and thereafter to make comments. Ideally, the customer will simply approve your design; a more likely outcome is that he or she will tell you what changes are required. Document these comments as action items and update the use cases. In most cases, if the changes are not too extensive, record conditional approval; that is, ascertain that approval is assumed once certain changes have been made. Once you receive conditional approval, you do not need further review. If the required changes are planned and do not interfere with further progress, then you can declare that the interface is sufficient to move on to the elaboration phase.

Top-Level Class Diagrams

During the inception phase, the top-level architectural diagram moves from being a planning tool to a critical part of the system design. The lead architect should update it based on further insight. The diagram must be captured in the design tool.

In addition, the design needs to be *unitized*; that is, the design file is divided into a set of separate design files. One file, sometimes called the *model file*, is for the overall design; separate files are kept for each of the top-level packages. Unitization of the design permits the individual packages to be updated individually under version control.

Each package symbol in the top-level design diagram has to be documented, to describe the role the package plays in the design and what sort of messages it is expected to generate and service.

The diagram should be updated throughout the phase. It is very possible that a better top-level diagram will emerge during this phase. Should this occur, you may need to redistribute the package ownership across the teams.

Assigning Responsibility

The top-level diagram is maintained solely by the lead architect. He or she will enter and maintain the diagram in the object design tool. Further, only he or she can modify the top-level design. In fact, the diagram should be kept under configuration management, with only the architect granted write access. If other members of the team want to change or update the diagram, they must bring their changes to the lead architect for concurrence. In practice, the changes will occur as a matter of course in the activities of the design team, headed by the lead architect.

Phase Exit Criteria

For the purposes of this phase, the top-level diagram is complete when it accounts for all the anticipated functionality. The most you can achieve during the inception phase is the confidence that all of the use cases appear to be implementable by the packages. A thorough analysis of this issue does not occur until the next phase. Nevertheless, the design team should review the diagram for completeness and adequacy.

You may decide not to present this artifact during the requirements review meeting, because it is not part of the requirements, but an early view of the design. Postponing the presentation of the diagram until the design review at the end of the elaboration phase, when it is more stable, may result in less confusion for the customer, who does not need to be concerned about the changes. Also, by holding off the review, the distinction between requirements and design remains clear.

System Test Plan

The system test plan shares the task of determining the system scope with the use-case database. But where the use cases describe the dynamic functionality of the system, the system test plan contains performance characteristics such as data capacity, the number of simultaneous entities, and the system response time. It should account not only for all the use cases, but also capture these performance requirements. The system test plan describes how the planned system tests will determine whether the functional and performance requirements are met.

Your team goal is to deliver a system that passes the system tests. In some cases, these tests extend to operational tests in the customer environment, therefore, the system test plan should cover both. With both the use cases and the system test plan in place, everyone has a complete view of what will be delivered.

Begin writing the system plan during this phase. Recall that your sole concern for the system test is to confirm as accurately as possible that the system is operational. In particular, a system test asks whether the system:

Is usable. Can the use cases be executed, and have the stated performance requirements been met?

Is stable under operational conditions. Does it crash, lose data, or affect its host platform integrity?

Promotes user efficiency. Does the system meet unstated but essential performance requirements?

The system test determines whether the system performs *as the user expects*, not whether it was built as designed or intended. Other test levels address these concerns. The system test should not have a view of the implementation, so it follows that it should be written in a *clean room* setting; that is using only the customer requirements and, more important, the use cases as input. The system test writers should not have access to or be concerned with the system architecture.

Finally, the system tests must be traceable to the use-case scenarios. (Recall that a use-case scenario is one of several possible paths through a use case.) In particular, every use-case scenario must be included in one or more system tests. A test may also include more than one use case. A system test plan should include:

- Requirements summary
- Test list
- Required resources
- Traceability matrix

A brief description of each follows.

Requirements Summary

Include in the system test plan a brief section explaining the developers' understanding of the assumptions underlying the test plan. This might include a description of the operational requirements of the system and how they affect the test plan, such as the number of entities, data items, open windows, and open files that the system will have to handle. For example, if you are testing a drawing program, you should know the number of graphical elements (lines, polygons, Bezier curves) that users typically include in a drawing. Ideally, from market studies you will have a histogram of the number of entities determined by percent of drawings for each graphical element. An example of customer usage research is shown in Figure 5.1, where 60 percent of the drawings have between 50 and 200 lines; 1 percent have more than 1,000 lines. In addition, from the tabular data, you can conclude that .01 percent of the pictures contain 100,000 lines.

If you plan to sell this as a shrink-wrapped product, verify that the program can handle 10,000 lines comfortably. Do the numbers: If you expect to sell 100,000

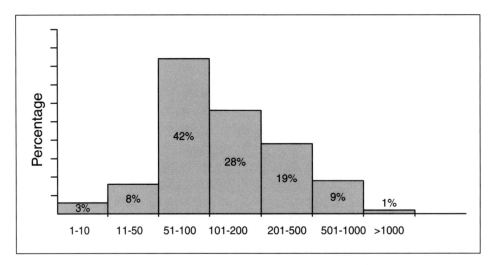

Figure 5.1 *A fictional histogram of the number of lines in user drawings.*

copies and, on average, each copy generates only one picture a day, your users will generate 1,000 pictures a day with 1,000 and 10 pictures a day with 10,000 lines. Unless you meet the 10,000-line standard, your service department will be bombarded by telephone calls and your product will get a poor reputation. Your test plan must include a way of testing the ability of a system to handle a drawing with at least 10,000 lines.

You also must describe and account for performance requirements, of which there are two types:

- Turnaround time for programs that handle a large amount of data—credit card postings, weather simulations, and the like
- System response time to user interactions

The first kind of performance requirement is often very explicit; for example, a bank must update its accounts overnight, every night, in order to conduct business in an orderly way. If the bank handles 100,000 transactions a day, your system must be able to deliver 100,000 transactions in about four hours. Anything less will not be able to accommodate days with an uncharacteristically large number of transactions or time to respond to a system outage. (Recall the program that could accurately predict the next day's weather. Unfortunately, it took two days to run.)

Response time to user interactions is just as important. If the system takes five seconds (or even one second) to respond to a mouse click, users will get annoyed. Productivity will suffer. In our drawing example, if the artist is capable of drawing a line in six seconds with a tablet, but the system takes two seconds to respond, the artist's productivity is diminished by 33 percent! Further, the artist will complain that his or her rhythm has been broken. As a rule of thumb, all responses should be less than one-third of a second, but one-tenth of a second is a good target. In our drawing program, the system response time to adding a new line should not increase with the number of lines. This design point affects the program design.

Putting these system and test criteria in front of the team and the customer *before* the elaboration phase ramps up is important. It is inefficient and potentially disastrous to have the team learn the performance requirements late in the development.

Test List

The heart of the plan is a list of test cases, which like use cases, should be maintained online in soft copy form. A database format is best. Each record in the database should contain the files shown in Table 5.2.

Table 5.2 Transition/Test Case Database Structure

Field	Test 1	Test 2	Test 3	...
Test Name*				
Identifier (Unique Number)*				
Brief Description*				
Use Cases Covered*				
Expected Execution Time*				
Performance Criteria (Acceptable Performance for Passing the Test)*				
Instructions (for Running the Test)				
Test Writer				
Revision History				

*At this point, not every field needs to be filled in; just those with asterisks. You will fill in the others as the tests are written throughout the next phases.

> **Simulator Test Planning**
>
> The system test lead points out what should have been obvious: Your system test requires a pilot. Fortunately, you realize this in time to adjust your plan. You decide to work with the customer to find a retired pilot who can serve as a tester. (Of course, many of your staff are eager to volunteer to learn to drive the simulator.)
>
> The test cases are derived from the same set of missions that were used for the use-case diagrams. This way traceability to the customer requirements and to the use cases is achieved.
>
> In addition to a pilot, system testing requires a test facility. The plan includes a lab layout and a schedule for installing all the required equipment. The transition/test lead will oversee the setup of the system test facility. The team agrees that the test lab needs to be in place before completion of the elaboration phase.

Required Resources

This section of the document describes the staffing, equipment, and facilities required to conduct the tests in the allocated time. The description serves two purposes. The first is to aid in your planning, allowing for the limited time and resources available. There is no point in writing a test plan that takes a year to execute or requires 100 people. You should use the expected execution time field from the test database to estimate how long each system test run will take in order to ensure your plan is executable.

The second use of this section is to help you manage your dependencies. List the availability of the required resources on your macroschedule, and communicate your dependencies clearly, then take the actions required to bring them onboard. For example, part of the system test may include operational testing at the customer site; in this case, your customer needs to provide facilities and staff. The last thing you want is to be unable to complete delivery because the customer did not realize he or she was expected to supply the resources.

Traceability Matrix

The system test database includes a field that shows the use cases addressed by each test. For each use case, also list which test confirms that the use case is executable by the system. If you are maintaining the system tests in a database, this *traceability*

> **NOTE**
>
> One source of error in system testing results from the fact that humans are creatures of habit. When carrying out a task which may be completed in more than one way, we often use the same way every time. Alternate ways of carrying out the task are not ever tested. However, if the methods exist, the customers will find them. Users are notorious for finding ways to legitimately use programs in ways never imagined by the designer.
>
> In a drawing, for example, the tester may draw the polygons by assigning the fill color as they are drawn, whereas the customer may draw each polygon, then go through each of them and assign the colors. A bug may be lurking in the second method. Clearly, it is impossible to test for all possibilities, but your test methodology should include a mechanism for testing more than one path. When you write the test instructions, be on the lookout for tasks that have multiple paths and institute mechanisms for randomly picking the path the tester should take.

matrix can be created using a report generator. The matrix is required to ensure and document that the system test plan covers all the use cases planned for the release. Table 5.3 shows an example traceability matrix for a drawing program. Note that one requirement may generate more than one use case. On occasion, you may want to generate the inverse requirements matrix. An example is shown in Table 5.4. This matrix is useful in determining which requirement is affected by the use case.

Process Tasks

Competent development staff is the most valuable resource to any project. As a manager, you must ensure that your team has the tools and procedures that they need to do their work efficiently. This is a critical dependency. Every hour your team spends struggling with tools, creating their own versions or working around them, is an hour not spent on development. Squandering their time exacerbates cost and schedule risk. In short, it is a management failure.

Identify and track process tasks in your macroschedule. Assign resources to put the tools in place. The associated macroschedule milestone is that the tools are installed and accessible to whomever needs them. Table 5.5 lists the type of program development tools you should be tracking. It is not complete; your specific project may need additional tools.

Table 5.3 Requirements Traceability Matrix

CUSTOMER REQUIREMENT	USE-CASE NUMBERS	USE-CASE NAMES
The program will save and restore files in a variety of standard formats.	121	Save File
	122	Open File
	123	Close File
Drawing entities may be grouped and ungrouped.	72	Group Selected Entities
	73	Ungroup Entity
	74	Regroup Entities
The following primitives will be supported: lines, circles, quadrilaterals, polygons, ellipses.	30	Draw Line
	31	Draw Circle
	32	Draw Quadrilateral
	33	Draw Ellipse
	34	Draw polygon

...

During this phase, you also ensure that all your procedures are defined and documented. The procedures include:

- Version control/configuration management
- Quality assurance
- Code and design style guides

In addition, update the SDP if there is any change in plans.

Assigning Responsibility

Your toolsmith is responsible for putting all the tools in place. This may be too much for one person to handle during the time allotted to the inception phase, so depending on the size of the project, assign others from your information services group to assist. Once the tools are in place, they will need constant attention. Plan to keep your toolsmith on your project on at least a part-time basis throughout the entire program.

Table 5.6 shows the owners of the other processes that need to be in place by the completion of the phase.

Table 5.4 Inverse Requirements Traceability Matrix

Use-Case Numbers	Use-Case Names	Customer Requirement
...		
30	Draw Line	The following primitives will be supported: lines, circles, quadrilaterals, polygons, ellipses.
31	Draw Circle	The following primitives will be supported: lines, circles, quadrilaterals, polygons, ellipses.
32	Draw Quadrilateral	The following primitives will be supported: lines, circles, quadrilaterals, polygons, ellipses.
33	Draw Ellipse	The following primitives will be supported: lines, circles, quadrilaterals, polygons, ellipses.
34	Draw Polygon	The following primitives will be supported: lines, circles, quadrilaterals, polygons, ellipses.
...		
72	Group Selected Entities	Drawing entities may be grouped and ungrouped.
73	Ungroup Entity	Drawing entities may be grouped and ungrouped.
74	Regroup Entities	Drawing entities may be grouped and ungrouped.
...		
121	Save File	The program will save and restore files in a variety of standard formats.
122	Open File	The program will save and restore files in a variety of standard formats.
123	Close File	The program will save and restore files in a variety of standard formats.

FOR FURTHER READING

More discussion on the standard software processes such as configuration management may be found in Scott Donald's and Stanley Siegel's *Cultivating Successful Software Development,* published by Prentice-Hall in 1997, or Luke Hohmann's *Journey of the Software Professional,* also published by Prentice-Hall in 1997.

Table 5.5 Program Development Tools

TOOL	DESCRIPTION
Development Hardware	PC's, workstations, file servers, compilation and network equipment, and special input or output devices. If you are compiling and linking files across a network, verify that you have sufficient bandwidth to maintain productivity.
Development Software	Design tools, toolkits, code editors, compilers, debuggers, linkers, and version control tools. In some instances, you will need to configure the software after it has been installed. Plan for this.
System Directory Structures, Makefiles	The directories for source code, design files, documentation, libraries, and executables must be defined, made available across the network, and placed under version control. Once the directory structure is in place, the system makes those files needed to specify automated compiling and linking.
Code-Generation Property Files	Customize your design tools so that the code is generated into the right directories.
Test Hardware	Identify system test machines. Usually, you will have a system test lab, and depending on the network traffic your product generates, it may need its own network segment. Also, identify *victim machines* for package integration testing. Set these machines aside from the development machines so that testing can run in parallel with development. Be aware that your partial product may take the victim machine out of commission for a while, say by overwriting an important system file. This is death to a development machine, but is a planned-for contingency for a victim machine.
Test Tools	Your project may rely on automated test tools. Examples include protocol generators and software that captures and plays back user interactions (mouse clicks, typing, and the like).
Libraries	Either commercial products or internal code that you are reusing. Examples include code libraries (code that can be compiled into your product), frameworks (base object classes from which you can derive inheritance classes for your project), persistent storage services, and object request brokers.

Table 5.6 Process Owners

PROCEDURE	OWNER
Version Control/Configuration Management	Configuration Management/Test Lead and Toolsmith
Quality Assurance	Program Quality Assurance Lead
Code and Design Style Guides	Lead Developer
Development Procedures	Development Manager

Phase Exit Criteria

The result of the process activities during this phase is to have everything necessary for the elaboration phase in place. Generally, your team should not enter the elaboration phase until the tools are established. This dependency must be a constant for you and your team. Deciding to officially enter the elaboration phase before all the tools are in place is a judgment call that depends on your situation and your team. In any case, putting the tools in place is a very high-priority item.

Coordinating Activities

Project activities must be tracked and coordinated differently in each phase, as each has a different microschedule; the agenda of your weekly program meeting will vary phase to phase. This section explores how to coordinate the inception phase.

Microschedules

You will maintain three microschedules during this phase:

Use-case completion. Maintained by the design team lead.

System test plan. Maintained by the test lead.

Process tasks. Maintained by the toolsmith.

Throughout this phase, direct your design team to maintain a microschedule list of use cases and use-case diagrams that are expected to be developed. On a weekly basis, the design team lead should schedule:

- Which use cases to complete
- Which use-case diagrams to complete

- Which use cases to prototype in the user interface
- Who is responsible for the completion of each of the efforts

This weekly schedule serves as the development microschedule for the inception phase. A similar microschedule is maintained by the test lead, and contains those test cases that will be detailed in the system test plan each week. The toolsmith will maintain a detailed schedule of the tool installation and tailoring tasks.

Program Meetings

Throughout the inception phase, hold weekly program team meetings. Do not confuse these with the more formal tracking and oversight meeting, which will be discussed in Chapter 9. The purpose of this weekly program team meeting is to review the progress of the previous week, reset short-term priorities, and coordinate the activities of the upcoming week. The attendees of this meeting should include, but not be limited to:

- Development manager
- Development lead
- Lead architect
- Toolsmith
- Development team leads
- Quality assurance lead

Choose a facilitator to take responsibility for keeping the meeting on track and for focusing the discussion. In general, resolve any problems outside the meeting; during the meeting simply add the issue to the action item list for tracking. A sample agenda is shown in Figure 5.2.

Schedule the meeting at a regular day and time and for a fixed duration. I like to hold my program teams on Thursday afternoons, to give the team a chance to assess how the week's efforts are proceeding while leaving a day to make adjustments and to set up the work for the following week.

Customer Communications

Customer communications in this phase should be both formal and informal. Formal in that you will hold scheduled program reviews as well as process milestone meetings such as the requirements review meeting. The formal meetings tend to involve management. Informal communications are more likely to occur among the technical staff. It is almost essential that your more experienced staff be in contact with their counterparts on the customer side.

Time	Item	Presenter
9:00	Previous Action Items	Development Lead
9:20	Overall Status and Risk Areas	Development Lead
9:30	Tool/Infrastructure Status	Toolsmith
9:35	Development Microschedule	Design Team Lead
9:50	System Test Plan Microschedule	Test Lead
10:05	Upcoming Program Events/ Macroschedule Review	Development Manager
10:20	Action Item Review and Assignment	Development Lead
10:30	Adjourn	

Figure 5.2 Sample inception phase program team meeting agenda.

NOTE

This meeting is not for setting the microschedules. They should be in place for presentation at the meeting.

During the inception phase, this is particularly true. Involving the customer to resolve questions about operations is going to be imperative during use case development. In fact, it is a great idea to have a customer representative on the design team. Your goal here is for the customer to be happy with what he or she sees at the

---

CAUTION

There is one drawback to ongoing customer communication. The customer may try to bypass management by exacting from you commitments or agreement to changes from the technical staff. To guard against this, clearly identify the staff members empowered to make such commitments. It may be you or someone else with sufficient experience on your team. Everyone else must learn to say, "Yes, we could do that, but we have to check with (the empowered one)." Informal commitments do not count. Program changes must be formally accepted and reflected in an updated requirements document. At this phase, the requirement could be accepted by the design team. Eventually though, you will institute an even more formal change control process, described in Chapter 7.

requirements review meeting—there should be no surprises. Second, during the inception phase you want to be encouraging a sense of teamwork between you and the customer.

I have also found it useful to explain the lifecycle model and its associated activities to the customer. Otherwise, the customer may think you are following a waterfall lifecycle, and this can lead to confusion when discussing status. Educating the customer is particularly important if he or she is involved in the oversight meetings. You cannot be too heavy-handed about this. Sharing the software development plan is a good start. You can reinforce the discussion at the various review meetings.

Managing Deliverables

I recommend strongly that whenever possible, don't deliver hard copy documents; instead, give your management and customers access to your artifacts online. Adopting this strategy sends the message that the program is activity and content-driven, not document-driven. Delivering formal documents gives the impression of finality; this is the wrong message at this stage.

Employing soft copy artifacts, however, requires establishing version control with timestamps. You must be able to go back to any version of any artifact that served as a basis of discussion or agreement.

> **TIP**
>
> If you must deliver hard copy documentation, limit their contents to references to the soft copy artifacts and high-level discussions, such as program overviews and working assumptions. Avoid printing out a paper version of the soft copy.

In my experience, customers are more than comfortable with soft copy. The last thing they want to carry home is a few hundred pages of use cases. So, for example, if you decide to deliver a system requirements specification, it should contain:

- Front matter
- Tracking and traceability descriptions
- Pointer to the use-case diagrams
- Pointer to the use-case database
- Use cases staging

Note, for this strategy to work, your customer may need a version of your design tool, suitable for browsing. You can make Java-based prototypes available for the user to execute across the network. Then the customer can easily view the updates without having to install anything at his or her end.

Holding the Requirements Review Meeting

The requirements review meeting is really a ceremony to mark the completion of the phase to the team and the customer. It is held to announce that the goals of the inception phase have been achieved. By ceremony, I mean a big deal, lasting at least a full day. The attendees are the program management team members, including the customer. (Recall the customer can be an actual customer or a customer representative, such as the marketing organization.) You may also want to include a higher level of management, both from your and the customer's organization.

At the review, be ready to deliver, present, and discuss:

- Use-case diagrams
- Use-case database, including which use cases are allocated to which build
- System test plan
- Prototyped user interface
- Updated macroschedule

A sample agenda is shown in Figure 5.3. The process of preparing for the meeting provides focus and discipline to the preparation of the artifacts. The team benefits from knowing that their material will be reviewed—that what they've done in the last 90 days matters.

It is important to make the distinction that the meeting is not to *achieve* approval, but to *mark* approval. The wise manager never lets the meeting go forward unless the approval is a foregone conclusion. You should have been involved in ongoing communications with customer representative throughout the inception phase so that there are no surprises during the presentation. For example, the design team might have included a customer representative.

Do not treat this meeting lightly. The smooth and professional handling of the meeting and its outcome is a reflection of your management capability. As a manager, you should be in charge, but you should not be doing most of the talking. It reflects better on you if your management and the customer see how well the team works together. So let them present their material. Put as many of the team in front of the customer as is practical.

Continue to resist delivering hard copy. Keep your use of viewgraphs to a minimum. Instead, connect projection monitors to computers and review the databases,

Time	Item	Presenter
9:00	Welcome and Introduction	Program Manager
9:15	Review of the Agenda	Program Manager
9:30	Development Overview, Status, and Plans	Development Manager
9:45	Use-Case Diagrams	Lead Architect
10:45	Break	
11:00	Use-Case Database Action Items	Members of the Design Team
12:00	Lunch	
12:45	Use-Case Database (continued)	Members of the Design Team
2:00	Break	
2:15	Prototyped User Interface	UI Designer
3:00	System Test Plan	Test Lead
4:00	Action Item Review	Program Manager
4:30	Adjourn	

Figure 5.3 Sample inception phase requirements review meeting agenda.

prototypes, and diagrams online. If possible, give the customer an executable version of the user-interface prototype to exercise at his or her office. Also, provide the customer with online access to the reviewed materials.

If the meeting goes well, the customer will leave with confidence in you and your team, believing you understand the problem and have a workable plan to deliver. In addition, you and the team will have gained confidence that the customer understands and will be happy with what you intend to deliver.

Phase Completion

"Are we done yet?" We are when all agree that that the goals of this phase have been met; that is, everyone has a clear understanding of what is to be built, and the team is ready for the elaboration phase. Reaching this point requires leadership. It is best to reach a consensus that the goals are met and that it is time to move on. That said, realize that agreement need not be absolute. Acknowledge that the program requirements or the even the current build requirements may change. Moving

> ### The Simulator Requirements Review Meeting
>
> You hold a one-day meeting for formal requirement review. All of your artifacts are in place. You choose to use a PC productivity database to maintain your databases. The contractor participates and appears to be onboard. The entire team attends, including those who do not present.
>
> The customer generally appreciates your approach. He likes the use-case approach and having traceability back to his planned curriculum. He also likes the team approach.
>
> He has numerous comments on the trainer prototype, all of which are captured. You agree to update the prototype and the associated use cases based on these comments. You assure the customer the updates will be available in 30 days, and you agree that the prototype will be available on a password-protected Web site.
>
> However, the customer announces a new requirement. He has learned that the simulator will be expected to participate not only in pilot training, but also in operational war games. This means that there will have to be a more elaborate "real-time" command-and-control interface to the simulator. The good news is that you all agree that this interface is not required until the second build. The new requirement falls outside the current scope and so requires further funding. You agree to come back with a proposed contract modification in 60 days.
>
> All in all, everyone leaves the meeting with a good feeling that the project is underway and on a good footing.

out of the inception phase does not mean that the current understanding of the system's required behavior is fixed for all time, only that at this point in time an agreement has been reached as to the scope of the project. If things change, the scope may need to be revisited. Often, if there are a limited number of unresolved issues, they are best answered by proceeding with the development.

If this phase is not complete on larger projects, some members of the team may be ready to move forward with the design activities of the elaboration phase. Give them the go-ahead. Often, the more detailed analysis of the activities of the next phase is useful to resolve scoping issues. Similarly, if you feel that the 80–20 rule has kicked in, find a way to spur the team on.

> **Completing the Simulator Inception Phase**
>
> After the review meeting, you take some time to assess your situation. Generally, things are coming together: Your teams are in place; the use-case exercise has gone well; customer relations are on track; the development infrastructure is in place.
>
> You do, however, have some major planning challenges. First, you have to adjust your current budget to include a system engineer and a retired pilot.
>
> Finally, you need to review the architecture to account for the command-and-control interface and to adjust the sizing. You consult with the lead architect and conclude that the architecture can be adjusted later and that the new requirement should not prevent moving forward with the current build.

All that said, you must discipline the team in completing the phase. Do not let the calendar determine when you are done. Of course, it is ideal to be on schedule, but if you are not, do not pretend that you are. Instead, draw up an honest recovery plan. There is nothing more damaging to a project than a manager who pretends that his or her project is ready to progress when it is not. Such a manager loses the respect of his or her team, the customer, and occasionally management.

The operational criteria for completion of this phase are that all the development artifacts have met their phase exit criteria, the process tasks are complete, and the requirement review meeting has been held. You then hold an all-hands meeting at which you present your view of the requirement review meeting. You thank the team for their efforts and announce the transition to the elaboration phase.

From Here

This chapter identified what outcomes you need to accomplish in the inception phase. It also described how to achieve these outcomes. The chapter itemized the associated activities and how to coordinate them. Finally, it delineated specific guidelines for completing the phase. The next chapter does the same for the elaboration phase.

6 MANAGING THE ELABORATION PHASE

Any solution to a problem changes the problem.

R. W. Johnson (b. 1916), *Washingtonian*, November 1979.

This chapter continues the detailed discussion of how to apply the controlled iteration lifecycle model to object-oriented projects. In the inception phase, much of the activity is focused on reaching agreement with the customer regarding what will be delivered. In the elaboration phase, the focus turns inward. Most of the activity is geared toward reaching a common awareness of exactly what software will be built.

Recall that this lifecycle model is based on the idea that software development is an exercise in group problem solving. The outcome of each phase is the completion of a problem-solving stage. In the previous phase, inception, the emphasis was on problem scoping. During this phase, you turn your attention to project design. However, scoping continues as the design efforts proceed. It is inevitable that a clearer understanding of the delivered product will emerge from the design activities.

The outcomes for the successful completion of the elaboration phase are:

Project design. Initial agreement by the team as to what exactly will be built.

Preparation. Ensuring all is in place for the construction phase.

The first outcome reflects the internal focus of this phase. In the inception phase, the hand-off of the project from the customer to the team was completed. As you enter this phase, you should have full confidence that you have captured in your use cases and other artifacts what the customer wants and needs to be delivered. With this understanding, you begin to turn the customer requirements into a system design. This process requires less communication with the customer and more among the team members. Thus, as a manager, you will be more concerned with team communications during this phase than during inception. The leadership task moves from building consensus with the customer to building consensus within the team.

> **NOTE**
>
> The leadership task moves from building consensus with the customer to building consensus within the team.

For object-oriented projects, a system design is a specification of all of the attributes and methods of the classes. The major challenge of this phase is the translation of the use cases, a dynamic view of the system, into classes, which are static. This transition is best done using some intermediate artifacts, such as the generation of package-level use cases and sequence diagrams.

With the completion of this phase, you must be ready to start the process of generating, writing, compiling, and integrating the system code. Therefore, all of the required development tools and libraries must be in place before you complete this phase. This chapter discusses how to achieve the outcomes of this phase; it addresses the artifacts generated and highlights the communication issues.

Management Overview

With the onset of the elaboration phase, your project should be fully underway and you should be fully staffed. With the increased understanding of the system, it's time to review your sizings and time and effort estimates. Remember, with each phase you have more information on which to base your estimates. It is very likely that you overlooked something and your original estimates are low. Rarely are the time and budget more than you need. If your revised estimate to complete is greater than your budget, you have four choices:

- Ignore the situation and hope for the best
- Figure out how to stay on budget and on time by spending reserve and cutting corners

- Adjust the content

- Find a way to increase your budget

Adopting the first approach is of course folly. By ignoring the situation, you forsake your responsibilities—you stop managing. You leave yourself and your team vulnerable to an eventual disaster.

The second approach is preferable. Everyone appreciates a manager who can bring in a project on the original budget schedule. But going down this path has consequences. Cutting corners can mean less testing or fewer reviews, and result in lower quality. Decide to ship a lower-quality product with care. Be sure that doing so to make a market window or to meet a critical need is the best decision. Realize that, in the end, the costs of shipping a poor product will probably exceed the cost of doing it right. For a commercially shipped product, service costs can be very high. (Of course, you also have to contend with the losses caused by your product earning the reputation as being inferior.)

If you decide to manage your budget very carefully and spend all your reserves, you may be putting your project at risk. You are betting that there will be no other surprises down the line. By trying to contain the shortfall, you may be unnecessarily adding risk. If adjustments are inevitable, the sooner you make this known, the better. Further, the customer and management usually prefer hearing bad news early, when there is time to regroup. The last conversation you want to have with your manager is: "Boss, I have good news and bad news: The good news is that we will be able to ship on time in three months; the bad news is that we are out of money today." Expect your manager to ask how long you have known about the situation and why he or she is only hearing about it now. A disciplined tracking and oversight process will help prevent this situation. I will discuss this in more detail in Chapter 9.

It is always tempting, and occasionally justified, to move content from the current build into the next one to protect the schedule. However, unless you have a recovery plan for the next build, you may just be putting off the inevitable. Beware of the bow-wave effect, whereby required content development keeps stacking up to the end of the schedule.

Sometimes the only method of protecting your budget and schedule is to simply reduce the scope of the project. Of course, discovering this just after the requirements review is a little awkward. You will have to manage customer communications carefully. Fortunately, the use-case database provides a common basis of discussion for prioritizing content.

Entering the Simulator Project Elaboration Phase

You are feeling good after the review meeting. Your team is fully staffed. Your project is defined. The process is underway. Now you ask your design team to focus on dealing with the new real-time interface requirement. They go through the affected artifacts and report on the impact to the overall design. Fortunately, many of the internal interfaces already were time-critical, so the impact is not as great as it might have been. A few new interface classes need to be added.

A week after the successful requirements review meeting, you get a telephone call from the customer. He congratulates you on your team's performance at the review meeting, then mentions that he just got out of a meeting in which the new airplane was discussed. He has learned that the aircraft will have a newly developed color-enhanced digital radar display, and it is an absolute requirement that this display be delivered in the simulation. He goes on to say that this should not be a problem. After all, the requirements specification included a radar system.

You stay calm. At this point, you do not know the impact. You ask the customer to send you all of the specifications on the new radar. He agrees. You tell him you will get back to him.

You call in your lead architect to discuss the situation. She has just completed her review detailing what the hardware contractor is providing. It does not include a radar model. In fact, all that will be provided by the contract is an IBM-compatible personal computer and color monitor to serve as the radar. Based on this discussion, you realize that the radar has fallen between the cracks. You assumed that the instrument interfaces that the contractor was providing included the radar, but there is no mention of radar in the contract with the customer. You call the contractor. He explains patiently that instruments and radar are different things. Clearly, your project's scope has increased.

You ask the architect to assess the impact and get back to you in two days. She comes back with a revised top-level diagram, shown in Figure 6.1; it is a revised sizing and effort estimate. The revised effort requires two people for the two years for development, plus another person for six months for testing. She also discovered that your company *does* have a radar simulation that can be adapted to meet the new requirement. After a rough estimate, you determine that you are short $650,000. Meanwhile, you review the use cases to determine your commitment to the customer concerning radar. You discover that the use cases refer to conventional radar. You ask the design team to flesh out the radar use cases.

You call the customer and ask to meet. At the meeting, you point out that the original estimate was based on the assumption that you could reuse an off-the-shelf radar model. The new radar is a new requirement that expands the scope of the effort. You make your case by providing the new top-level diagram and use cases, then ask for a $700,000 budget increase. He takes the data and says he will get back to you. He has to find the money. You hope that his management has reserved some money to cover such a contingency. You proceed as if the funds are forthcoming.

As the problem is primarily the display of data, you assign the task to the out-the-window team. You ask the team lead to find the staff. In addition, you ask for a way to stage the functionality.

At your program meeting, your staff takes all this in stride; after all, they are professionals. It is business as usual. However, in private your new hire has expressed severe misgivings about the customer, suggesting that the customer screwed up the requirements. "Why don't we just execute the contract as written?" he asks. If it doesn't work, it is not our fault. You explain the business context of the deal and how everyone wins if the customer gets what he *needs*, not just what he asked for. While talking, you learn that the new hire has just come from a start-up with "cool" technology. (Unfortunately, the customers did not appreciate the product as much as the developers.) The employee thinks that customers in general are morons. You clearly have some work to do. You ask to meet with the new hire once a week to see how things are going.

200

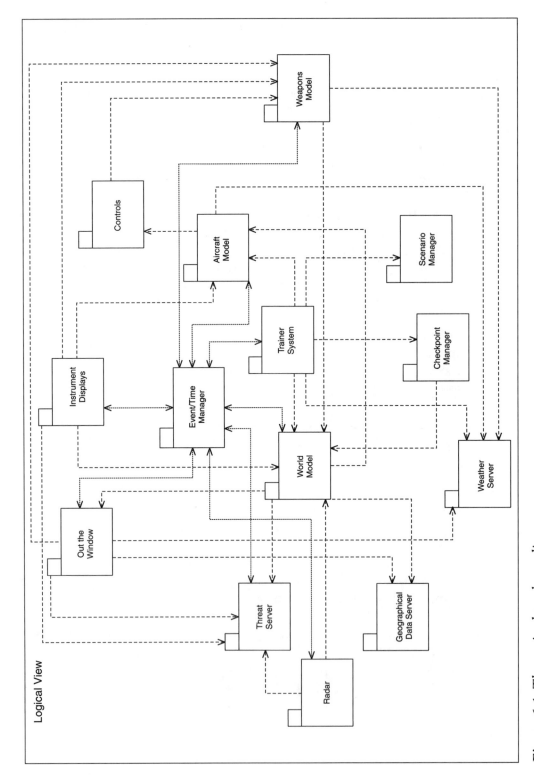

Logical View

Weapons Model

Controls

Aircraft Model

Scenario Manager

Trainer System

Checkpoint Manager

Instrument Displays

Event/Time Manager

World Model

Weather Server

Out the Window

Threat Server

Geographical Data Server

Radar

Figure 6.1 The revised package diagram.

Team Issues

The elaboration phase is often the hardest time for the team, because it is during this phase that consensus may be to the most difficult to achieve. There are two reasons for this:

- The class design task is particularly difficult.
- The team might be in the storming stage.

The object design is probably the most daunting task of the project. It takes experience and creativity to develop a robust class design, and often there are numerous alternatives and opinions to consider. Some will result in design trade-offs. For example, some designers prefer deeper inheritance. Other designers like abstract interfaces with façade classes; they appreciate the improved modularity. Still others, more concerned with performance, are uncomfortable with such an approach. And sometimes very little is at stake. Certain designers may have more experience with one set of utility classes than another. I had one team spend two weeks debating the right way to handle Boolean types in a design. I called it the "one-bit problem."

Disagreements may arise out of different levels of experience. More experienced developers often approach design differently from those less experienced. Developers new to objects tend to design large complex objects with too much state. Some may not understand the object paradigm at all; nevertheless, they may defend their designs fervently.

Ironically, just when there is the greatest potential for disagreement, the team may be the least prepared to deal with it. If your team is in the storming stage, some of the developers will try to establish their roles, their status, by insisting the team adopt their approaches. Ego interferes with reason. Consequently, during the storming phase, you and your leads will spend more time working with the team members than during the other team forming stages. Once the team moves into the norming and performing stages, you should be able to step back and let the team do its job. For now, you have to help the team come together.

Leadership

I am always impressed by the difference good leadership makes to a team. The elaboration phase is your opportunity to provide leadership and make good things happen. Here are some techniques to keep in mind as you manage through this phase.

- *Assign ownership and exact commitments.* Use your team's concerns to your project's advantage. During the storming phases, when team members are concerned about establishing their status, you can reward them by assigning clear responsibilities. Their part of the bargain is to be willing to make and keep commitments. When individuals meet their commitments, increase their roles on the team; when they do not, diminish their roles.

- *Share the vision.* Explain to the team what the fruits of their success will be; better yet, tell them what is at stake. Detail what the project's success means to the customer, to the business, and to the team. Describe the opportunity for follow-up efforts to make the program better, to be able to build something they will be able to take pride in. Keep them informed about the business and customer side of the program. And don't forget to share the importance of the schedule. Try to achieve buy-in that meeting the schedule is essential. Share your understanding as to why the customer and management need the product on the named date.

- *Set expectations.* You will have to deal with developers who take the position that you cannot force creativity. They will say a design takes as much time as it takes. In response to this, do not waver on the need to hold the schedule. Point out that you and the team have been entrusted to deliver and that you firmly believe that the assembled team can deliver. Make it clear that failure is not an option.

- *Focus on bringing issues to closure.* Do not let the team get bogged down. If you sense the team is not making progress, step in and use your consensus-building skills to break the deadlock. In many cases, you can empower the appropriate technical lead to handle team problems. Let him or her resolve the issue. Only as a last resort, resolve an issue yourself. But remind them that holding the schedule is usually more important than how a technical issue gets resolved. Having a good design is very important, but most issues take more time than they are worth. In most instances, if it becomes clear that another alternative is needed, there will be time to make the adjustments.

- *Build trust and loyalty.* Unless the team trusts you, they will not share with you the information you need to successfully manage the project. You need honest, accurate assessments of the project's status and progress, so the team must feel comfortable in sharing bad news as well as good. Treat bad news constructively. Do not focus on blame, particularly in public. Instead, immediately turn attention to recovery plans. Be flexible, while being firm in the goal of making the schedule. If you respond to schedule slips or other bad news with personal abuse, you are not as likely to hear the next round of bad news.

- *Make yourself available to help.* At every meeting, I ask if anyone needs management assistance to help them meet their commitments. I counsel staff that they should use all the available tools to meet commitments, including the management. For example, if they cannot proceed because some dependency is not being met, they are not off the hook. They need to bring the concern to someone who can help; in most cases, their team lead or manager. When problems are brought to you, either resolve them quickly; or, if possible, counsel the employee on how he or she can solve the problem. If you criticize an employee for bringing a problem to you, you will betray his or her trust.

- *Do not be a hero and usurp an employee's work.* Taking work away from a team member is devastating. You will lose the employee's commitment to the team forever. If the employee cannot do the work, get him or her help. Over time, gently move the employee to a different assignment or different team.

- *Always give credit.* Let employees present their efforts to the customer. You can take credit for how well you managed the team and how well they performed, but not for the individual efforts of your staff.

- *Never show panic.* The staff has to trust that, even in a crisis, they can count on you to keep your cool and lead the team to a resolution.

- *Support your staff.* Once you have assigned ownership and responsibility, give your staff room to make their own decisions. Reinforce their ownership. If an individual raises an issue that lies in the domain of another staff member, refer the problem to that person. If there is a disagreement regarding the decision of one your staff members, your initial response should be to support that person even if you have misgivings. If you have serious doubts, discuss them with the responsible staff member, in private. Address your concerns without usurping authority.

- *Depersonalize discussions.* Foster an atmosphere of free and open discussion. People need to feel secure to explore alternatives without a fear of reprisal. Set the ground rule that criticism of approaches is allowed, but criticism of people is not.

- *Be willing to move people off the team.* It is inevitable that certain team members will not work out. They might not have the required technical ability, or perhaps they consistently fail to meet their commitments. Many managers will try to work with such employees, hoping to make them useful members of the team. But do not jeopardize your project by continuing to carry staff who are adding risk. Eventually, other members will complain. Hesitating too long to let the ineffective person go is not fair to the other employees, to your customer, or to yourself. Take the person off the project. Do it quickly and with as little upheaval as possible. Ideally, you can find the employee a position in which he or she will succeed. Even if you cannot, firing an employee is preferable to having a project fail. With the correct timing and execution, you will actually earn your team's trust by stepping up to doing what is required to support the project.

- *Use overtime sparingly.* Plan to have your staff work regular hours. If your plan relies on your team working 80 hours a week, you will experience a well-deserved failure. Extra hours should be regarded as a kind of management reserve to be used sparingly. If everyone is already working too many hours all the time just to stay on schedule, there will be no reserve when an extra push is needed. Under these circumstances, productivity suffers and morale plummets. It is fair and reasonable to ask the team to put in the extra hours every so often in order to make a deadline, but it should not be business as usual. When overtime is required, buy the pizza. Having these extra hours available gives you room for recovery from unexpected setbacks.

- *Say thank you.* It amazes me how often managers fail to thank the staff when given an opportunity. It is also amazing how far a sincere expression of appreciation goes. Develop the habit of saying thank you often and meaning it. Realize that your career depends on the performance of your teams. When they perform, be truly thankful.

FOR FURTHER READING

There are several good books on leadership. For a more complete discussion of management leadership techniques, I suggest you read Neal Witten's *Managing Software Development Projects*, 2nd ed. published by John Wiley & Sons, Inc. in 1995, or Luke Hohlmann's *Journey of the Software Professional* published by Prentice-Hall in 1997.

Simulator Team Issues

All teams are on board. You take time out to review the leadership concerns for each of your package teams. Table 6.1 summarizes your observations and includes how you plan to address each of the teams.

Each of your package teams has a different set of management issues and so requires different kinds of leadership. You are particularly concerned about the core services team. You wonder when the team members will start visiting the office.

You are also concerned about how well the program team and the design team will come together. Your lead architect shares this concern. You agree to attend the design team meetings to serve as a facilitator until you are comfortable that the team can proceed on their own.

Table 6.1 Simulator Package Teams

TEAM	STATUS	LEADERSHIP APPROACH
Trainer Team	Newly formed team with competent, experienced team lead. Numerous enthusiastic younger programmers.	You meet with this lead every couple of weeks to discuss how the team is coming together. You are confident that he can bring his team through the various phases.
Core Services	New team with representatives from teams from the various servers. No one has built a world model before. Your new hire team lead comes from a start-up with real-time computer game experience.	This new hire will require a lot of attention. Given his technical competence but lack of team skills, he may have trouble effectively delegating the work. Further, with a set of programmers from different server teams, the opportunity for competitive behavior is very strong. In fact, it is likely that your new lead will find himself being competitive with his team. He will require a lot of counseling.
Weapons Model	You added the exiting weapons team to the project. They are servicing another project as well. There has always been some tension between you and the team lead. She is very secure, having led this team for six years.	You are concerned that the team lead is not fully committed to your project. However, she has technical integrity—she can be counted on to do the right technical thing even if she does not like you or the project. You decide to maintain a healthy distance. You do meet occasionally, when you ask for her advice on finding the best technical solution. Her advice is usually reliable, so you follow it when you can. You always work through her when dealing with one of her team members.
Controls	This team is led by one of your senior engineers, about five years from retirement. He is reliable, with a focus on details. Although he is short on vision, he is just the sort of person to work with a contractor. His staff is a mixed bag of programmers.	You meet with the lead on an as-needed basis. You give him lots of room and authority to work with the contractor. You pray he does not leave the project.

(continues)

Table 6.1 Simulator Package Teams (*Continued*)

TEAM	STATUS	LEADERSHIP APPROACH
Instrument Display	This team is led by an up-and-coming programmer. This is her first team lead job. She has shown leadership in the past and you believe she can meet this challenge. She is given a staff with a combination of younger and older programmers.	You suggest that the lead meet with you on a weekly basis to discuss how things are going. In addition, you try to enlist the controls team lead as a mentor for her. She is to accept guidance from the controls team lead in working with the contractor. Fortunately, she is willing to try this arrangement.
Out the Window	You pick up an existing team with graphical skills. The team lead is very strong technically. About half the team takes the transition point between projects to find other opportunities.	You are pleased to have this team onboard. You wonder why the turnover is so high. You make some informal inquiries to learn that the lead, while a good person, drives many of his team members crazy. You decide to send him to a leadership class and to do some mentoring.

Development Activities

From the cognitive model perspective, the elaboration phase is devoted to designing—developing the approach to solving the problem. It follows that during this phase your team will focus primarily on translating the requirements into a software design. From the point of view of object-oriented design, the activities of this phase consist of deriving the static view of the system, classes, and their interaction. The desired outcome of the development activities of this phase is the completion of the initial software design, which is sufficient to start construction.

As you enter the elaboration phase, you have two development artifacts:

- Top-level package diagram—static view of the total system
- Use-case database and diagram—a dynamic view of the total system

By the end of this phase, you need to have a view of the system that includes detailed static and dynamic views of the modules—that is, the packages.

Recall that one technique of designing a solution to a problem is to divide a larger problem into smaller sections. To partition the system view into a modular view, you have to accomplish two tasks:

1. Modularize the dynamic view into dynamic view of the packages.

2. Develop the static view of the packages.

With the completion of this phase's development activities, the team will have a complete, consistent initial design. The new artifacts of this phase are the:

- Development-level use-case database and diagrams
- Package-level use-case database and diagrams
- Sequence diagrams
- Detailed class and package diagrams
- Integration and unit test plan

Figure 6.2 shows how these artifacts fit together. The initial top-level package diagram is analyzed to create the package-level and development-level use cases. These in turn are used to create object sequence and class diagrams, the combination of which constitute the object design. Note that the use cases are maintained at two levels of abstraction: the system level and the package level. The package-level use cases are the basis for the subsystem integration tests, and the class specification are the basis for the unit tests. I will go into the different artifacts and activities in more detail in the following sections.

Looking ahead in the next phase, you will focus on capturing the design in a form that facilitates the efficient construction of the code. Along with the new artifacts, the activities of this phase may result in the updating of the previous phase's artifacts.

Use-Case Elaboration

The first step in the design process is to describe the dynamic view of the packages and their interactions as the user-level use cases are executed. Two artifacts can help you achieve this goal:

- Development-level use cases, which capture the package interactions
- Package-level use cases, which capture the individual package behavior

Both are elaborations of the development-level use cases in the sense that they add details and are the result of the further analysis. Treat them as tools on your shelf, not as rigid steps. Recall that the user-level use cases developed in the inception phase described the system from the users' view. User-level use cases, by design,

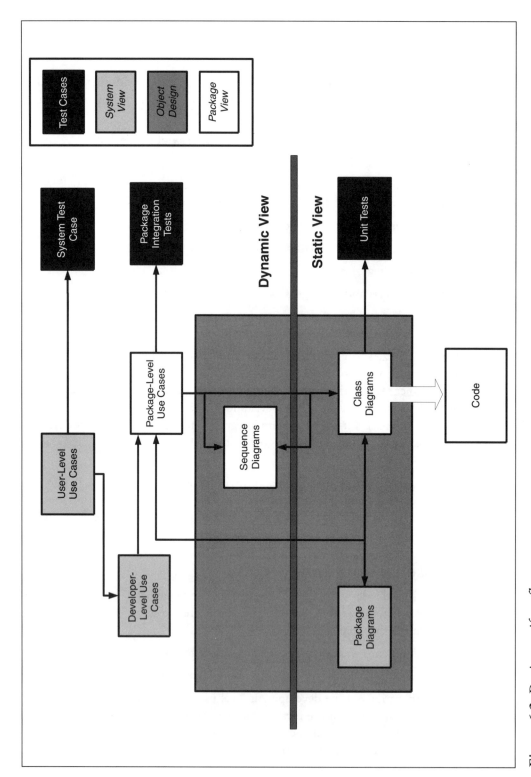

Figure 6.2 Design artifact flow.

avoid discussion of system components. The development-level use cases, described in Chapter 2, take the development-level uses to a lower level of detail by adding how the system achieves its responses, including subsystem interactions. Recall that in the development-level use cases, the actors can include subsystems.

Like user-level use cases, development-level and package-level use cases are kept in databases. Ideally, these databases are available online for browsing to anyone who has a legitimate interest.

Development- and Package-Level Use-Case Databases

The development-level use cases may map one to one to the user-level use cases. Each development use case is simply an elaboration of the underlying user-level use cases. However, if the team finds it helpful to divide the user-level use cases into more than one development-level use case, that is fine. The database structure should allow for it. An example of a database structure for the development-level use cases is found in Table 6.2.

Package-level and development-level use cases were introduced in Chapter 2. I strongly recommend you build the development-level or the package-level use cases or both, although the package-level may be the more important. In my experience, they serve as an essential mechanism for both interteam and cross-team communication regarding how their part of the system is supposed to work, and provide a basis for discussion and understanding of what will be built. The development and

Table 6.2 Development Use-Case Database Structure

FIELD	USE CASE 1	USE CASE 2	USE CASE 3	...
Unique Name				
Unique Identifier, a Serial Number or Label				
Identifier of Underlying User-level Use Case				
Use-Case Text				
Use-Case Owner				
Revision History				
Use-Case Identifier				

Table 6.3 Package Use-Case Database Structure

FIELD	USE CASE 1	USE CASE 2	USE CASE 3	...
Unique Name				
Unique Identifier, a Serial Number or Label				
Package				
Identifier of Underlying User-Level Use Case				
Use-Case Text				
Use-Case Owner				
Revision History				
Use-Case Identifier				

package use cases serve the common understanding of the design approach for meeting the systems requirements. They are a form of agreement—you design your part to do this, I will build my part to do that. With these understandings, the team can be comfortable in proceeding to detailed class design. A suggested database structure for maintaining the package level use cases is shown in Table 6.3.

Package-level use cases provide other essential benefits. For one, they serve as a basis for designing the subsystem integration tests. Further, since they bridge to the user-level use cases, they are a way of ensuring that the eventual system design will in fact be capable of carrying out all of the required use cases. Recall that the user-level use cases benefit from being structured and presented in use-case diagrams. This is true of the package-level use-case diagrams as well.

Assigning Responsibility

All the development staff should get into the act. The lead architect and the design team should be responsible for the elaboration of the user-level into development-level use cases. The team members will enter and modify the development-level use-case database and ensure that every user-level use case has been addressed.

Partition the package-level use cases to the subsystem teams. They will maintain their use-case database. The team leads will in practice take ownership of their team's package-level use cases.

Phase Completion Criteria

Development-level use cases are complete when each of the user-level use cases has been addressed; that is, each of the user-level cases should have at least one derived development-level use case. Package-level use cases are complete when each of the user-level use cases has been investigated from the point of view of the package interfaces and services.

The desired outcomes of creating the development-level use case are:

- The team can proceed to class design with a clear understanding as to what the classes in the various packages are supposed to do.

- You are comfortable that if the class design carries out the development-level use cases, the requirements captured by the user-level use cases will be met.

If the desired outcomes are achieved, the development- and package-level use cases are complete. If, however, the team seems insecure about the class design, it often is a symptom of inadequate understanding of what the code is supposed to do, which means the development use cases will need more work. Later, you will trace the sequence diagrams back to the user-level use cases for completeness. In the meantime, it is very valuable to review the set of developer-level use cases to determine whether they exhaustively cover all planned user-level use cases. This audit should be the responsibility of the design team.

Class Design

With the dynamic view of the packages in place, your teams can comfortably get on with class design. The required outcome is to have a competent class design of a program capable of executing all of the developer-level and package-level use cases. In practice, this means discovering the objects from the analysis of the use cases. The artifacts resulting from this activity are:

Sequence diagrams. The dynamic view.

Class diagrams. The static view.

which are two views of the same design. Both are required. Recall that class diagrams describe the classes' static relationships. The static view is used to generate the code. Sequence diagrams describe how objects of the classes can be used to carry out a task. The dynamic view is used to establish that the classes are sufficient to meet the system requirements. Some inexperienced teams will attempt to go directly to class design without maintaining the dynamic view. This is a mistake and will only lead to frustration. In a typical scenario, the team walks through a use case and drops classes and methods into the diagram. Everyone leaves the meeting

Stealth Simulator Use-Case Elaboration

The simulator design team proceeds with the task of analyzing the use cases. First, the team members, consisting of the lead architect and the susbystem team lead, review the use cases as rapidly as possible, identifying the role of each of the top-level packages in the use-case scenarios; for example, every use case that involves storing data identifies the persistence. To work as efficiently as possible, the team divides into two teams: One looking after flying-missions use cases and the other looking after training use cases. For example, use cases that involve maneuvers describe how the controls, aircraft model, event/time manager, and instrument displays packages collaborate. Each of the subsystem teams reviews these use cases as they are developed, then build their own set of use cases to drive their package design. For example, titles of the use cases for the aircraft model include:

- Report Orientation

- Report Velocity Vector

- Query Control Settings

Three weeks into the process, the design team decides to meet daily to review the separate package use cases to be sure they are consistent. For example, in the meeting it is decided that querying all of the control settings either one at a time or all at once will introduce a performance bottleneck. The lead architect asks the core services and controls team leads to meet and design an efficient grouping of control queries. They readily agree.

happy with the work they accomplished. A few days later, they come back to the design and cannot remember their reasoning behind the class design. Further, the confidence in the adequacy is lost. By keeping both views in sync, you can capture the reasoning behind the design.

TIP

Adopt the rule that no static design is complete without an accompanying dynamic view.

There are two levels of detail in a class design: *architectural* and *unit*. The architectural level is defined by the package diagrams and the identification of method calls allowed between objects of different packages. The packages and the method calls between the packages define the software architecture of the system. At this level, the design is seen as a modular set of services. How the services are actually accomplished is encapsulated within the packages. The architecture is the responsibility of the architect and the design team.

The unit level of detail captures the behavior within a package. Unit-level design is the identification of object classes, their relationships, and the method calls between classes within a package. It captures how the packages perform the services specified at the architectural level. The unit level is the responsibility of the package team.

Clearly there is interplay between the two levels. As the elaboration proceeds, the design team needs to look after the architectural level as the package teams develop the unit level design.

FOR FURTHER READING

If you or your team is new to the process of class design, I recommend *The CRC Card Book* by David Bellin and Susan S. Simone published by Addison-Wesley in 1997. Also see Craig Larman's *Applying UML and Patterns: An Introduction to Object-Oriented Analysis and Design* published by Prentice-Hall in 1997, and the classic, *Object-Oriented Analysis and Design with Applications* (2nd edition) by Grady Booch, published in 1994 by Addison-Wesley.

There is no automatic way to generate the class design, but there are two approaches to class design of the packages.

Bottom-Up. Finding the classes by analyzing the use-case text in detail.

Top-Down. Finding the classes by recognizing the opportunity to use recurrent class patterns.

Gain familiarity with both approaches as most projects will benefit from using a combination.

Bottom-Up Class Design

In the bottom-up approach, the use cases are reviewed in detail, noting each noun and verb; this is known as noun-verb analysis. Each noun is a candidate to be an object and each verb is a candidate to be a message. The candidate objects and methods can be captured as sequence and class diagrams or on Class Responsibility Collaborator (CRC) cards, an artifact used by the developers to represent object classes.

The candidate objects and methods need to be analyzed further in order to discover classes that can be used to instantiate the objects. It is not acceptable for every object to have its unique class. If you use the CRC cards, the team jointly sorts them into piles with the intent that the objects in any one pile will be combined as instances of a single class. If you use a design tool, the same sorting and combining needs to take place. Some teams use the initial sequence diagrams to generate the CRC cards and do the sorting; and then they go back into the design tool and update the classes.

Class Responsibility Collaborator cards are used to assist, document, and communicate the results of object analysis, design, and implementation. They are useful when deriving the sequence and class diagrams. Kent Beck and Ward Cummingham introduced them as a brainstorming tool in 1989. Since then, no standard CRC format has been adopted. There are two recent books which explain their use: *The CRC Card Book* by David Bellin and Susan S. Simone published by Addison-Wesley in 1997 and Nancy Wilkinson's *Using CRC Cards: An Informal Approach to Object-Oriented Development (Advances in Object Technology, No. 6)* published by Prentice-Hall in 1995. I prefer a CRC variant called Class Responsibility Operator Collaborator Cards (CROC), created by a colleague, Martin Svedlow, shown in Table 6.4. The CROC version extends the more common CRC format by including operations. I have found that capturing the designers' thoughts about the class op-

Table 6.4 CROC Card Format

CLASS	
Responsibility	
Responsibility	
Responsibility	
Operation	Collaborator Class
Operation	Collaborator operation
Operation	Collaborator operation
	Collaborator Class
	Collaborator operation
	Collaborator operation

erations while defining the classes is more efficient than waiting until later. The ground rule for using the cards is that the operations will most likely change at a later date.

The elements of the CROC cards are:

Class

Derived from the "objects" on the sequence diagrams.

A class is a generalization of the objects shown in the sequence diagrams; objects are instances of a class.

Responsibility

A high-level statement (description) of what the class does.

Operation

Derived from the message on the sequence diagrams.

Message-service request among classes.

Corresponds to a class method.

Collaborator Class

Another class from which this class requests services.

Important because this collaborator class will be referred to in the class code.

Collaborator Operation

The specific operation invoked in the collaboration class.

Important because this method invocation will be included in the class code.

Once you have the initial class and sequence diagrams in place, you will continue to refine them as the design and implementation evolves. They must stay in synchronization throughout the development. Failure to do this will result in your inability to trace the impact of the design of requirement changes, and you will lose the ability to confirm the adequacy of the design.

Top-Down Class Design

Top-down class design differs from the bottom-up approach in that it takes advantage of object design patterns introduced in Chapter 2. To use this method, first

Stealth Simulator Class Design

Different teams take different approaches to class design. The trainer team decides they are building a new application and so adopt a bottom-up approach to their class design. The other systems decide that their subsystems are enough like other systems to enable them to take a top-down approach. They reuse past design decisions and couple them with some of the patterns found in *Design Patterns, Elements of Reusable Object-Oriented Software* by Erich Gamma Richard Helm, Ralph Johnson, and John Vlissides published by Addison-Wesley in 1995. For example, the core services team decides that the world model package is concerned with managing the external view of the state; and rather than have different classes handle state inquiries, they feel it will be more robust to define a single class whose sole purpose is to maintain the world model's public state and handle state inquiries. They adopt the façade design pattern from that text as a starting point for their class design.

identify a design pattern found in one of the design pattern books listed in Chapter 2 as meeting the needs of a given package. Often, the packages will cross package boundaries to specify objects in more than one package. The decision to adopt a pattern that crosses package boundaries is a design-team decision. The package team decides whether to adopt a pattern within a package. Once a package is adopted, it is tailored and refined by the package team to ensure that the package-level use cases and sequence diagrams are executable.

After the classes have been entered and found adequate, they will need further refinement. The design should become simple and more elegant, and the classes need to be reviewed for their potential for inheritance and reuse. Large classes with too many methods should be divided. And if you have many small classes, evaluate them to determine whether they can be combined. Consider using aggregation. Finally, review the overall modularity of the design and make any necessary changes.

Performance Budget

When defining classes, be concerned not only with their behaviors, but also with their performance. One way to address this is to have the design team assign a *performance budget* to each of the objects. Include this in the class specification documentation. The unit tests for the objects of this class should confirm that they meet their performance budget.

For example, if the system has to respond in a predetermined amount of time to user input, allot some of that time to each of the packages that collaborate to provide the user service. For example, if the acceptable response to a user updating a drawing is deemed to be .3 seconds, the designer can allocate .01 seconds to the user interface package, .09 seconds to the drawing model classes (which maintain the data description of the drawing), and .2 seconds to the rendering package. The assignment is possible in this phase as the design comes together.

Sequence or Collaboration Diagrams

As discussed in Chapter 2, your team can adopt either sequence or collaboration diagrams to capture the dynamic behavior of your system's objects. The sequence or collaboration diagrams serve three roles. First, they are the pivotal artifacts that connect the static class view with the dynamic use-case view. Second, they confirm that the classes are sufficient to meet the requirements captured in the use cases. Third, they provide a mechanism for tracing the design elements back to the requirements. To fill these three roles, the following criteria must be met:

- There is a sequence or collaboration diagram for every development-level use case.
- Every object and method in the sequence diagram is an instance of a class entered into the class diagrams.

By meeting these criteria, you demonstrate exactly how the program will carry out the use cases with the class definition. Certain of the object design tools enforce the second rule. You are on your own on the first.

Document the Classes

You need to ensure that each of the classes is fully documented. Only by enforcing the discipline of documentation can you be sure the designers have considered all the issues. Further, the documentation serves as a guide to anyone who needs to maintain the system. The required class documentation includes:

- Role and responsibility of the class
- Sequence diagrams it participates in
- Performance requirements it is expected to meet
- Function of each operation
- Role of the variables and return value of the class methods

Most developers have been trained to include this information in their source code. Direct them to enter it in the object design tool instead.

Assigning Responsibility

Developing the class design is the responsibility of the subsystem teams. Each team does its own class design, and each must respect the package associations specified by the package diagrams. Further, each team must review the class diagrams in the context of the package interfaces. The package team allocates the performance budget to the package classes.

Phase Completion Criteria

Recall that the desired outcome of this phase is for the team to understand the design to the point at which they are ready to construct the solution. In practice, this means that the class design is complete and detailed enough so that you can start focusing on coding. It follows that for the purposes of the elaboration phase, the class design is complete when:

- The package-level use-case database is sufficient to account for all user-level and development-level use cases.
- There is a sequence diagram for every package-level use case.
- Every object and message in the sequence diagrams are instances of classes specified in the class diagrams.
- All of the performance budgets have been allocated.
- Every class in the design is fully specified, including all methods, attributes, and documentation.
- Each of the artifacts has been reviewed for quality and traceability.

Completion of this phase does not, however, mean that the design effort is over. All should acknowledge that the class design will be refined and modified during the construction phase. As the program is built, the implications of the design will be better understood, so it makes sense to allow the team to take advantage of the lessons learned during elaboration.

System Design Specification

You may be required to generate a system design document. Although using object design tools obviates any real need for the system design specification, architecture and interface documents are very useful (see Chapter 8). If you must write a system design document, keep it short and make references to the design and use-case files. Include a narrative describing the design considerations, alternatives considered, and decisions. You might want to include the top-level diagram, along with a brief discussion of the roles and responsibilities of each of the packages. Finally, refer the interested reader to the design files.

Subsystem Integration and Unit Test Plans

Recall from Chapter 2 that there are three levels of tests in a large software project:

System. Tests whether the system performs as the user expects.

Subsystem integration. Tests whether the packages, once integrated into the subsystems, work as the architect expects and whether the subsystem interfaces have been properly implemented.

Unit. Tests whether the classes work as the developer expects, and that the class objects perform their intended behavior.

System test plans are derived from the user-level use cases, whereas the other two are derived from the class and package specifications. Once your class and package design is far enough along, it's time to initiate the writing of the integration and unit test plans.

A sound subsystem testing strategy has a positive effect on the team's efficiency. If a package team's members know that the other packages are well tested and reliable, they will feel better about their chances of success. They can be confident that they will be able to fix any problems that arise, and that the packages they depend on will work as advertised.

Subsystem Integration Test Plan

Each package should have an associated integration test plan. The purpose of the subsystem integration tests is to determine whether the project's architecture has been properly implemented and that each of the packages plays the appropriate role in the overall system. They also test the calls across package boundaries to verify that the total package provides its external services exactly as expected. The system test cases are specified by the user-level use cases, and the package test cases are generated by package-level use cases.

An advantage of writing package-level use cases and test plans is that they support reuse of the package by other projects. When the package's use cases, design, and test cases have been captured, they can form a basis for inclusion in other programs, intact or modified for derived efforts. Assuring reuse at the package level adds value to your development. Not only will you delight the customer by delivering a modular, adaptable program, but you will also be providing your organization an intellectual asset. Having your package available can make your organization more effective in the next development.

The subsystem integration test plan describes how the planned package tests determine whether the package's functional and performance requirements are met.

You can start writing the integration plan during this phase. Recall that the sole concern of the subsystem integration test is to confirm as accurately as possible that the architecture has been implemented. In particular, the package tests should confirm that:

- The package use cases can be executed within the performance budget allocation with expected results.
- The package implementation does not crash the system, cause data loss, or affect host platform integrity.

Conversely, the subsystem integration tests should *not* be concerned with whether the packages were built as developers intended—they should have no view of the implementation; they should only test the package interface. Similar to the package tests described in Chapter 5, the subsystem integration tests should be written in a *clean room* setting, using only the package-level use cases as input. The system test writers should not have access to or be concerned with the class implementations.

The subsystem integrations tests must also be traceable to the package-level use cases. In particular, every use case must be included in one or more system tests, and a test may include more than one use case. Each package team's integration test plan should prepare a:

- Test list
- Description of required scaffolding programs or test fixtures
- Description of required resources
- Traceability matrix

A brief description of each follows.

Test List. The heart of the plan is the list of test cases. The structure is very similar to the system test use cases. Each record in the database should contain the fields shown in Table 6.5. All of the data are text fields with the exception of the Unique ID, which may be a sequence number generated by the database tool.

Scaffolding Programs. Most packages are not intended to function as standalone programs. For that reason, they cannot be tested in isolation from the total system without some special interface program. Such test programs are often called *scaffolding* or *test fixtures*, thin programs whose sole purpose is to exercise the package interface. For example, if your system graphically displays the results of a complicated analysis, you must test the rendering subsystem in isolation, for which you will need to write a special program that exercises the rendering system.

Table 6.5 Subsystem Integration Database Structure

FIELDS	TEST 1	TEST 2	TEST 3	...
Subsystem Name				
Test Name				
Identifier (unique ID of the test)				
Brief Description				
Use-Cases Covered (a list of the package-level use cases that the test verifies)				
Performance Criteria (expected execution time for parts of the test)				
Instructions (how to run the test, including the names of Test Fixture)				
Test Writer				
Revision History				

Different packages call for different scaffolding systems. For one, the scaffolding may be an automated version of the entire test case. This approach should be used when the services provided by the package are not user interactions. For example, the test case may involve a series of long computations or a large number of transactions. The scaffolding should return a log of what was run, the capability to examine the result of the test, and a measure of performance. This strategy is particularly important if performance is a criterion. The tester simply launches the test case and later analyzes the results.

A second scenario is when the package provides user-interaction services and is directly accessed by the system user interface. In this case, you do not need scaffolding, but can use the prototype system user interface as the test driver. An advantage of this approach is that it moves the integrations forward. The decision to use the system's user interface as a test driver should be identified in your plan.

A third possibility occurs when the package testing calls for user interaction, but the package is not accessed by the system's user interface. In this case, have the package team prepare a scaffolding program that provides a graphical interface to the subsystem's services along with provisions for displaying the result. This is reasonable given the efficiency possible with modern user-interface builders. A benefit of this approach is that it enables more flexible and robust testing than an automated test fixture. The scaffolding program is used to exercise the test cases.

Required Resources. As for the system test plan, it is useful to think through and document the staffing and resources required to exercise package-level testing. As always, you need to achieve the right balance of ensuring quality within a limited time and budget. However, keep in mind that if you scrimp on package testing, you may be defeating its purpose by adding cost and schedule risk to the entire project. Recall that package-level testing takes advantage of the modularity of the system; if there is a package bug, it is more efficient to isolate it in a package test than in a system test.

A Traceability Matrix. Again, the analogy to the system test holds. The package test list database includes a field that shows the package-level use cases addressed by each test. But you also need the inverse: For each use case, list which test confirms that the package-level use case is executable by the system. If you are maintaining the system tests in a database, this traceability matrix can be created using a report generator. The traceability matrix is required to ensure and document that the package test plan is sufficient, and that the package requirements are met.

Unit Testing

Each class should have an associated unit test. Generally, each unit test exercises all of the external methods of the class in a random order to confirm that the class behaves as the developer expected. It is good practice not to add a class to the subsystem or system builds unless the unit test has been executed successfully.

Unit test planning is very straightforward. Each class developer is responsible for writing, conducting, and documenting the successful completion of unit tests of his or her class. (Note: The class developer writes the unit test.) The function of this test is to ensure that the objects of this class perform as the developer intended. There is no point in the developer and the test writer communicating their common understanding of what the class is expected to do; the quality assurance team audits the adequacy or the unit testing and the reports. As a manager, you need to ensure that this expectation has been set and that the audit processes are in place.

Of course, you have to allow the time to write and conduct the tests. As for package testing, it is risky to try to save time on unit testing. The overall impact on productivity of a defective class added to the build is much greater than any effort spent to adequately test the class.

> **Stealth Simulator Test Planning**
>
> You find a former fighter pilot to add to your transition team. He starts writing a set of system test cases for the simulator pilot, which consist of a set of flight maneuvers based on his understanding of the mission requirements of the fighter.
>
> The subsystem testing is a unique challenge. Some of the packages can be easily tested in isolation; others cannot.
>
> Your team decides to build scaffolding for the more easily tested components: the weather and data servers, the event/time manager, the checkpoint manager, scenario managers, and the aircraft and weapons models. A special hard-wired data file will be built to test the out-the-window system. It is agreed that building fixtures to test the display and controls is too costly. Instead, they will be tested using the simulator hardware as part of the incremental system integration testing in the construction phase.

Assigning Responsibility

Package-level tests are the responsibility of the package teams. The package team lead, along with his or her team test liaison is responsible for his or her package test plan. It is reasonable, however, that some of them may ask for help from the user-interface experts to generate the scaffolding. The design team should review the plans.

Individual developers write the unit tests, but it is the team lead's responsibility to confirm that the unit tests are planned and executed. The entire package and unit testing function is monitored and audited by the quality assurance team.

Phase Completion Criteria

The subsystem-level test plans may be considered complete for the purposes of this phase when they account for every package-level use case. They should be reviewed for completeness and traceability.

Updated Artifacts

In the course of the elaboration activities, you and your team will achieve a deeper understanding of the system you are building. Thereafter, review the artifacts created in the previous phase to ensure that they are still complete and accurate. Revise and update the following artifacts throughout the elaboration phase:

- Top-level class diagram
- User-level use-case database
- System test plan
- User interface

It is likely that the top-level class diagram may also be modified in this phase. Further, the roles and responsibilities of the packages may be reallocated. Of course, changes at this level cause a ripple effect throughout the program and so should be subtly discouraged or implemented with care. One reason for having the lead architect onboard is to lower the likelihood that the top-level diagram will change. For example, the staffing of the package teams is based on the initial concept of the package's purpose. That said, if your design team insists that a change at the top-level is required, listen and support the change if you agree. Then be sure that the assignments are adjusted accordingly.

As mentioned at the end of the previous chapter, one of the outcomes of the requirements review held at the end of the inception phase is that the user-level use cases may need modification. In fact, you may need to add some user-level use cases. Occasionally, the team discovers that the user-level use cases are not sufficient to specify the design. Perhaps there are interactions allowed by the design that are reasonable for the user to carry out, but were not discovered during the inception phase. These use cases, of course, should be added to the use-case database. Further, the system test plan will have to be updated to reflect the new use cases.

The user-interface development that started in the inception phase will continue naturally into the elaboration phase. The user-interface designers, armed with comments from the requirements review, will refine and fill out the interface to more closely match the users' needs. In addition, during this phase, the user interface must be augmented to account for any new user-level use cases. Finally, during elaboration, the system test team can proceed with writing the cases identified in the elaboration phase.

Process Tasks

At the onset of the elaboration phase, the design has been modularized to a point at which separate teams can work on their packages independently, negotiating their interfaces as necessary. But for the different teams to be able to work simultaneously on the various parts of the system, the system design must be *unitized*, divided into separate files that can be updated independently. These files must be kept under version control. How you divide the overall system design into separate files depends on the tool you're using. Some of the leading design tools support integration with configuration managers so that the design files can be checked in and out within the tool.

You, as the manager, have a stake in how the design is divided into units. The units defining the work can occur simultaneously, and establish a basis for enforcing responsibility and ownership. A good place to start is to unitize along package lines, whereby each package is a separate file. However, you may decide to further divide some of the packages into subpackages so that a given team can work on aspects of a package separately. I allow the package team lead to make this decision. Each package team may take ownership of one or more files that contain the class and subpackage design for that package. Along with the package design files, there are also files that link the entire system. For example, a file specifies the top-level diagram and a file may contain the user-level use case. The design team owns these files, and everyone on the team must be able to view everyone else's files.

Importing off-the-shelf class libraries and frameworks into your design is another important process support activity. These libraries and frameworks contain classes that are a part of your design and must be reflected in it. Any version of your design that does not reference these classes is incomplete. Once the classes are included, your team can document the messages that their classes use. In the case of frameworks, they need to document the methods and attributes of the classes they are using as a base for deriving new classes. Fortunately, most design tools have the capability to traverse the header files of a class library or framework, determine the class structure, and import that structure into the model.

By definition, a class library is a modular subsystem with a set of external messages, so they are easy to capture as a package in your design. Once they are in the system as a package, the associations between the library and those packages that use the library can be represented.

Frameworks need to be treated a bit differently. Since they provide base classes, the derived classes in your design will inherit from the framework. In practice, this means you have to identify which classes you use as a base from the framework and include surrogates in your design. These surrogates are abstract classes, classes that are never implemented through code generation, but contain the framework methods and attributes that the derived classes use. Your team may need to enter the surrogates into the design by hand.

After this phase, code construction happens in earnest, for which you need to ensure that everything necessary to generate, edit, debug, compile, link, execute, and test the code is in place. Many of the process activities are tied to the creation of the physical view of the program—the directory structure of the code files. Therefore, you must create the directory structure for the source files and enter the directories into the configuration management tool. Update the design tool properties so that the tool generates a class code into the right directory. Finally, complete files to support compilation and linking.

Coordination of Activities

The elaboration phase may require more coordination than the other phases, as it takes leadership and focus for a team to come together on a design. It is during this phase that the architecture is firmed up, the package interfaces are initially negotiated, and the class design is filled out. The team will also meet for design reviews.

The focus of the design effort moves from the design team to the package teams. The members of the design team will be spending most of their time overseeing and reviewing the package design efforts.

Internal Design Reviews

Design reviews are essential in the elaboration phase. Accomplishing the joint design is one of the chief outcomes of this phase, so it makes sense that finding a means of bringing people together to discuss and agree upon the design is necessary. Design reviews are often very difficult. In fact, if they are not handled well, they may discourage, rather than promote, team communication. Unless the meetings are well structured, with a clear purpose or agenda, the developers may leave feeling they have wasted their time and that meetings interfere with "real" work. Unstructured meetings also leave room for storming behavior. There is nothing like a design discussion to bring out the egos. But if the meetings are productive, team members will learn that such gatherings can promote the design work and make the team more efficient.

Design reviews, too, must be well prepared and managed with discipline. They must facilitate communication. Organize the reviews around two goals:

- To reach agreement on the adequacy of the proposed design
- To identify and track design issues as they arise

Note the meeting is not held to *discover* a design, or even to *fix* a design. When issues arise, track them and assign action items. Schedule reviews regularly, and make them of fixed duration. Identify the portion of the design under review and publicize it to the team before each meeting.

For larger projects, you should hold system design reviews in addition to package design reviews. In the system-level meetings, review the package interfaces. Cri-

Internal Design Review Agenda		
Time	Item	Presenter
9:00	Previous Action Items	Lead
9:20	Introduction of the Part of the Design under Review	Lead
9:30	Relevant Use-Case Review	Designer
10:15	Review of Class Design And Sequence Diagrams	Designer
11:00	Discussion and Issue Identification	All
11:45	Action Item Review and Assignments	Lead
12:00	Introduction to Next Design Review Topic and Adjournment	Lead

Figure 6.3 *Elaboration phase design review meeting agenda.*

tique the class interfaces within the package in the package-level reviews. In the meeting, identify design issues by first reviewing the relevant development-level use cases—system-level for the system meeting, package-level for the package meeting. Then present the detailed static design. The presenter shows how his or her packages collaborate to carry out the use cases. Sound design concepts such as granularity, size of the classes, and modularity of the design are fair bases for discussion, as are any concerns that the design fails to meet project standards. In particular, root out any design that violates the package associations defined by the lead architect.

The lead architect should take the responsibility for the preparation and leadership of the system reviews. The attendees should be the design team, including the package leads. The package lead should run the package-level reviews, which all the package team should attend. The lead architect may decide to attend all of the package meetings. An agenda for a design review meeting is shown in Figure 6.3.

Microschedules

Throughout this phase, have your package team leads maintain a microschedule of the development-level use case and class design. On a weekly basis each team lead should schedule and coordinate the artifacts that will be developed that week and by whom.

The package leads should replicate the process the design team used during the inception phase. At the beginning of the phase, they create their list of package use cases and schedule their completion. Once classes are identified, the package lead schedules the completion of the specification. The package team microschedules should include development of:

- Package-level use cases
- Class diagrams
- Sequence diagrams
- Subsystem integration test cases

Given the volatile nature of the package-level use case list and classes, the lists and schedules must be updated weekly and be reviewed at the program meeting. The microschedules can be maintained as simple tables. Ideally, they should be maintained on Web pages. An example of a microschedule is shown in Figure 6.4. The system test team can start tracking the writing of the test cases identified in the inception phase.

Program Meetings

Naturally, you will continue the program meetings started in the inception phase. The program meeting purpose stays the same: to review the progress of the previous week, reset short-term priorities, and coordinate the activities of the upcoming week. As before, the attendees of this meeting should include, but not be limited to:

- Development manager
- Development lead
- Lead architect
- Toolsmith
- Package team leads
- Quality assurance lead

Choose a facilitator for the meeting to take responsibility for staying on track and focusing the discussion. Generally, any issues raised should simply be added to

ARTIFACT	ASSIGNED TO	PLANNED COMPLETION DATE	DONE?	COMMENTS
Line Class	Fred	10/1/97	Yes	
Rectangle Class	Mary	10/8/97	No	
...				

Figure 6.4 A microschedule table.

Program Team Meeting Agenda		
Time	Item	Presenter
9:00	Previous Action Items	Development Lead
9:20	Overall Status and Risk Areas	Development Lead
9:30	Tool/Infrastructure Status	Toolsmith
9:45	Package Teams Microschedules	Package Team Leads
10:45	System Test Microschedule	Test Lead
11:00	Upcoming Program Events/ Macroschedule Review	Development Manager
11:20	Action Item Review and Assignment	Development Lead
11:30	Adjourn	

Figure 6.5 Elaboration phase program team meeting agenda.

the action item list for tracking and resolved outside the meeting. A sample agenda is shown in Figure 6.5.

The meeting ground rules remain as set in the inception phase. Note that this meeting is not used to set the microschedules, as they should be in place, ready for presentation at the meeting.

Customer and Manager Communication

The elaboration phase can be the most difficult time for the customer and management, for those intent on staying involved. The customer or manager may have trouble perceiving progress, and may often express impatience; they want to see more code and less design, or does not appreciate the value of the elaborated use cases and class diagrams. They often measure productivity by lines of code. If your team is not writing code, how can they be productive?

If this happens, remind them that much of what formerly was coding—writing header files and the like—is actually being done during this phase, that the design tool will generate the code from the design specification. Assure the customer/manager that not only has coding begun, but it is being captured in such a way as to make the team more productive. Also, making the class and sequence diagrams available may be reassuring. The customer or manager can see that the design is progressing as the diagrams come together. Finally, if you decide to do some initial

> **Stealth Simulator Activity Coordination**
>
> Each of the teams conducts the activities with different levels of maturity. The trainer team acts as a separate application, making assumptions as to which messages the rest of the system will provide. They document these assumptions in the package use cases and sequence and class diagrams. The team lead reviews them at the design meetings. The other package leads review the requirements and update their use cases and class and sequence diagrams. Joint class diagrams are created to reflect how the classes across the packages cooperate to service the trainer package. This scenario is duplicated many times.
>
> As you expected, the core services team is struggling. The lead seems to be doing more development than leading, and as a team, they are complaining about too many meetings and not enough time to do real work. When you wander into their offices, you find them writing code instead of creating designs. The other teams are complaining that they are not getting much help. You decide that the problem is inexperience, that they are more comfortable coding than participating in team design. No amount of yelling at this team will fix this problem. They are doing what they know how to do. You decide to step in. First, you review the team member's roles and responsibilities with the lead. You ensure that the lead is not doing all the work, but is leading and coordinating the work. Second, you start holding daily meetings with

integration during the elaboration phase, you can share these with the customer. In addition, sharing the revised user interface is always a good idea.

Holding the System Design Review Meeting

This meeting marks the transition from the elaboration to the construction phase. Probably, the team has already been easing into the construction activities. Some integration of the user interface with other parts of the system may have occurred. Nevertheless, it is important to have the formal overall system design review meeting.

Like the requirements review, the meeting should be an occasion, lasting a day. The attendees should include the program management team, the customer, and possibly someone from your management. As this meeting is more technical than the requirements review, the customer might want to bring members of his or her technical staff.

the team. You do not berate the team; you take a positive approach, while insisting that the process be followed. You review on a daily basis what each member is expected to do and remind them the assignments are designed to bring them into the process. By providing the increased guidance, you are teaching them what is needed, and for the moment have assumed responsibility for their participation in the team. You are raising their comfort level. There is grumbling at first, but you are confident they will come around. They appreciate the leadership. By doing what you ask, they become part of the overall project team; the complaints stop. Over the next two or three weeks, you participate less and less, essentially handing the team back to the lead. Eventually, you decide to stop attending the team meetings, although you do continue to meet with the team lead on a daily basis until you are comfortable the team is really on track.

As you expected, the contractor reps simply will not participate. They have their own processes and will supply what they always do. You decide to form an ad hoc team consisting of the domain expert, the instrument package lead, the control package lead, and the system engineer to coordinate all issues related to dealing with the contractor. They are added to the program meeting agenda. This team will serve as buffer and ensure that the hardware interfaces are folded into the design. The other teams are all doing fine and the design does move along.

At the review be ready to deliver, present, and discuss the:

- Top-level architecture diagram
- Class and sequence diagrams
- Updated user interface
- Updated macroschedule
- Updated system test plans

A typical agenda is shown in Figure 6.6.

Like the review meeting, this meeting is not held to win approval. If you have doubts that your team's approach will not be acceptable to the customer, resolve those issues *before* the meeting. If, as recommended, you have had ongoing communications with customer representatives throughout the phase there will be no surprises as to what will be presented. Maintain the policy of keeping hard copy

System Design Review Meeting Agenda		
Time	Item	Presenter
9:00	Welcome and Introduction	Program Manager
9:15	Review of Agenda	Program Manager
9:30	Development Overview, Status, and Plans	Development Manager
9:45	Top-Level Architect	Lead architect
10:45	Break	
11:00	Class and Sequence Diagrams	Package Team Leads
12:00	Lunch	
12:45	Class and Sequence Diagrams (continued)	Package Team Leads
2:30	Break	
2:45	User Interface	UI Designer
3:30	Review of Previous Action Items	Program Manager
4:00	Review of New Action Items	Program Manager
4:30	Adjourn	

Figure 6.6 *Elaboration phase program team agenda.*

distribution to a minimum. Present your viewgraphs and design artifacts from soft copy using a projector.

A successful meeting will renew the customers' confidence in you and your team. Your goal is that they will leave impressed with the technical insight and professionalism that you have brought to the problem. The customer should be confident that if anyone can build this product, your team can.

Phase Completion

This phase is complete when the design is sufficiently complete that you can start building the solution. Note, the design need not be perfect. It is not necessary to remove all doubts. In fact, you should count on design changes occurring during the phase.

There is good news and bad news about ending this phase. The bad news is that it is often difficult to have the team reach a comfort level regarding the design

Simulator System Design Review Meeting

You hold a one-day design review meeting. Again, the entire team attends including those who do not present. The contractor reps participate, too, and appear to be onboard, but have nothing to present. You insist they be represented in order to answer questions. Of course, you have to discuss whether this meeting was included in their original budget.

The radar issue is not fully resolved. You present the design, including the provisions for the new radar requirement, but make the point that the implementation is out of scope with the current budget. Since the new radar is required in the first build, you emphasize the urgency of coming to closure on the issue. Outside the meeting, the customer announces that he has $500,000 to add to the project. After some negotiation, you agree to contain the new radar and the real-time interface to $750,000.

You include your former pilot in the review, and he presents his mission- and maneuvers-based test plan. You follow the agenda from Figure 6.6. Each package team presents their package-level uses cases and the class diagrams. The customer is reassured that the team has been productive and busy.

state. The good news is that it does not matter. Often, the best way to resolve lingering issues is simply to move on to the construction activities. In most cases, the decision to move to the construction phase is a judgment call, but here are some signs that it's time to move on:

- Productivity has slowed; the schedule is at risk.
- The same issues keep arising without resolution.
- The 80–20 rule has kicked in.
- The team has a solution, but is concerned that it not optimal.

These are all symptoms that the team needs more data to agree on a decision. The missing data will bring the system together. The best way to settle the outstanding issues is to go ahead and start building. If you have an initial class design that contains the majority of the attributes and methods specified, and the above symptoms have set in, move the team forward.

Give the right message to the team, that you are moving forward not only to protect the schedule, but because in your best judgment the team needs to go to the next phase. Explain your reasoning and try to get their buy-in. Your lead architect may need to make some arbitrary design decisions to move forward. Support those decisions.

If you go ahead, you will discover that:

• Morale will improve; teams like to progress

• Some of the issues will disappear

• Other issues will resolve themselves in the course of the construction activities

It is important to remember that a suboptimal solution is better than no solution, and that you may not have the time and budget to find the optimal solution. Again, this decision is based on your understanding of the business context of your project.

> **NOTE**
> Remember, a suboptimal solution is better than no solution.

The operational criteria for completion of this phase is that all the development artifacts have met their phase completion criteria, the process tasks are complete, and the system design review meeting has been held.

> **Completing the Simulator Elaboration Phase**
>
> After the system design review meeting, you take some time to assess your situation. Your teams are more or less functional. You are confident that the design is sound. You expect that the design will change as you go through the construction phase. You are hopeful that the build's content is fixed. Your budget is tight, as usual. Nevertheless, your sizing is still in line.
>
> You hold a second all-hands meeting at which you present your view of the system design review meeting. You give a frank assessment of the status and challenges facing the program. You thank the team for their efforts and announce the transition to the construction phase.

From Here

With the initial design in place, it is advisable to again reassess your sizings, the schedule, and budget. Your ability to estimate is significantly better now than at the beginning of the project.

A successful system design review signals a good break for the team. The design effort is usually difficult. The team has solved some difficult problems. There have been some emotional meetings. Hopefully, the storming period is over. On the positive side, the team believes they have gone through the hardest part of the program. All that remains is to finish the details and implement the system. Success seems very likely, and the team is ready to make it so.

With the completion of the design phase, your team is ready to move to the next problem-solving phase. It is time to build the solution. In the next chapter, I discuss how to manage the construction phase—the building of the system.

7 MANAGING THE CONSTRUCTION PHASE

Ah, to build, to build! That is the noblest art of all the arts.

Henry Wadsworth Longfellow (1807–82), poet.

The construction phase is the next step for your team in the software development as problem-solving process. During the first two phases, your team's efforts consisted of understanding the problem and finding a solution. In the construction phase, your team builds the solution. As you enter this phase, you have:

- A complete class design, including a full specification of all the methods
- A dynamic view of the design tied to the user-level use cases
- A fully functional development environment

It might appear that the only remaining tasks are to implement the methods, compile and link the code, test the integrations, and prepare for delivery. But appearances can be deceiving; keep in mind that class definitions may change, new methods may be defined, and some of the interfaces may change. Your job is to achieve a balance between accommodating the changes and meeting the schedule. For larger projects, coordinating the construction activities is a significant challenge.

The outcomes for the successful completion of the construction phase are:

Complete system build. All the anticipated functions for the current build have been implemented and integrated.

Preparation. The basis for the transition phase has been established.

237

All the functionality that will be delivered in this build will be completed in this phase. In order to exit this phase, your team must have built a fully operational system and be ready to start the process of delivering the system to the customer. Further, the system must be ready for testing in an operational environment. In the next phase, you will continue to develop the code, but not add functionality. All development in the next phase will be in response to defects discovered during system testing. This chapter discusses how to achieve these outcomes. I will address the artifacts generated during this phase and highlight the communication issues.

Management Overview

The construction phase of an object-oriented software project is a bit like David Copperfield performing a magic trick: The hard part is done long before he performs on stage. The risk of performing a magic trick is mitigated through elaborate preparation and teamwork. To the audience, the smooth execution is magical.

Depending on the sophistication of your customer or your superiors, your management of this phase may seem a little magical. Every time they check, you

---

Entering the Stealth Simulator's Construction Phase

As you enter the construction phase, you again assess your situation. As usual, it is a mixed bag. On the plus side, your team is working well; it has reached the performing stage. Your intervention has turned around the core services team's productivity and morale problems. Your relationship with the hardware contractor is good enough that you do not anticipate problems. In addition, the team is comfortable with the design. More important, they have learned to resolve design issues without conflict. Finally, the development environment is in place. In fact, a fair amount of code was built during the elaboration phase, confirming the design as well as the tools.

On the negative side, you are worried about the budget and the schedule. Because of the previous problems with the core services team, you are four weeks behind schedule. Your financial reports show you are over budget. At some point in the future, you will evaluate the cause of the slippage. For now, you must deal with the situation. You realize it is impossible to make up all of the time. You decide to reset the program baseline.

have more of the project to show. Because of the careful design effort and the leveraging of the design tools, it seems to them to come together easily. If they are used to the usual pace of a software program, when the crises occur in the system integration toward the end of the development, your crisis-free delivery of a working system will make you seem like a magician.

From your team's point of view, the hardest part—solving the problem—is over. Your attention now turns to managing the actual construction of the system. At this point, your customer has an pretty fair idea of what will be delivered, and your team has a good idea of what they need to build. A productive development environment is in place, and the team is working well together. There should be nothing stopping you now.

Unfortunately, it is not that simple. While David Copperfield has absolute control of the conditions on stage, you do not. The following distractions and challenges may add risk to your schedule:

- New requirements from the customer
- New approaches generated from the team
- Unexpected mismatches of the interfaces
- Unexpected behavior of the integrated subsystems
- Failure of some of your team members to perform

Your job is to handle all of these impediments and get the job done. The price of a successful project is eternal vigilance. Your raison d'être at this stage is to get the code built.

> **TIP**
> In the construction phase, the leadership task moves from building consensus within the team to maintaining focus.

Resetting the Baseline

It is useful to revisit the three major risk areas at the beginning of each phase because, remember, your early estimates of the scope, effort, and cost were informed guesses. Recall that a 20 percent error in the planning stage estimates of effort and cost is common. As you proceed with the project, however, the uncertainty is replaced by solid information. Armed with this information, you can reset the program's baseline—that is, adjust your program and your customer's expectations to reflect the reality of the project. Do not reset baseline too often, though. The phase transitions provide a perfect opportunity; they occur at the right frequency. In addition, the customer or management may be more open to the discussion following the successful completion of a phase.

Keep in mind the three risk areas: cost, schedule, and customer satisfaction. At this point in the project, address the cost and schedule risk by revisiting your sizings. Do a detailed sizing analysis. You have what you need to calculate a *cost-to-complete* within 10 percent. There are various ways to determine the estimate. One approach follows these steps:

1. Count the number of classes to be completed. Do not include the constructors and destructors generated by the code generators.

2. Assign duration and resources to the development of each of the methods. Recall that a method needs to be coded and unit tested. Your estimates will vary, but realistically, approximately one method per day per developer is reasonable. If your estimates vary considerably from this, revisit the design.

3. Assign duration and resources to the subsystem and system integrations. These activities are discussed in more detail next.

Share the cost and schedule estimates with your program team, and discuss the implications. With any luck, you will not have a problem. If you are short on time for the current build, your best approach is to review the content of the build with the intent to minimize risk. As a guide, I suggest that you and your lead architect sort the project's use cases into four categories determined by two scales: customer priority and development (cost and schedule) risk.

Create a graph like that shown in Figure 7.1 Customer priority increases along the *x*-axis, and the development risk along the *y*-axis. The graph is divided into four categories:

Low-risk, low-priority. These features are candidates for *lowering resources*. It is possible that the resource is better spent on the higher-risk items.

Low-risk, high-priority. In this case, leave well enough alone; *stay the course.*

High-risk, low-priority. These use cases are the *first to go.* Consider eliminating them from the build.

High-risk, high-priority. These candidates may require more resources. At the very least, these use cases require more attention.

Place each of the use cases on the grid. For example, high-risk, high-priority items will be in the upper right-hand quadrant. An advantage of the grid is that you can visualize the relative position of the use cases. Figure 7.2 provides an example.

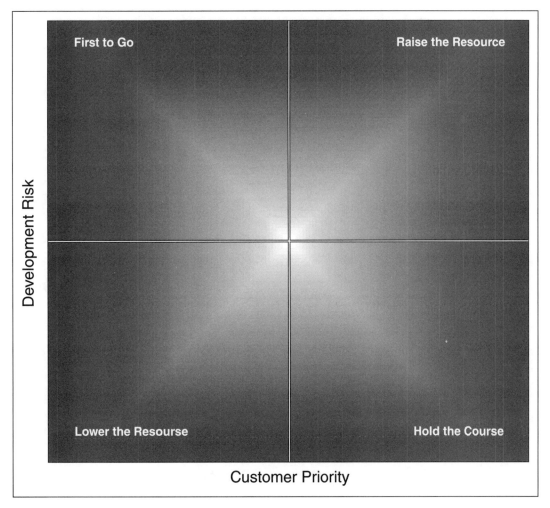

Figure 7.1 Use-case priority grid.

If you cannot get the schedule lengthened or the budget increased, you have only three options:

1. Try to increase productivity by lengthening the hours.

2. Move resources to increase overall efficiency.

3. Negotiate for less content.

After you have computed your cost-to-complete and sorted your use cases on the grid, stay on plan by exploring these options.

Figure 7.2 A risk/priority matrix for the simulator.

Staying on Plan

Many managers opt to increase productivity by lengthening the hours; 60- or even 80- hour weeks are far too frequent in this business. I say use this option sparingly and carefully. A project may need extra effort down the road, and you want to be able to count on the team to deliver. Managers who require long hours as a matter of course risk losing their team's commitment. Further, it is a sign of weak management. Experience has shown that extended periods of working long hours eventually lowers productivity and leads to a low-quality product and to loss of valuable staff.

> **Resetting the Simulator Project Baseline**
>
> With the new commitments and budget, you still are on a tight budget. You put together a risk-priority table to assess your situation and ensure your resources are allocated correctly. Admittedly, given the variety of skills and the functionally focused subsystem teams, you do not have much leeway. Nevertheless, it is useful to go through the exercise. An abbreviated version is shown in Figure 7.2.
>
> You discover that there are a few low-priority/high-risk use-case scenarios, including the ability to play back the missions in reverse, and providing weather–based tactile feedback to the pilot via the controls in addition to the visual impact. Both of these exceed the customer's specifications, but were added to the requirements as functionality within required use cases.
>
> You call your program team together and go over the results. The team agrees to remove first-to-go items from the build. Plans are instituted to direct the staff in response to the other results. In a follow-up meeting, your team estimates the cost of completing the build. Fortunately, with the adjustments, your budget seems to be adequate and you do not have to go back to the customer.

If a period of extended hours is required, share the reasons with the team. Ask for a commitment from them to meet the schedule. Never discuss the hours per se, only how quickly the work needs to be completed. I leave it to the individual members to set their hours to meet the commitment. Of course, if someone falls behind, then the discussion must become more serious.

If you have low-risk, low-priority items, consider moving resources from these use cases to the high-risk, high-priority ones. But use this option with caution; moving resources will only take you so far, and as we have discussed, it can make the problem worse. Moving the wrong person onto an assignment can derail the effort. The team may have to spend its valuable time bringing the new member onboard instead of developing the code.

If you have any low-priority, high-risk items, you can go back to the customer and negotiate their removal from the build. Explain the use cases are unnecessarily adding risk and that the time is better spent on ensuring a successful build.

Team Issues

Generally, the construction phase is an easy time in the build. Most of the team formation issues have been addressed, roles and responsibilities have been well established, and the right level of communication is supported. The team members know who is supposed to do what, what they own, and to whom they need to talk to discuss a design issue. They have made whatever accommodations are necessary, and know who can be relied upon to deliver. Further, they see real progress as the integrations come together, so they can take pride in being part of the team.

All that said, team coordination still requires support and focus. Most of the team members will be intent on filling in the methods of their classes and supporting the integrations. During this activity, some may have a tendency to revert to "let me hide in my office and do my work" behavior. After all, they are responsible for building their classes. They may feel that further communication is a distraction and so avoid dealing with over developers. They would rather work around a bad design than ask someone to fix it. Alternatively, they may not be responsive to the requests of other developers who want to discuss interfaces of mutual concern. The result will be a less-than-optimal design, so such behavior must be discouraged. Continue to emphasize the need for collaboration in order to tune the internal interfaces.

The use of object design tools makes it easy to contain the impact of interface changes. Teach team members to use the tools to their mutual advantage. In fact, supporting changes in attributes and methods well into the development cycle is one the tool's chief benefits. When the team members want to make changes to the design, support their decision. By doing so, you set the tone that it is the overall solution that matters.

Leadership

Two leadership skills are required for the successful management of this phase. The first deals with filtering communications from outside the project. The second deals with promoting internal communications and eliminating conflict.

Be a Low-Pass Filter

One of the important roles of a program manager is that of a *low-pass* filter, who relays only the facts to the team and filters out speculation or information that does not directly involve the team. In signal processing, a low-pass filter removes the high-frequency noise from a signal, allowing the low-frequency content to pass. Similarly, messages to the team from the upper management and the customer contain low-frequency content—involving program content and plans—as well as high-frequency content, consisting of requests of the moment—support an unplanned demonstration, consider a new market, and so on. Both, your team members and management expect you assess the impact of the high-frequency content on the project and to provide the discipline and decide which requests can be accommodated. The low-frequency content remains—regardless of the distractions, you must deliver the project. It is your responsibility to filter out these requests and distractions and keep the team on track. Remember that if you respond only to the noise, your project will be a failure. If you protect your project by limiting the impact of the noise, you will in the end gain the respect of your team, your management, and your customer.

> **TIP**
>
> When I receive a request from the management or the customer that I feel cannot be supported without adding unacceptable risk, I never say no outright. Instead I say something like, "Yes, we could do that, but the project would be delayed a week. Also, it would blow the budget." This makes the point that nothing is free, and demonstrates that you are in control of your project. What should follow is a discussion as to the importance of the request and whether it is worth the impact. You and the customer end up making an informed, deliberate decision. The project is not put at risk.

Your role as a low-pass filter is especially valuable to the team. Teams rightly denigrate a manager who resonates with the requests, detracting focus from the project delivery. They feel their efforts are wasted—and they are probably right.

If, during this phase, the customer comes to you with new requirements, it is good news. It shows the customer cares about the project even though it might mean more work for the team in the end. However, with rare exceptions, the construction phase is not too late in the build to accommodate new requirements. The requirements should be captured as use cases, added to the database, and be folded into the content priority discussion for the next build.

> **TIP**
>
> Be flexible in executing the plan. Be rigid in protecting the plan.

If the team gets wind of some of the high-frequency content—a possible change in plans, an unplanned visit—they are likely to become distracted and very concerned. When this happens, share as much information as appropriate. Explain the issues and how you plan to respond. Emphasize that completing the project is the first priority and that their efforts are still valued and appreciated. As the situation evolves, keep them informed. Your job is to protect your team from such high-frequency distractions and to keep them focused on the low-frequency mission.

Conflict Resolution

Things will go wrong: Integrations will fail, tools will break; code that worked yesterday and has not been touched, will fail today. When these crises occur, never panic. Stay calm; be decisive and deliberate. Never use such an occasion to make personal attacks. Nothing is more pathetic than a manager who responds to crises by screaming and blaming his or her team. The crisis will pass. Your relationship with your team is an ongoing concern. Follow these steps to resolve any conflicts that may occur.

1. Gather information. Determine the root cause of the problem. Listen to all sides.
2. Ask the affected team members for alternatives in dealing with the problem.
3. Make a decision. Any decision is better than no decision.
4. Put a plan in place; get agreement and buy-in from the participants.
5. Follow up. See if the plan is working as desired.
6. If there was an instance of individual failure, deal with it privately and discretely.

If you are able to successfully lead your team through a crisis or two, they will follow you anywhere.

Development Tasks

The development tasks of this phase consist of building, testing, and integrating the code. In particular, your teams will:

- Fill in methods of the classes
- Unit test the classes
- Complete the user interface
- Integrate the subsystems
- Test the subsystems
- Conduct a series of incremental system integrations
- Test the system builds
- Complete the user documentation

Simulator Team Conflict

In one of your few quiet moments, you assess the status of your team formation. You realize that many of the issues result from the fact that you are managing two linked applications: the actual cockpit simulation and the trainer workstation team, and they have different sets of development constraints and priorities. There is not much to be done about this, other than to make the teams aware of the need to work together to address the issues. You share the insight with the teams and encourage them to be flexible.

Meanwhile, everyone is angry with the core services team. The other team leads are not comfortable that this group will be able to make their commitments during the interim integrations. As they are providing the services that link the other subsystems, any failure on their part puts the entire project in serious risk. As much as you would like to have the new lead succeed, you decide that it is time to make the difficult decision: You quietly start making plans to replace the lead. You make the move within two weeks.

Meanwhile, the hardware subcontractor reps are rigidly holding to their own way of doing business. That said, they continue to deliver; they meet their schedules. Your decision to add a program team to represent the hardware function is working. Although they have done little to affect the contractor's behavior, they have served to facilitate the communication and to fold their status into the overall project.

At the completion of this phase, the entire integration will be completely built and system tested! The transition phase, discussed in the next chapter, is focused on operational testing and customer delivery.

Note the primary development focus is on the static artifacts. The dynamic artifacts are updated only as needed to stay in synchronization with the inevitable design changes. The dynamic view is reflected in the test cases generated in the previous phase. Of course, if the interfaces change, so must the unit- and subsystem-level tests.

Integration Strategy

The primary activity of this phase is the generation of a sequence of incremental integrations. There are two approaches to building a system: big bang and incremental.

Big Bang Integration

The big bang approach is illustrated in Figure 7.3. In this figure, time proceeds to the right. Prior to any integration, each of the development teams develops and tests their code separately. At the end of the development activity, the separate subsystems are brought together for a single integration. The presumption underlying this approach is that if they meet specification, the assembly will come together smoothly. In practice, this rarely happens.

Many programs, using some of the more traditional development methodologies, adopt the big bang approach. Not surprisingly, it fails for several reasons. First, there are too many interactions introduced into the system at once. Integrations usually fail because of unexpected interaction between the states of the classes. If all the classes are brought together at once, discovering which pair of classes is at fault is difficult. For example, if the defect leads to a system class during initiation, you have little to go on in finding the flaw. Once the program initializes, plenty of bugs will be found to be corrected. Of course, every correction must be followed by an entire system test to be sure that no new bugs have been introduced. If on the other hand, classes are introduced a few at a time, it is easier to narrow the problem. The new classes participate in the problem.

TIP

Code may be so poorly designed that it can never be successfully integrated and tested. The symptom of this is that, after a while, every fix introduces a new bug. Such systems are called *brittle.* The integration of brittle code literally drags on forever. Brittle code arises from insufficient modularity: A problem with one part of the system cannot be addressed without affecting other parts; fixing one problem affects the system state in such a way that another problem develops.

If you discover during a big bang integration that you have a brittle system, there is little you can do. The best course of action is to throw away the code and start over. (This explains the maxim that, in software, you build the first system, throw it away, and deliver the second. I don't accept this.) Even better, do not develop a brittle system in the first place. Object design per se will not prevent such a catastrophe, but a good class design will. An experienced architect can usually detect a brittle system while browsing the class diagrams. In addition, integrating incrementally will help enforce modularity and lead you to discover unfortunate state interactions while there is an opportunity to address the problem—before it gets out of hand.

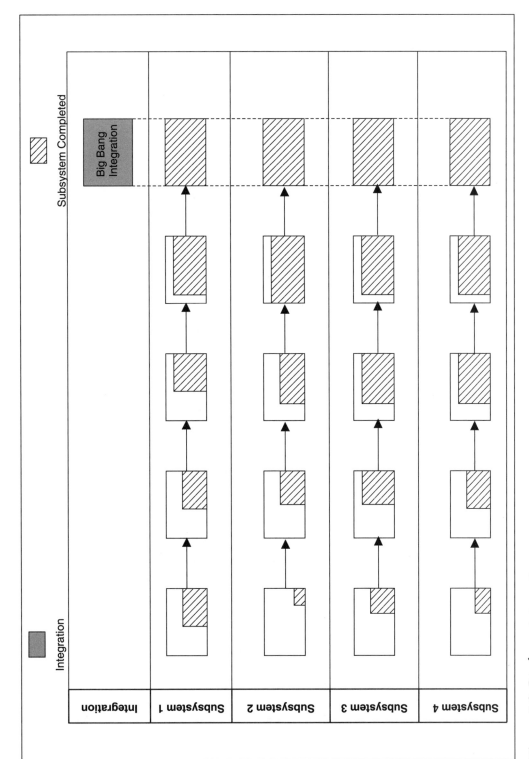

Figure 7.3 Big bang integration.

249

A second problem with the big bang approach is that it occurs too late in the process to allow recovery. By putting off the integration until the end of the development cycle, you have little time to deal with the inevitable defects. Some bugs can be found only during system integration so it makes no sense to wait until you are up against the end of the schedule to find and address these subtle errors. To make the problem worse, correcting errors found during integration often requires a re-design. By adopting the big bang approach, you are forced to do a redesign under severe time pressure. It is hardly surprising then that it is during this activity that projects blow their schedule, or lose control of their design, or both.

Finally, big bang integration interferes with your ability to accurately track the program. Because of the uncertainty of what will be found during the integration process, you have no idea of the true state of your development. There is no way to estimate how long the integration will last, and you are thus unable to estimate the cost to complete with any certainty.

Teams and their managers come to dread big bang integrations. The time pressure, the uncertainty, the difficulty of debugging, and the resulting long hours and occasional panic turn the otherwise well-run program into a crisis. The program ends with much stress, and success is not assured until the very end. Fortunately, there is an alternative.

Incremental Integration

The incremental integration approach is illustrated in Figure 7.4. As time proceeds to the right, each of the subsystems develops more function. The existing functionality is integrated and tested in a series of interim integrations. Each integration extends the previous one. In the diagram, the dark rectangles in the integrations represent the previous integration, the light gray the incremental function. Note that in the big bang integration the amount of newly integrated code to debug is large, while in incremental integrations, at any one time the amount of newly integrated code is relatively small.

Though incremental integrations require more ongoing coordination between the development teams than the big bang approach, carrying them out during the construction phase has none of the difficulties found with the big bang approach. The defects resulting from class interactions are more easily discovered and addressed; there are relatively few classes in the first integration, making debugging the smaller system easier than debugging the full system. And since there are fewer interactions, there are fewer places to look. Once the initial integration is debugged, you add a few more methods from the same classes or new classes. When things break, the problem is clearly due to the new code. Again, there are fewer places to look and fewer state interactions to understand.

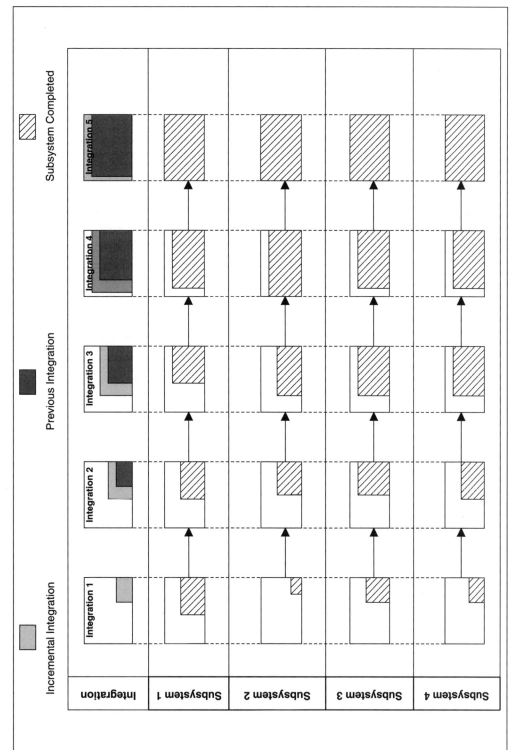

Figure 7.4 Incremental integrations.

If a design flaw is discovered during an integration, it can be addressed in an orderly manner. Recall that one of the premises behind the use of objects and the controlled iteration lifecycle is that new requirements and necessary interface changes will be discovered as the code is built and integrated. While I have emphasized many techniques—use of design tools, modularity of design—that enable the ongoing design activities, correcting the designs as an anticipated activity during the construction phase rather than as an unplanned activity during a big bang is clearly preferable.

One of the chief advantages of the incremental integration technique is that it ensures greater certainty and accuracy in tracking progress than the big bang technique. With the big bang approach, though you know how far along the parts are, you do not know how far along your assembled product is. This explains how some projects spend 60 percent of their time being 90 percent complete. With the incremental approach, you have precise knowledge as to what has been accomplished. There are two useful measures of completeness:

- The percent complete is the measure of the planned use cases that are executable in your current interim integration.

- The percent complete is the measure of the planned class methods that have been implemented and linked into an interim integration.

The first provides your level of completeness from the customer's point of view, the second from the implementers' point of view. Both are useful. With the two views, there is little uncertainty as to where the effort stands. I will come back to this discussion in Chapter 9.

Finally, interim integrations have a very positive effect on your team. As they go into the later phases of the development, the team is confident that they can and will succeed. They can see the integration coming together, and they harbor no lingering doubts as to the viability of the project or that the integration might fail. No crisis looms ahead. With the integration in place, the team enters the transition phase without a hitch. Like the magician on stage, they make it look easy.

Levels of Integration and Testing

Recall from Chapter 2 that there are three levels of testing:

Unit tests, which determine whether the class works as the developer intended.

Subsystem tests, which determine whether the subsystem works as the architect expected.

System tests, which confirm that the entire system behaves as the user expects.

All three are conducted during the construction phase.

Assigning Responsibility

The developers conduct unit tests to ensure that the code is ready for subsystem integration. As mentioned in Chapter 2, the subsystem teams may need to do subintegrations and conduct subsubsystem tests. From the point of view of the program manager, this is the subsystem teams' problem. They interact with the other teams by providing tested, integrated subsystems. Recall that the transition team leads the system integration and testing, and the subsystem integrations are the responsibility of the subsystem teams, directed by their test leads. The unit tests are the responsibility of the individual developer.

Class Development

Class development consists of:

- Implementing the methods of the classes in the design
- Documenting the classes, attributes, and methods in the design tool comment files
- Writing scaffolding and unit test code to exercise the classes prior to integration into the subsystem
- Compiling and linking the class and the test code
- Testing the methods to prove they perform as designed
- Debugging the class
- Documenting the unit test
- Dropping the source files into the subsystem and system integrations

All of the artifacts, including the unit tests, must be kept under version control.

The class owners do all these implementation tasks. Their responsibilities include not only delivering tested, working code, but also ensuring the code is consistent with the design. The attributes and methods of the source files must be the same as those in the design. This concurrence is possible using two facilities of the design tools: *forward code generation* and *reverse engineering*. In my experience, neither is infallible.

In forward code generation, the design tool overwrites the current version of the source file, preserving the bodies of the methods. The source files are updated to reflect the changes in the class specification without losing the method bodies. The tools do this by inserting tags in the body as comment fields. It makes for ugly code, but it is a very useful feature, as it preserves the design tool, rather than the source code, as the place where the classes are specified. However, the tools cannot perform miracles. If the changes in the specification are too extensive, some cutting and pasting of the source files may be required, so it is essential to keep your files under version control to preclude the danger of losing work through a mishap in this process.

To use reverse engineering, the developer updates the source file. The reverse engineering feature reads the source file and creates the class diagram. The challenge in this method is that the associations to all of the other classes that invoke the method may need to be reestablished. Reverse engineering is most useful if you have let the design get out of control, that is, out of synchronization with the code. You can reverse engineer the current code to capture its class design back into the tool. This way you can document the as-built design. But this use of reverse engineering should be a last resort; it should never be necessary. In my projects, I use reverse engineering only to bring off-the-shelf class libraries into the project design.

In theory, a unit test report should be generated every time a class unit test is run. However, during debugging, a test may be run many times. A more reasonable standard is that the unit test report be generated every time a new defect is found, and when there are no defects found and the class methods are ready for inclusion in the subsystem integration. The unit test report can be hard copy or, preferably, soft copy. Figure 7.5 contains a sample unit test report form. The quality assurance organization should audit the unit tests and the reports.

In order to carry out the development activities, the developers need to maintain three views of the code: design, source, and debug. The design view is maintained in the design tool; the source view is maintained in a code editor; and the debug view is maintained in the debugger. The views offer different perspectives of the code. For example, when updating a class, the developer may need to update the design, generate the code, reload the source view into a code editor for further update, rebuild the test, and enter the new executable into the debugger in a matter of minutes. Some development environments have these tools integrated. If you are not using these integrated tools, then your toolsmith will have to lash your separate tools together to create a productive environment.

During class development, it is very likely that the developer will discover a need to change the interface of one or more of the associated classes. If the developer owns the associated classes within his or her team's package, and no one else is depending on them, he or she simply updates the class specification, regenerates the code, and goes on with life. The design tool can report which classes are dependent on the updated classes. If, on the other hand, the developer is changing the interface to a class that affects another developer's code or if he or she needs another developer to change a class interface, then a discussion is necessary. He or she should contact the owners of the associated classes, discuss the changes, and reach an agreement. I prefer these discussions to be informal, developer to developer. However, if there are other stakeholders, they should be involved. You need some

```
┌─────────────────────────────────────────────────────────────────┐
│              Simulator Project Unit Test Report                   │
│                                                                   │
│                                                                   │
│  Developer _____      Date _____          │
│  Subsystem _____                                        │
│  Class _____        Methods Tested _____  │
│                                   _____    │
│                                   _____    │
│                                   _____    │
│                                   _____    │
│                                   _____    │
│                                   _____    │
│                                   _____    │
│                                   _____    │
│                                   _____    │
│                                   _____    │
│                                                                   │
│  Defects Found _____   │
│  _____   │
│  _____   │
│  _____   │
│  _____   │
│  _____   │
│  _____   │
│  _____   │
│                                                                   │
│  ☐  Class is ready for integration                                │
└─────────────────────────────────────────────────────────────────┘
```

Figure 7.5 *A sample unit test form.*

mechanism to ensure that these small changes do not accumulate to alter the roles and responsibilities of the packages. Any interface changes that affect the architecture should be reviewed with the design team. In any case, treat these sorts of changes as business as usual. Do not impede these changes; facilitate them while maintaining the integrity of the architecture.

Internal Code and Design Reviews

Every project manager is faced with the question of how much code review to conduct. Reviews are essential to:

- Confirm that the code respects the architecture
- Ensure that sound coding and design principles are maintained
- Determine that the code is sufficiently documented to be extensible and maintainable
- Establish that the unit testing is sufficient
- Enforce the project's coding standards

There are those who argue that code reviews are a good tool for detecting and preventing errors in a cost-effective manner; they have experimental data to back up this contention. But this has not been my experience. I find that code reviews are a very expensive method of locating errors in anything but small efforts. For one thing, much of the benefit of code walkthroughs has been attained using sequence diagrams. I prefer to rely on the scrutiny of the design and the interfaces, and less on the code. I trust good design, competent developers, the tools, and the multilevel testing to detect and remove the errors.

FOR FURTHER READING

Watts Humphrey, the former director of the Software Process Program at the Software Engineering Institute, is a strong advocate of the use of code reviews to reduce errors. His 1995 text, *A Discipline for Software Engineering*, (Addison-Wesley) describes his theory in further detail.

Younger team members may not fully buy in to the extra overhead required to keep the source and design consistent, the code documented, and the unit test reports written. They may feel it adds unnecessary effort and risk to their individual efforts. Under these circumstances, it is all too likely that the code will become disconnected from the design. These members need to be educated as to their role in the larger effort; they must support the big picture. That said, code reviews are essential to ensure that the overall development goals are met.

TIP

Review all code to ensure that the architecture is implemented and that the project's standards are respected.

Have each of the team leads review each of the classes against the given set of criteria. Review the code as a condition of entering the subsystem and system integrations.

Assigning Responsibility

Throughout the class development activity, the individual developers design, implement, document, and unit test the classes. In general, they negotiate the interface changes with oversight from the design team. The quality assurance staff ensures that the classes and unit tests are reviewed and that the test reports are adequate.

In the section on coordination of activity, I will discuss how to determine the order of implementation of the class methods.

Phase Exit Criteria

Very simply, the class development phase is complete when the current build is *functionally complete*; that is, all of the planned use cases can be executed in a stable build.

Horizontal and Vertical Development

There is a simple system model that can aid you when planning the order in which classes are implemented. Consider the system as a two-dimensional set of layers, as shown in Figure 7.6. The top layer is the user interface. The lower layers are functional classes that provide the system services and the underlying base classes. The horizontal dimension of the system represents the breath of its functionality. The

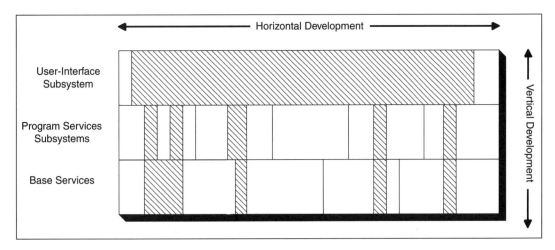

Figure 7.6 Horizontal and vertical development.

Simulator Interface Development

The horizontal and vertical strategy applies to both the cockpit and training workstation development. The simulator hardware itself provides the horizontal view of the cockpit simulator development—it is the user interface. The order of integration you adopt for the cockpit simulation is:

1. Install the simulator.

2. Fill in the basic flight controls and instruments to support flying, take-off, and landing—in that order.

3. Bring in the out-the-window functionality, emphasizing display first, realism later. For example, it is preferable to have the initial integrations include out-the-window display, composed of simple filled polygons. The texture maps, weather effects, shadows, and the like can be added in later integrations.

4. Add the weapons and threat systems once the initial flight capability is in place. However, be careful not to wait too long to do this.

The training station has its own user interface. By now, your team and the customer have agreed on the interface design. At the first integration, you simply include the interface with little or no functionality. The first vertical slice in your plan is the ability to save and restore a scenario. This slice shows that the connections from the user interface to the middle layers of the database services are in place. The next round of integrations connect the training subsystem to the cockpit. The first integration of the two major subsystems contains the ability to initialize the cockpit from the trainer workstation. Your team plans to add the abilities to capture checkpoints and have the trainer intervene in the succeeding integrations.

vertical dimension represents the depth of implementation of each specific functionality. The horizontal development represents filling in the user interface. The vertical slices represent the functionality needed to carry out user-level uses.

One practical way to organize the system development is to fill in the top layer in a horizontal direction, then follow with vertical slices until the entire system is complete. Taking this view of development has several advantages.

- Functionality is integrated to support use cases.

- The user interface is in place to drive the design of the functional classes.

- The user interface is in place to exercise and test the functional classes as they are developed.
- The system tests may be used to test the interim integrations.

User Interface Development

The prototype user-interface effort that began in the inception phase evolves during this phase into the actual system user interface. It stops being prototypical and starts being the real thing. Prior to entering this phase, you should have had adequate customer reviews of the interface so that you can proceed in confidence with the development. In this phase, you focus the user-interface activity on completing the design of all the windows, implementing the methods in the underlying classes, and integrating the design into the system. The user interface plays two special roles in the construction phase:

- Establishes the horizontal view in the integration strategy
- Provides an interface for system testing the vertical slices

Incremental Subsystem Integration and Testing

As the classes are developed, they are integrated into subsystems, which are linked to form the system. Recall that the subsystem test plan was created from the subsystem scenarios during the elaboration phase. As the class methods of a subsystem are implemented, they are tested as a whole in a subsystem test, before inclusion in the system integrations. Recall, too, that the subsystems are made up of one or more packages, and have well-defined external interfaces derived from the package interfaces. The subsystem tests demonstrate that the subsystem interfaces perform as expected.

The artifacts generated by this activity are the subsystem test reports and defect records. The subsystem test reports look much like the unit test report, as shown in Figure 7.7.

Defect Tracking

Maintain defect reports in a database, because various team members will need access to the records at different times. For tracking purposes, generate reports on the number, status, and disposition of the defects. Handle defects, once they are discovered, as in most development processes. The details may vary from organization to organization, but for most, the process works as follows:

1. The tester who finds the defect enters it into the database.
2. Once entered, an architect prioritizes the defect.

Simulator Project Subsystem Test Report

Tester _____   Date _____

Subsystem _____

Integration Number _____   Test Cases Run _____

_____
_____
_____
_____
_____
_____
_____
_____
_____
_____

Defects Found _____

Number:	Name
Number:	Name
Number:	Name
Number:	Name
Number:	Name
Number:	Name
Number:	Name
Number:	Name

☐ Subsystem is ready for integration

Figure 7.7 A sample subsytem test report.

3. Project management assigns the person to work the defect and sets a due date for completion.

4. Once fixed, the original tester confirms that the defect has been removed.

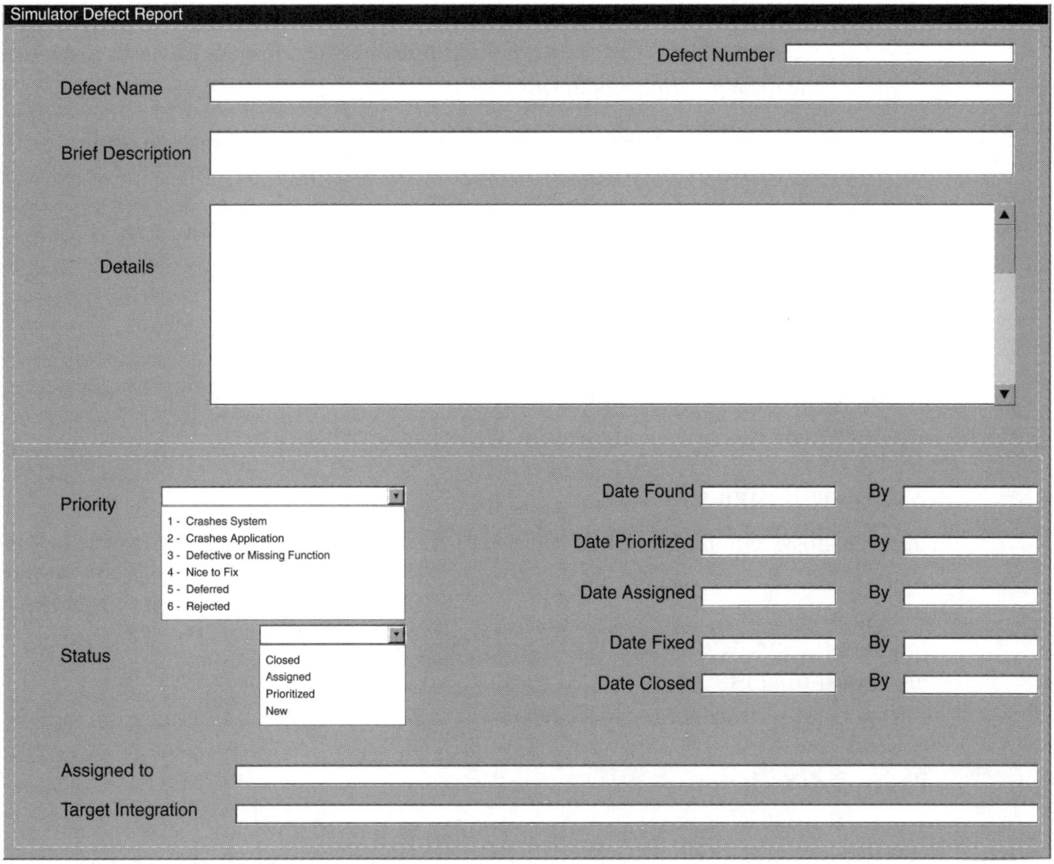

Figure 7.8 A defect record entry format.

A sample entry from the defect database is given in Figure 7.8. The database fields are:

Defect Number. A unique number assigned by the database tool.

Defect Name. A text name that identifies the defect, entered by the person initiating the record.

Brief Description. A synopsis (up to 256 characters) of the problem, useful for reports. The person initiating the record enters the brief description.

Details. An open-ended text field that can be used for a fuller description of the problem, reasons for status changes, and the like. Anyone can update this field.

Priority. The determination of the importance of fixing the defect, chosen from a predetermined list. The lead architect or his or her delegate, usually someone from the design team, fills in this field.

Status. The status of the defect as it moves through the evaluation and disposition processes. The status may be chosen from a finite list. The date of the status change and the person responsible are entered into the appropriate fields.

Assigned to. The name of the person assigned to lead the correction of the defect. The development lead or the team lead fills in this field.

Target Integration. The integration number or date that the correction is to be dropped into the system and tested. The development lead or the team lead fills in this field.

Assigning Responsibilities

Interim subsystem integration and testing is the responsibility of the package teams' leads. They are responsible for delivering stable subsystems to the project's transition team. They do the integrations, conduct the subsystem tests, and generate the test reports and defect records. You may also want to assign some of the development staff to assist the leads on a part- or full-time basis. The system architect and the team leads process the defect records.

Phase Exit Criteria

The exit criterion for this activity is similar to that of the class development: the creation of a stable, functionally complete build. In addition, all of the priority 1, 2, and 3 defects should be closed.

Incremental System Integration

As discussed, the transition team links the interim subsystem integrations into interim system integrations throughout the construction phase. This team also assembles and conducts the integrations. They use an abbreviated version of the system tests to confirm that the integration works effectively. If errors are discovered, the team enters them into the defect database. Each integration adds greater functionality, and more of the use cases are executable.

The Final Integration

As you approach the end of the phase, your team should become increasingly conservative in allowing content into the integrations. This principle is particularly critical as your team completes the final integration of the build. You and they will feel pressure to deliver all that you promised. Inevitably there will be some function that the team wants to add hours before your release manager kicks off the last integration. The function, while not critical, will benefit the product. You will be tempted to "go for it." My advice is *don't do it. Just say no.* It is inevitable that in the developers' haste to institute the new function, a bug will be introduced, leading to rounds of fixes and integration testing. If you are careful, you will be able to back out the function. But, that will take extra time and a new integration. In any case, your team will be compelled to work around the clock to fix the problem. You will deliver a system that you are less sure of than you should be. Ultimately, you and your team will question your judgment.

Likewise, as you approach the final integration, be increasingly strict regarding which defects you address. Naturally, you cannot ship a system that harbors level 1 or level 2 defects. However, you cannot afford to risk fixing a level 4 defect. In approaching a level 3 defect, you might consider backing out the functionality rather than attempting to fix it. My goal in any build is to complete the last integration early and take the team out for beer.

TIP

To finish the phase cleanly, avoid the temptation to add just one more method to the final integration.

Phase Exit Criteria

The phase ends when all of the planned class methods have been integrated and tested successfully in a system integration. At the end of the phase, a system has been built that supports all of the use cases. The entire system test suite executes correctly.

User Documentation

Depending on the nature of the system, your deliverables might include:

- Help files
- User manuals
- Reference manuals
- Tutorials
- Installation manuals
- Developer manuals

One of the challenges you will face in using the controlled iteration lifecycle model is coordinating the design and the user-level documentation, which needs to be consistent with the system design. However, the system design continues to evolve until late in the cycle. The requirement to develop user documentation places some constraints on how much change is permitted in the system. For example, context-sensitive help files are intimately tied to the user interface, but the interface may continue to change throughout the construction phase. Your challenge is to deliver the documentation without unduly restricting the development. If you adopt a process that requires the user documentation content to be pinned down long before delivery, you will end up developing a system to meet the documentation, not writing documentation to describe the system. This reversal of roles is unlikely to lead to the best system.

The documentation must be developed concurrently with the system. In terms of phasing, put off beginning the documentation until the construction phase, and finish it during the transition phase. Adopt a production method that supports this schedule. In particular, deliver as little hard copy as possible. Of course, the help files will be developed in soft copy, but I suggest that you go further and deliver the user manuals, tutorials, and reference manuals in soft copy as well.

> **TIP**
> Deliver as much of the documentation in soft copy as possible.

Producing lengthy hard copy documents adds time, cost, and satisfaction risk to the program. Printing large books is costly, requires a long lead time, and makes physical packaging more expensive. Further, large books eat up paper and require more energy to produce and ship. Save the Earth; use soft copy. Equally serious is that the odds of shipping a document with an error are very high. Nothing annoys a customer more than having a system that does not behave as documented. Shipping a buggy user document can result in many service calls from upset customers. Finally, the schedule to support a large hard copy document will not give users the opportunity to review the documentation in conjunction with the system, further adding to the satisfaction risk.

Delivering the documentation in soft copy addresses these risks. In fact, in most instances, the documentation can be delivered in the same medium as the executable, and so can be delivered to manufacturing at the same time as the system, thus reducing cost and schedule risk. If you finish the documentation along with the code, it is more likely that it will be accurate—which explains why the major software providers are moving toward soft copy delivery. That big box of documents that used to come with a spreadsheet is outdated.

Consider, too, the use of HTML formats for soft copy user documentation. With HTML, you can take advantage of the hyperlink capability to develop highly interactive documentation, including links to a centrally maintained Web site. Take this concept one step further and make most of the documentation available on a Web site. This choice brings with it the lowest distribution costs and allows you to update and correct the documentation as needed, at minimal cost.

There are two kinds of help files: *context-sensitive help*, which explains how the user interface works; and *reference* help, which provides a reference to the system's functionality. Context-sensitive help is usually implemented by a movement on a user-interface icon (such as a right mouse click), which results in a description of what the icon does. Usually context-sensitive help consists of only one or two sentences, written by the user-interface team. Reference help files typically are more extensive, usually consisting of several paragraphs provided as HTML files or through the application framework's help file capability; they are drafted by the technical writers under supervision of the design team. The technical writers also compose the other documentation, such as user and reference manuals.

The bulk of the technical writing is done during this phase. At the beginning, the design is sufficiently in place to support efficient production of the documentation. (Recall that the documentation planning occurs during the elaboration phase.)

Avoid using developers as document writers. They generally do not write well, they cost more per hour than document writers, and in any case, should be doing development. Writing documentation is a specialty, and so it should be done by professionals who respect the task. And you will spend less money for a better product.

Phase Exit Criteria

By the end of this phase, a complete initial draft of all of the documents should be in place, and read and approved by the design team. Editing and polishing takes place in the transition phase following review by users.

Updated Artifacts

Throughout the construction phase, the artifacts developed in the elaboration phase will need to be maintained and updated. As the implementation of the classes proceeds, there is some likelihood that the design will be updated. It follows that you should review the earlier artifacts to ensure they are current. You can do the re-

Planning Simulator Transition

The customers plan to implement their training operation during the second build. They want to use the first build to support system shake-out, development of training materials, training the trainers, and extensive testing of materials and the system, using potential students. For that reason, they want to take delivery at the end of the first build. By doing so, they will be able to supply comments and defect reports to the development team during the second build.

You remind your team that formal acceptance of the build requires that the system tests be run at the customer site by customer employees. After discussions with the customer, your transition team institutes a plan to deliver the initial system during the transition phase. The transition team works with their counterparts at the customer site and the hardware contractor to develop a plan that results in an installed version of the system at the beginning of the transition phase. You plan to put two of your staff members at the customer site for two weeks to get the system up and running. In addition, you finalize the defect reports and service plans during this phase.

view as a part of the code reviews. At the review of a given class, the reviewer can ask about and log which of the following artifacts need to be updated:

- User level use-case database
- System test plan
- Development-level use cases
- Subsystem scenarios
- Class and sequence diagrams
- Integration test plan

Construction Process Tasks

The primary process tasks of the construction phase involve version control and configuration management of the interim integrations. Each system integration is an opportunity to break the system. As you proceed from integration to integration, you will need to reconstruct to a previous version. For example, if a defect is detected during a system test, it is useful to determine during which integration the defect entered the system. It is usually, but not always, the most recent integration in which a newly detected error was introduced. If you have a demonstration, be able to reconstruct the previous version, as the current version may not work. This ensures a disciplined version control process.

As discussed in Chapter 4, you must have a version control/configuration management tool that maintains previous versions of all of the source, object, and execution files. Your staff must be familiar with the use of the tools. Follow these guidelines for each subsystem:

- For a class to be included in subsystem integration, it has to be unit tested, reviewed, approved for inclusion, and checked into the version control tool.

- The integration is assembled from checked-in files. The versions of the included files are locked and labeled with the integration number.

- Every subsystem integration must be documented with exactly which version of which classes were included.

- The subsystem tests must be included with the version of the subsystem.

- Create and maintain a release record documenting the contents of the integration.

The package team test leads are responsible for carrying out the integration process and for delivering subsystems ready for integration into the system. System integration guidelines are similar:

- For a subsystem to be included in system integration, it must be tested and approved for inclusion, and its object file must be checked into the version control tool.

- Document each system integration with exactly which version of which subsystem was included.

- Include the system tests with the version of the subsystem.

- Create and maintain a release record documenting the contents of the integration.

Assigning Responsibility

System integrations are the responsibility of the transition team. A release manager from the team is assigned and is responsible for working with the subsystem test leads and for assembling the system integrations. The release manager leads the build meetings described next.

Coordination and Tracking Activities

As you enter the construction phase, your activities move from facilitating the concurrent design to coordinating the integrations. Your major role is to give structure and order to the integrations. In particular, you need to plan and track the order the of class methods as they are implemented.

As in the other phases, closely track the progress of the new artifacts. There are two views of the integrations status:

- The number of planned user-level use cases that can be delivered to the customer
- The number of planned class methods implemented by the developers

Both are important and should be tracked. Throughout this phase, track how many of the planned use cases are complete, and how many of the class methods have been integrated. By maintaining this data, you have the information you need to intelligently manage this phase, accurately measure progress, and estimate the remaining effort. You also have the information to manage the content and to set development priorities. (Tracking and oversight are addressed more explicitly in Chapter 9.)

Of the two views, the first must prevail. To meet the customer's priorities and address his or her business needs, you must explicitly manage which use cases are delivered in which order. The customer does not care how many methods you deliver; he or she cares about which of the promised use cases are in place. Success of your project is determined solely by the number of promised use cases you deliver.

> **TIP**
> I implement the class methods to support completion of use cases, not simply to complete the classes.

If the class methods are developed in a random order, there is no way to test them at the system level. On the other hand, since the system tests are derived from the use cases, if the methods are chosen to support the use cases, the interim system integrations can be tested using (possibly abbreviated) versions of the system tests.

Risk Management

The microschedule is your primary risk management tool. At this point in the development, you can only address risk through managing the system's content and resource allocation. By setting the microschedule, you accomplish two main tasks:

- The sooner a capability is scheduled for integration, the more likely it will be delivered. Probably some of the content in the final integration will be thrown overboard in order to save the system.
- The developers' activities will be devoted to addressing the content of the earliest integration in which their class participates. The integration order implicitly prioritizes their efforts.

With this in mind, set the order of the use cases to be integrated to manage both schedule and customer satisfaction risk. Managers use two approaches to set the order: content-driven and risk-driven. In the content-driven approach, the manager sets the order to lock down the easy stuff before addressing riskier components. The reason behind this approach is that you might as well lock down the content you know you can deliver. If you spend your team's time on riskier content, you might not deliver anything at all. The problem with this approach is that it almost guarantees that the risky material will not be delivered. You will not have time at the end of the phase to include the more challenging content.

In the risk-driven approach, you face the riskier material at the beginning, the underlying assumption being that the riskier material will take more time and so should be started sooner. In addition, by completing the riskier material, you and your team can be comfortable that the build will be a success. Anxiety is removed as soon as possible.

Of the two approaches, I prefer the second. However, before you choose an approach, I suggest that you use the risk-priority matrix introduced at the beginning of this chapter. Focus your team's development efforts on the content in the following order of priority:

1. High-risk, high-priority.
2. Low-risk, high-priority.
3. Low-risk, low-priority.
4. High-risk, low-priority.

By adopting this strategy, you reap several benefits. You increase the probability of customer satisfaction by scheduling enough time for producing what the customer really cares about. Later in the phase, you can add nice-to-haves, which also can be abandoned if necessary. Regardless, you have set the efforts so that you have maximized the number of affordable low-priority items in the build.

Setting the Microschedule

It follows that you must coordinate the class method implementation so that the use cases become integrated. The ideal way to organize this phase's activity is to:

1. Plan the order of use-case implementation.

2. Derive the order of class method implementation to meet the use-case implementation plan.

3. Sort out the dependencies and resource leveling of the class method implementation and schedule the implementation of the classes based on the effort and the dependencies.

4. Reset the use-case order to meet the development realities.

5. Review the new use-case order.

6. If it is acceptable, set the microschedule.

If the derived use-case order is not acceptable, go through another iteration. This process is diagrammed in Figure 7.9. The output of the process is the phase microschedule and the Svedlow diagram, a cross-tabulation of the use cases and the class methods.

As in the previous phases, use the microschedule to coordinate and prioritize order of development. In this phase, it contains the schedule and content of the interim system integrations. As shown in Figure 7.10, the microschedule records the date and contents of the interim system integrations. The Functionality column is used to record any limitations on the functionality of the use case. For example, your team may decide to include a use case, but not all of its scenarios. Of course, in this situation, you need to include the rest of the functionality in a later integration or negotiate it as out of scope for this build.

Also as in the other phases, the microschedule is maintained by the development lead. I recommend the microschedule be maintained on your project's Web site as well, so that the most current version is readily available.

The Svedlow diagram is used to derive the class methods that need to be implemented in each system integration. A simplified version of the Svedlow diagram is shown Figure 7.11, and a more elaborate spreadsheet version containing tracking capability is available on the companion Web site. Each row contains one of the system's class methods. The columns list system use cases along with their target integration number from the microschedule. The X's signify which class method is included in each of the integrations.

The Svedlow diagram and the microschedule are maintained by the development lead. Update both on at least a weekly basis at the *build meeting*, discussed in more detail later in the chapter.

Finally, it is important to note that the use of interim integrations and the construction phase microschedule gives you with an unambiguous view of the phase's progress. A class and its methods are complete if and only if the code is successfully

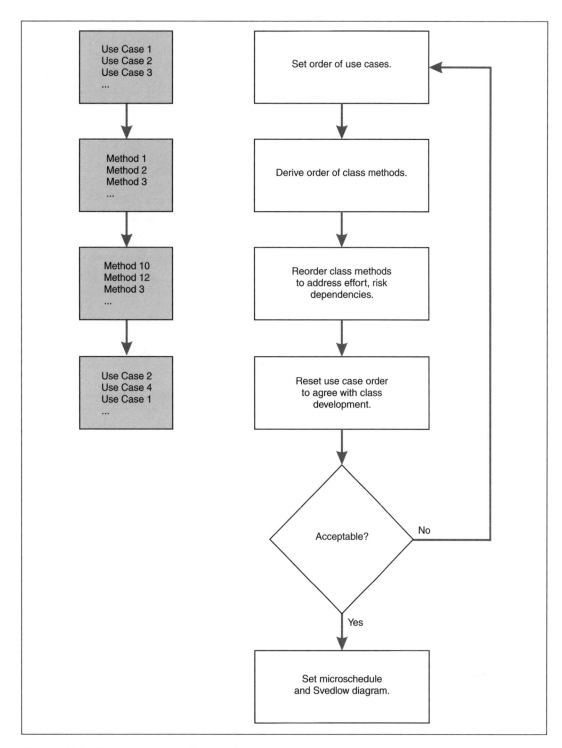

Figure 7.9 Coordination of class development.

Integration	Target Date	Actual Date	Use Cases	Functionality	Comments
1			Case ID Case ID Case ID …		
2			Case ID		

Figure 7.10 Construction phase microschedule.

			Use Case 1 *Int. Number*	Use Case 2 *Int. Number*	Use Case 3 *Int. Number*	Use Case 4 *Int. Number*	Use Case 5 *Int. Number*
Subsystem	Class Name	Method Name	X	X			
		Method Name	X		X	X	
		Method Name		X		X	
	Class Name	Method Name	X	X			X
		Method Name			X	X	
		Method Name					
		Method Name					X
	…						

Figure 7.11 A simplified Svedlow diagram. Each X is an integration number.

tested in system integration. Further, the overall system state of completion can also be determined. The system's progress can be measured by comparing the number of planned use cases to those that test successfully in an integration.

FOR FURTHER READING

See Alistar Cockburn's *Surviving Object-Oriented Projects, a Manager's Guide* published by Addison-Wesley in 1998 for another discussion of managing incremental integrations.

Change Control

During this phase, do not accept changes in requirements. Even if you have done an outstanding job on managing requirements and customer communications from the earlier phase, your customer will have new ideas and new requirements. Your job during this phase is to protect the build and the schedule. Changing requirements during this phase will have a major impact on your team's productivity, thus the success of your project depends on your ability to keep your team focused on the current build, to bring it to completion.

It is true that one of the strengths of object technology is that it enables design change well into the construction phase. However, the changes you should accommodate in this phase are those discovered in the process of developing the code.

TIP

During the construction phase, accommodate changes of design, not changes of requirements.

Manage customer initiated change requests very carefully. Be open to anything that might improve the acceptance of the product, but your first response should be to relegate them to the next build. Remember, any requests will impact the schedule and budget. Unless you are sure that you can accommodate the change, put it off until the next build. Too frequently, an agreeable manager will accept a new or altered requirement late in the process only to blow his or her budget, schedule, and respect from the team. In my experience, the customer would rather hear you say no than miss the schedule.

Put in place a formal *change process* to deal with changes. The change process for these projects is the same as for most software development lifecycles, so I will describe it only briefly here.

FOR FURTHER READING

A more extensive discussion of the change process may be found in Neal Whitten *Managing Software Development Projects,* 2nd ed., 1995 or Philip Metzger and John Boddie, *Managing a Programming Project*, Prentice-Hall, 1996.

The first step in the process is to create and maintain a database of change requests. Enter all those requests into the database. A sample form is shown in Figure 7.12. Its' fields include:

- Unique number
- Change request name
- Description of the change
- Business justification
- Defects status
- Scheduled integration, if any
- Dates when the status changed
- Staff members responsible for change of status
- Discussion of the impact

You may also want to include sizing fields in the change request record, adding fields for use-case development, system design, implementation, and integration. In my experience, however, these fields are not sufficient to discuss the impact. For example, sizing depends on assumptions about approach, therefore I prefer a more flexible text field for explaining the impact on the system.

The requests need to go through a gauntlet of reviews and assessments:

Accepted or Rejected for Sizing. Some ideas are so off the wall that no resource should be expended on sizing them. They may include a function that is out of line with the product (adding a 3D game engine to a spreadsheet, for example), add a function that only 1 percent of the customers might need (say, elaborate plumbing joins and end in a general drawing program), or duplicate an existing function.

Sizing and Impact Analysis Complete. The change should be sized and its impact on the project assessed. Sizing includes any effort spent to update all of the artifacts, including the use cases, test plans, system design, and class implementation.

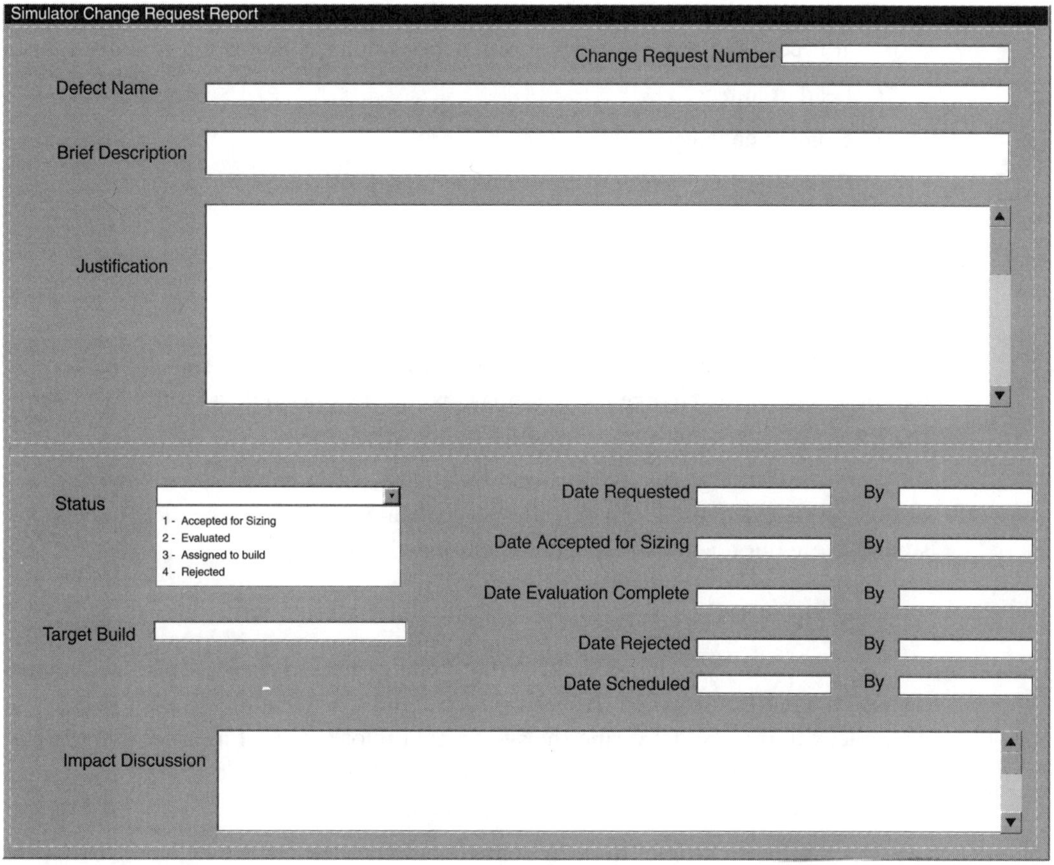

Figure 7.12 A sample change request form.

Scheduled for a Build or Rejected. Which build, if any, has been specified for the change integration. If the request's impact or expense is too high, it should be rejected. Note: It is possible, but unlikely, that the specified integration is the current one.

Assigning Responsibility

The change control board, an IPT whose responsibility it is to manage the change requests, handles the change requests. Its members are responsible for maintaining the database, accepting requests for sizing, assigning the sizing activity, and recommending the integration number for inclusion. The program team reviews the decisions of the board.

The membership of the change control board must be granted the level of authority it needs to effectively carry out its responsibility. Membership should include:

- Lead architect
- Domain engineer
- Customer representative
- Development lead
- Transition team lead
- Some or all of the package team leads

Choose a board lead and a database administrator to maintain the change request database. Direct the change control board to meet as needed to handle the change requests. The board chairperson should decide how often.

One more thing: It is very common for a customer to try to "sneak" in a change request disguised as a defect report. Train your team to be alert to this possibility, close out the defect report, and enter a change request.

Transition Preparations

In the next phase, you may be delivering your system to the field for operational testing, the nature of which depends on the nature of your business situation. For example, you may be delivering the system to a pilot group of internal users, a customer site for acceptance testing, or, if you are delivering shrink-wrapped software, to marketing for beta tests by potential purchasers.

What these situations have in common is that the system will be leaving the supportive, nurturing development laboratory environment to face the hazards of the real world. Smooth the journey by providing the customer what he or she needs to successfully install and run your system:

- Specification of the system platform (required hardware and software)
- Installation instructions
- Installation media (disks or CD-ROMs), including the system and required runtime libraries
- Install scripts
- Readme files

In addition, assume that there will be problems in the field. Be prepared to deal with these. The formality of your customer support and defect reporting depends on your situation. At the very least, provide a telephone number of someone who is prepared to help the customer troubleshoot the installation and accept defect reports. At the other extreme, you may need to coordinate with your company's customer support organization so they are ready for an onslaught. Identify a support lead who is responsible for managing the customer support function. This person can be a member of the transition team or someone from the customer support function.

Test the installation materials. Identify victim machines for the installation machines. It is important that these machines not have any of the runtime libraries already installed. Also, find a naïve surrogate customer, a developer who can test your installation materials and instructions.

Assigning Responsibility

The transition team is responsible for all of these activities. By the end of this phase, all the installation materials are ready and tested, and the support staff is trained and ready to take the calls.

Team Meetings

During this phase, your team will hold a variety of team meetings:

- Design meetings
- Change control board meetings
- Integration meetings
- Program team meetings

The design team meetings that were started in the elaboration phase will continue into this phase. They are the venue for discussing interface changes proposed during the construction. Further, they are a forum for discussing and settling technical disputes. The change control board should start periodic meetings during the construction phase, as set by the board lead.

Integration Meetings

The function of the build meeting is to coordinate the content of the interim integrations. Once the microschedule is in place, establish a setting in which the team leads come together and discuss in detail their development. In this forum, the team leads identify the content they intend to include in the integrations and what they will not. They discuss the dependencies and the impact of moving one team's content from one integration to another, and propose adjustments to the microschedule based on the realities of missed dates.

The release manager, chosen from the transition team, leads the meeting. The agenda is very simple: The release manager reports the results of the last integra-

Methods	Status	Comment
Restore record	Y	Bug in database still not resolved. Working with database vendor.
Create record	G	Unit test successful.
...		

Figure 7.13 A sample build meeting status report.

tion; each team lead, in turn, presents his or her status regarding content, along with previous action items. You may decide to adopt a color convention for reporting status, for example:

Red. Unlikely to make the date.

Yellow. Possible to make the date, but issues remain.

Green. On track.

And you can incorporate up and down arrows to communicate whether the situation is improving or worsening. For example, if one of the integration components, say a class, is not problematic and is currently on track, but you foresee a problem, you might report its status as green with a down arrow. See Figure 7.13 for a suggested status summary format.

There may be some brief discussion following the status report. If an issue is identified, log it as an action item. Report its resolution during the next meeting. In a disciplined build meeting, everyone comes well prepared. No one speaks for more than ten minutes. Figure 7.14 is a sample build meeting agenda.

Hold the meetings at least weekly. Commonly larger complex projects will have daily build meetings. Frequency aside, the key is for them to be highly focused and productive.

Program Team Meeting

Program team meetings continue throughout the program. In this phase, the agenda is changed to reflect the ongoing integration activities. An amended agenda is shown in Figure 7.15.

Customer Communication

During the construction phase, direct your customer communications toward achieving two goals:

Build Meeting Agenda

Time	Item	Presenter
9:00	Integration Status	Release Manager
9:20	Team 1 Status	Team Lead
9:30	Team 2 Status	Team Lead
9:40	Team 3 Status	Team Lead
	....	...
10:20	Adjourn	

Figure 7.14 Build meeting agenda.

- Ensure that the customer is pleased with what you deliver. At least make sure there are no surprises.
- Prevent the customer from adding risk to the build.

Program Team Meeting Agenda

Time	Item	Presenter
9:00	Previous Action Items	Development Lead
9:20	Overall Status and Risk Areas	Development Lead
9:30	Build and Defect Status	Release Manager
10:45	Change Request Status	Change Control Board Lead
11:00	Transition Preparations	Transition Team Manager
11:20	Upcoming Program Events/ Macroschedule Review	Development Manager
11:40	Action Item Review and Assignment	Development Lead
12:00	Adjourn	

Figure 7.15 Construction phase program team meeting agenda.

Thanks to all the use-case and user-interface review, you should be comfortable that the delivered functionality will in fact meet the customer's wants and needs. What remains to be discussed is how much functionality to deliver. The key to managing the communications is content management.

As a manager, you will be pressured from two directions. First, the customer will want as much content as possible—bug-free of course. However, your team and the realities of the project may require you to pare back content. Therefore, your challenge is to set the customer's expectations appropriately so that you can achieve your goals. Further, be comfortable insisting that any new content be deferred to a succeeding build. To achieve this level of communication, keep your customer informed as to your progress, development surprises, and the trade-offs. If there are hard choices to be made—planned content to be deferred—it is best to have your customer share in the decisions.

If your customer is already an active participant in the project—that is, participating in the program team and possibly one or more of the IPTs—you are halfway there. Even so, hold informal meetings to discuss what is expected at delivery. Use the use cases as a basis for customer discussions. On a periodic basis, review with your customer which use cases will be delivered. In addition, discuss any use cases that may have only partial functionality. I suggest you have this conversation at the end of each integration.

Protect your processes. Capture customer suggestions as change requests or defect reports, then treat them accordingly. In trade, give your customer full visibility to your process status. Since the customer should be participating in the program team meeting, he or she will have a view of the status reports. Supply summary defect and change request reports. Even better, give your customer access to the Web-based databases and tables so he or she can monitor status of the processes themselves.

Operational Test Readiness Review

As at the end of the other phases, mark the completion of this phase with a ceremonial meeting, in this case, to mark the agreement that the system is functionally complete and ready for operational and field testing. It is very significant to have your system achieve this status and be worthy of public acknowledgment.

If there is to be field testing, more is at stake in moving to the next phase than at the previous phase transitions. Field testing requires additional expense and resources from the customer. A beta test is very expensive, and a failed beta test can result in bad press as well as a loss of money. Acceptance testing requires time from the customer's staff, so hold a formal meeting to review status, thereby ensuring that all is in fact ready, and that the customer investment in the transition activities was justified. A suggested agenda for the operational test readiness review meeting

Operational Readiness Test Meeting Agenda

Time	Item	Presenter
9:00	Welcome and Introduction	Program Manager
9:15	Review of the Agenda	Program Manager
9:30	Development Overview, Status, and Plans	Development Manager
9:45	Integration Status, Known Deficiencies	Release Manager
10:45	Break	
11:00	System Test Content	Transition Team Lead
12:00	Lunch	
1:00	Installation Procedures	Transition Team Member
1:45	Support Plans/Defect Reporting	Support Lead
2:30	Review of Previous Action Items	Program Manager
3:00	Review of New Action Items	Program Manager
3:30	Adjourn	

Figure 7.16 *Operational readiness test meeting agenda.*

is shown in Figure 7.16. Consider ending the meeting with a ceremonial *handing over of the code*, accompanied by applause.

Construction Phase Exit Criteria

The construction phase is complete when:

- The system is functionally complete. All of the planned functionality for the current build is integrated and tested.
- All of the preparations for operational testing are in place.
- The operational test readiness review meeting has been held.

Note, the system does not have to be flawless. Defects can remain in the system if:

- They do not interfere with operational testing.
- There is a plan to address them without a system redesign.

If you have to redesign the system to address a level 3 bug, it is better to disable the function and bring it in to the next build. List the known deficiencies in release notes included in a readme file with the system media.

From Here

Completing the construction phase can be a hard time for the team, and so they may have mixed feelings. Probably they are pleased and relieved that this milestone has been reached; however, they are all too aware of the deficiencies still in the system; that in spite of their best efforts, they had to deliberately deliver the code with some level 3 deficiencies. They may feel that you pushed the code out the door "to make a date"' and that it is not their best work.

> **TIP**
>
> Help your team see the beauty of the system, not just its warts.

It is important to address this dichotomy immediately, *before* the problem reports start coming in from the field. I suggest you hold an all-hands meeting and face the issue head on. Reinforce the importance to the business of completing the phase. Acknowledge the remaining problems and state that in your judgment, it is time to begin the operational testing. Emphasize that the users are pleased with the system and that it is time to benefit from their experience. Remind them there is still time to address the defects, and that that is in fact your plan. And, of course, thank the team for all their good work.

In the next chapter, I discuss how to manage the transition phase—the delivery—and how to deal with inevitable series of small crises that follow.

> **Completing the Simulator Construction Phase**
>
> Well, you did it. At the readiness meeting, the customer accepted the system for operational testing on-site. It is not quite what they envisioned, but they agree that it will meet their needs—and you made the schedule!
>
> You move your attention to achieving customer acceptance.
>
> You are relieved, of course, and are only a little worried about how the system will perform at the site. Your team is functioning well. You throw a send-off party for the installation team.

8 MANAGING THE TRANSITION PHASE

"It ain't over til it's over."

Yogi Berra (1925–) sportsman.

There is only one goal in the transition phase: Customer acceptance of the system on time and within budget. All of your efforts come down to the customer finally saying yes. Your job is to make this happen. Beginning with the problem-solving paradigm introduced in Chapter 1, in the transition phase, you demonstrate that your solution solves the customer's problem, which is to deliver an operational system. In this phase, then, you confirm that the system you have built does in fact function in an operational environment. And you make any small changes required to finalize the solution.

An excellent theme for this phase is "no more functionality." Adding functionality at this stage will all but guarantee that you will not make the budget nor the schedule. In essence, agreeing to additions would be attempting to solve the development problem all over again. There is no time to develop use cases and bring a new function into the design in this phase. Again, your only purpose is to deliver the completed functionality.

TIP

Resist all attempts to add functionality during the transition phase.

The transition phase is, however, an excellent time to start the inception activities for the next build. Probably your domain expert and lead architect are now free to start capturing the change requests and the experience of operational tests of the user-level use cases, so you can start the process of planning the next build.

Management Overview

One of the strengths of the project management methods I have presented is that everything you have done to this point supports the customer accepting delivery:

- You and the customer have reached agreement at every previous stage.
- The interface and behavior have been reviewed several times.
- The customer has been involved in the requirement analysis and the design.
- The customer has agreed that the use cases adequately describe what is needed, that the design implements the use cases, and that the system is ready for operational testing.

There is little room for disagreement. The customer should be used to saying yes. You have every reason to believe that the customer will accept your code.

Nevertheless, you have yet to prove that you have fully solved the problem, that the code can withstand the rigors of actual use. The operational issues that remain include:

System reliability. The system does not crash or hang under operational conditions.

Data integrity. The system does not damage its own data or that of other programs when managing large data sets.

Performance. The system response does not impede the user from doing his or her job.

The only way to address these issues is in an operational setting. Examples of such settings include running stress tests at beta sites in your own lab or on your customer's premises. The idea is to log as much user time on the system as possible. Once the operational issues have been addressed, the code will be accepted.

For mission-critical systems, such as a bank's financial system, install a *shadow system*, a fully operational version of the new system that conducts the same data processing as the legacy system. Only when the new system has been shown to be fully accurate and reliable should the old system be shut down. For this, success depends on the customer moving to your system.

> **NOTE**
>
> The details of reaching formal acceptance depend on your business situation. If you have a formal contract with your customer, it is essential that you have the acceptance criteria in writing. Negotiate all changes to the acceptance criteria caused by changes in scope before entering the transition phase. If you are delivering shrink-wrap software, you will need a clear understanding of your corporation's approval procedure for product release. You may also have to obtain required sign-offs.

Leadership Issues

A natural tension usually permeates this phase. People may feel they have to act quickly to squash any bugs that arise in operational testing. Problems reported by the customer begin to come in at an overwhelming rate, and may require fast turnaround on bug fixes. It is easy for panic to set in. However, you must maintain discipline among your team. Developing fixes haphazardly results in wasting valuable time on the wrong fixes at best; at worst, you will lose control of your design and put the entire project at risk.

Therefore, every action you and your team take in this phase must be deliberate—whether to make a change, identifying the change to make, or whether to ship the change. As a manager, you need to ensure that a problem report process is in place and followed, along with the change control process. Above all, stay cool, stay positive. The team may bristle at some of the comments from users. After all, the problem report mechanisms are designed to collect negative input, and users can be cruel. But remember: They are not always right. The manager must provide the balance between positive and negative input that the team needs to be productive. Solicit positive input from the customer and convey this to the team. Reinforce that the team will soon deliver a successful, useful system—and that the lessons learned here will be folded into the next system.

Transition Development Activities

The transition process consists of the following development activities:

- Operational testing
- Generation and disposition of problem reports
- Prioritization and repair of defects

Figure 8.1 shows how these activities work together to meet the overall goal—customer acceptance of the build. Any concerns discovered are recorded in a problem report, a written record of the issue and how it will be addressed. The problem reports are then reviewed by the transition team, who decide whether the report should result in a defect report. The change control board then decides if the defect must be fixed. Each of these steps is described in detail in the following sections.

The Problem Report Process

The problem report process is the mechanism by which the testers notify your team of perceived problems. It is very important that these problems be addressed as soon as possible. The sooner you do so, the sooner you can achieve system acceptance. The process begins when either your service organization or your transition team receives a problem report. A sample problem report form is shown in Figure 8.2. The form is generated in two steps: The person reporting the problem fills out the top part of the form. He or she gives the report a name, describes the problem, and signs his or her name. I recommend that the reports be kept in a database, in which case the tool can generate the number. If not, the number should be generated by the transition team, who can ensure the number is unique. The transition team fills in the bottom of the form. They review the problem reports daily.

Problem reports can be sorted into the following categories:

Not Reproducible. The reported problem cannot be reproduced in the lab. Either the description was wrong or—more likely—incomplete, or the problem was not the fault of the program, but some weird interaction with another program running on the user's workstation. Another possibility is that the problem existed on a previous version, but cannot be reproduced using the current build. Often, these problems simply "go away" with the succeeding build. If they persist, the cause must be determined. Assign a member of the transition team to work with the customer to discover the cause of the problem. In some cases a tiger team (described shortly) must be assigned to the problem. Often, these issues are resolved by having the customer load a patch to the operating system or supporting runtime library. The experience is captured in the release notes. For example, the notes should include exactly which version of the operating system and supporting library is required. These reports do not result in a change of the system code.

Works as Designed. The perceived problem is not really a problem. The user may be requesting a change in design that has already been considered and rejected, or a feature that is simply out of scope. The report may describe an inappropriate action, such as, "When I open 100 copies of the same data set and

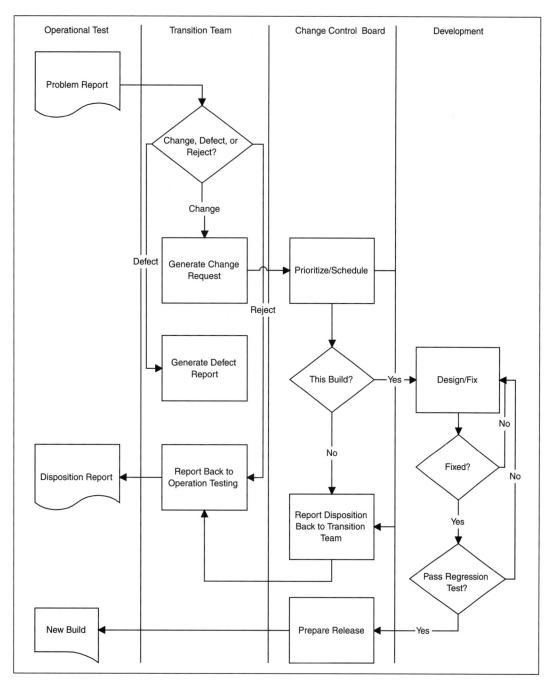

Figure 8.1 *The transition process.*

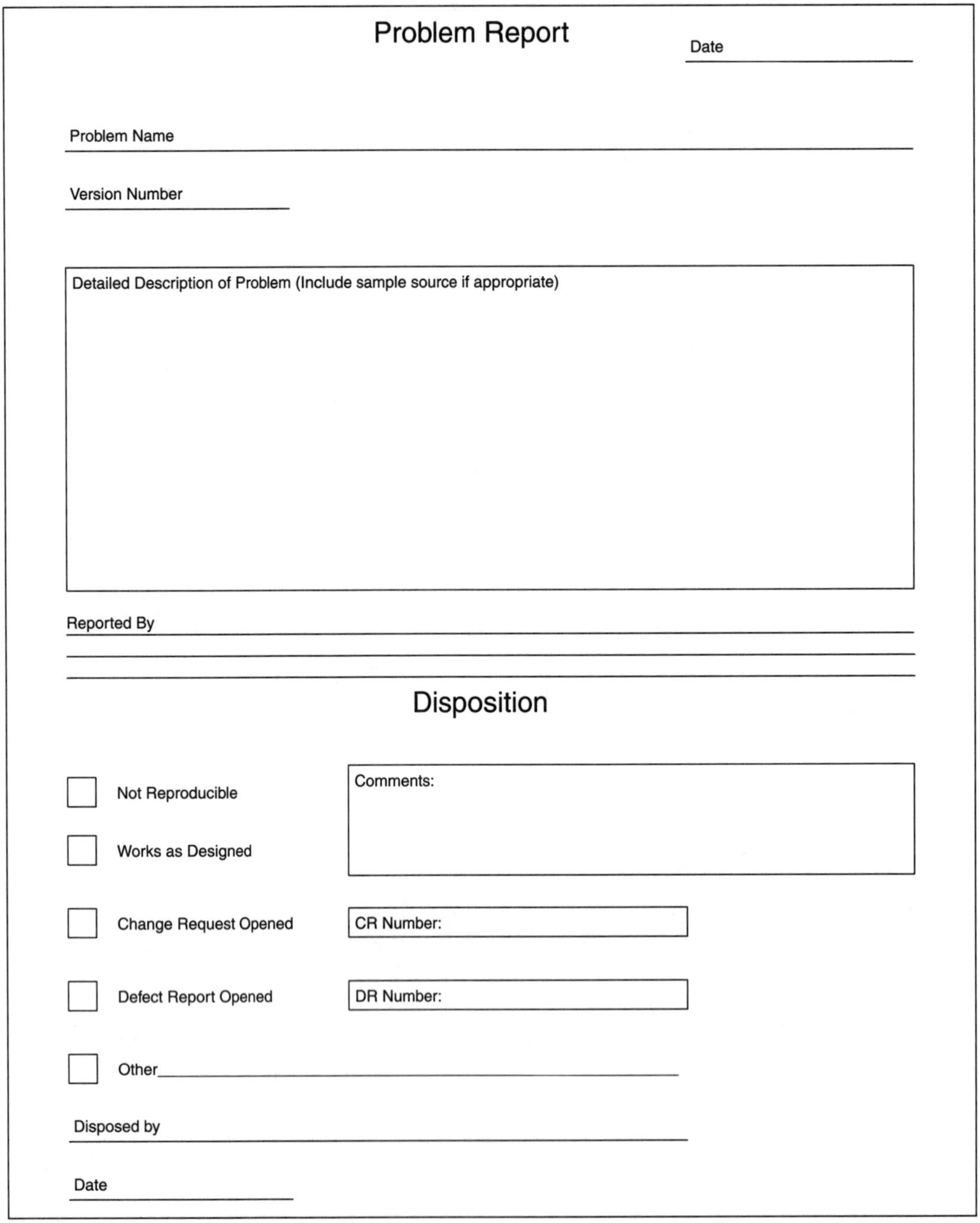

Problem Report

Date _____

Problem Name _____

Version Number _____

Detailed Description of Problem (Include sample source if appropriate)

Reported By _____

Disposition

☐ Not Reproducible   Comments:

☐ Works as Designed

☐ Change Request Opened   CR Number: _____

☐ Defect Report Opened   DR Number: _____

☐ Other_____

Disposed by _____

Date _____

Figure 8.2 A sample problem report form.

close them as fast as I can in random order, the system occasionally hangs." Well, don't do that.

Change Request Opened. The report contains a good idea that should be considered for a succeeding build. The report asks for new, and useful, functionality or a user-interface design change.

Defect Report Opened. The report contains a real defect, a flaw that interferes with the system meeting its intended purpose. A defect report is generated and handed off to the change control board.

Note that these categories may be found in the disposition section of the problem report form.

The transition team member who addresses the report checks the appropriate box and fills in the comments (hopefully polite). His or her comments briefly justify the decision. In addition, he or she enters the change request number or the defect report number if appropriate. And if a workaround is deemed appropriate, it can be described in the comment field.

It is important to distinguish between the decision to open a defect report and deciding to fix the code in the current build. They are not the same. Opening a defect report is simply bringing the defect to the attention of the CCB. The defect may not warrant cost or schedule risk. The change control board will decide whether to fix the defect.

Addressing Defects

A question that you and your team will facing during this phase is "Is the system good enough?" The answer to this question may not be as simple as you think. It is impossible to reach a state of zero defects for a system of any size. At a certain point in the defect removal process, the team will begin to add defects at the same rate they remove them. Attempting to reach a zero defect state becomes infinitely costly, both in time and money. The goal of successful software design is to build a system that is good enough before this minimal defect state is reached.

I have adopted a pragmatic point of view, that is: The code is good enough if the users like it. Generally, there are three aspects to achieving user satisfaction:

Accuracy. The system produces correct results. The algorithms are correctly implemented and the databases are maintained properly.

Reliability. It is highly probable that the system will continue to run, it will not crash nor hang, during the user's session. Reliability is often measured in *mean time to failure* (MTTF), the average amount of time it takes the system to fail in normal use. Put another way, expect that, when run, half of the systems would crash within the MTTF.

Performance. The system meets the performance criteria specified in the initial requirement scoping and set in the inception phase.

Must-Fix Process

Every fix has the potential to introduce new problems. During the transition phase, the change control board must put every opened defect to the "must-fix test," which asks: Can we ship this code if the defect is not addressed? If the answer is yes, then the defect must be deferred until after the release of the build. There are two criteria for deciding that a defect is a must-fix:

1. *Severity.* All level 1 and 2 defects must be fixed.
2. *Frequency.* If many of the operational testers find the same level 3 defect, it must be fixed.

Generally, you should fix only a few level 3 defects and no level 4 defects.

There may be some defects that your team feels do not fall into the must-fix category, but should be addressed as soon as possible. A common approach to this situation is to plan a patch for delivery shortly after product ship (sound familiar?). This option may be unavoidable, but always use it sparingly.

Depending on the frequency of defects discovered during the operational testing, the change control board might need to meet daily, to prioritize defects and schedule them within one day of being opened.

It is critical to gain customer concurrence with your must-fix decisions. After all, just because you decide something is not worth fixing does not mean the customer will agree. Hopefully, you and the customer are working well enough together to ensure agreement on status easily. Having a customer representative on the change control board is clearly a plus here. In any case, review the must-fix decisions with the customer and be sure you have agreement.

Remove any defects that make the system inaccurate. Fortunately, these tend to be easier to find and to remove than those that affect reliability. Removing defects that render the system unreliable is more problematic because you need to decide in advance the reliability requirement for your system. To do this, first determine (either formally or informally) how long the program has to stay up if it is to be useful. Some programs, such as word processors, must stay up for hours. Others, such as operating systems and bank data processing systems need to stay up for weeks. Airline reservation systems, for example, do not seem to be sufficiently reliable, as they are often down when I need them to be up.

Second, you need to decide how certain you are that the system will stay up as long as it should. For most systems, adopt a 99 percent standard, that is, the system will crash only one time in a hundred within the use period. That standard is a good balance between testing and service costs. Achieving more reliability is very costly; shipping lower reliability will result in a lot of phone calls. In some cases, like the software that handles the shuttle engines and controls during a space launch, reliability is a matter of life and death. One failure per 100 launches (99 percent reliability) is *not* good enough. NASA requires something more like 99.999 percent reliability.

FOR FURTHER READING

There are some excellent papers on software reliability at the NASA Web site: shemesh.larc.nasa.gov.

Continue removing defects that affect reliability until the system meets your reliability criteria. There is a statistical relationship between *density of defects* (number of defects per kloc) and the mean time to failure. Capers Jones, in *Applied Software Measurement*, reports the relationship found in Table 8.1. It is very unlikely that the actual numbers shown will apply to your system; however, the table illustrates a very important phenomenon: the fewer the defects, the more expensive they are to find. Testing costs money. As you remove defects, the time and, therefore, the expense of finding the next defect increases. Eventually, your project cannot afford to find the next defect. Only in rare cases, like NASA code, can you afford to find defects that take more than 160 hours (4 weeks) to discover, to get your density below one defect per kloc.

Table 8.1 Relationship of Defect Density to Approximate Mean Time to Failure

DEFECT DENSITY (DEFECTS/KLOC)	APPROXIMATE MEAN TIME TO FAILURE
More than 30	Less than 2 min.
20–30	4–15 minutes
10–20	5–60 minutes
5–10	1–4 hours
2–5	4–24 hours
1–2	24–160 hours
Less than 1	Indefinite

Even if your budget could support finding the rare defect, your schedule cannot. Using your limited system test staff, your team will not find the defects fast enough to ship on schedule. One solution to the dilemma of affordably and efficiently achieving highly reliable code is to create an *alpha release*, release the code to a limited set of real users who agree to generate problem reports—for free. Statistically, you can expect that some of these users will discover additional defects by going down some unlikely code path.

In summary, your goal is not zero defects but, useful software. So remove only those defects that you must to deliver a useful, operational system.

> **TIP**
>
> A zero-defect system is not a reasonable goal.

Dealing with Functional Deficiencies

A functional deficiency is an error in design resulting from a failure to adequately scope the system. The program works as designed, but it does not serve the customer's needs—the customer cannot use it. Using the methods in this book should prevent such a disaster.

If you discover a functional deficiency during the transition phase, it is a genuine crisis. The situation calls for a recovery plan; do not address a functional deficiency through normal transition phase activities. The recovery plan is this: rapidly repeat all four phases of the build. Do abbreviated versions of all the activities and all the reviews. Update the use-case database and the design files. Do system integrations—quickly. Maintaining this discipline of following the lifecycle process is the fastest way to recover. In addition, restrict your team's attention to fixing the problem. Set aside other development activity until the crisis is over.

> **FOR FURTHER READING**
>
> See John Boddie's *Crunch Mode: Building Effective Systems on a Tight Schedule* published by Prentice-Hall in 1987 for an excellent discussion of dealing with crises situations in program development.

At this point, it is important that the customer understands that any deficiencies that emerge from a lack of understanding the requirements is a shared responsibility. The customer needs to understand that implementation errors are different from functional deficiencies. Implementation errors are your team's responsibilities. Functional deficiencies at this point can only result from inadequate communications of the requirements from the customer.

The Tiger Team

As the system hardens, it becomes harder to determine the cause of a problem. Accordingly, it is difficult to assign the defect to the appropriate team for removal. For example, suppose the system unaccountably freezes after running fine for thirty hours. The system is restarted only to freeze again after twenty-one hours. With only this data, the bug could be anywhere in the code. One way to deal with this situation is to identify a small team of expert developers, the *Tiger Team,* whose function is to determine the cause of the bug and assign the fix to the appropriate subsystem. When a defect is not easily assigned by the transition team, assign it to the tiger team who will then work with the appropriate developer to have the problem fixed.

The members of the tiger team should be experts in the use of debuggers, trace tools, and the like. You may want some of the team members at the operational test site where the problem occurred and some at the development site to work where the system is built. Having team members at both sites facilitates both communication and rapidity of solution. The team members at the customer site can identify the problem while having full access to the exact configuration of the customer's system. By having the debugging tools on the customer system, the team member can quickly identify the cause of the problem and propose a solution. The person staying at the development site has full access to the development environment and can implement and test proposed fixes quickly.

Design, Code, and Test

When faced with the necessity of changing the code to fix a defect, adopt the maxim "First, do no harm." In practice, this means:

- Maintain the system integrity; do not change the system design, only class designs.

- Do not ship a new bug.

All code changes attempted during this phase should be minimal. You have to assume that the design is sound and that only small changes are needed to address any remaining problems. Ideally, contain the changes within the body of the class methods. For example, often a small change in a single class can address a performance issue. If you need to change a class design or the way two classes pass messages, that is acceptable. But draw the line there.

Review and unit test any changes before integrating them. Even after the fix has been included in integration, do not ship the system until you can confirm that the defect has in fact been removed and the system has been *regression* tested. A regression test is used to verify that the fix has not introduced a new bug. It is usually an abbreviated version of the system test, run by the system test team.

If possible, reintegrate the system on a daily basis. This minimizes the content change from one integration to the next, which in turns makes the regression testing more meaningful. It also makes it easier to back out of any fix that introduced a new problem.

NOTE

During the transition phase, you will be rewarded for having a good modular design. In my first object-oriented project, I expected that the result of all the effort my team put into the design would be an abbreviated period of operation testing. I believed my design efforts would pay off in fewer initial defects and more time to make corrections. I was disappointed when the discovery rate of the defects was as high as usual. However, I was surprised and pleased to note that the work-off rate (the rate at which the defects were corrected) was higher than usual and that the fixes rarely, if ever, introduced a new defect. The net effect was exactly what I had hoped for: The code passed operational testing in record time.

I now understand this sequence of events. Ironically, the rapid discovery of defects was a sign of the quality of the code. It is easy to find a large number of defects in more stable code than in buggy, unstable code. Bad code does not stay up long enough to reveal its defects. The work-off rate is also easily explained. Because of the modularity of the design, the defects were easily found. The impact of any change was contained to a single class. None of the other classes was affected by the fix. The single class was sufficiently simple to make it a straightforward matter to fix it. No new bugs were introduced. I have seen this phenomenon several

---

Transition Process Tasks

There are two transition phase process tasks:

- Manage version control and configuration
- Assemble and archive the program's internal deliverables and process artifacts

The version and configuration management tasks are similar to those in the construction phase. However, in this phase, configuration management includes tracking the releases and patches (partial releases) to the customer. Tracking includes which defects are addressed by which release.

Recall from Chapter 4 that the process artifacts and internal deliverables include the use-case databases, object model design files, design documents, source code, make files, and the requirements, design, and test plan documents. At the end of the transition phase, archive the artifacts to provide a record of the development and to establish a resource for further development.

Assigning Responsibility

As in the construction phase, the process tasks are the responsibility of the configuration management lead in the transition team.

Coordination of Activities

Since the activity of this phase is the removal of must-fix defects and the integration of the fixes into the system, the microschedule in the transition phase consists of tracking those must-fix defects, identifying in which integration of the system they will be delivered, and the team assigned to do the fix. Review the microschedule on a daily basis. A sample microschedule is shown in Table 8.2.

Depending on the pace of your program, the microschedule may need be updated daily. For example, as the defects arrive, some of the new ones may take priority over previously scheduled defects. If they require the same resource, the schedule may need to be adjusted.

Build Meetings

Build meetings continue into this transition phase. In fact, if you have daily integrations, you will need daily build meetings to review the status of the previous integration and decide what is ready for the next integration. And, as you would expect

Table 8.2 A Transition Phase Microshedule

DEFECT NUMBER	TARGET INTEGRATION DATE	ASSIGNED TO
121	7/16	Core Services
134	7/17	Out the Window
157	1/17	Tiger Team
...	...	...

from the microschedule, the focus of the build meeting changes from tracking use cases to tracking defects.

Program Meetings

As you bring the build to closure and to customer acceptance, remove the last must-fix defect. To achieve this on time or to reset the acceptance date, track the status and progress of the defects closely. This requires weekly program meetings whose main purpose is to review defect status and other acceptance issues. Maintain and review a chart like that shown in Figure 8.3 to assess how soon you will achieve system acceptance.

On a daily basis, you track:

- Number of open must-fix defects
- Number of closed must-fix defects
- Number of newly discovered must-fix defects
- Number of newly fixed must-fix defects

The most convenient way to maintain the chart is in a spreadsheet. And if you are tracking MTTF, add a chart showing the MTTF for the current release to the agenda.

Maintaining the chart allows you to thoroughly understand how the project is running. Both the values and the slope of the graphs should be of interest to both you and the customer. From the chart, you can determine if the rate of discovery of new must-fix defects is increasing or decreasing, whether the backlog of defects is approaching zero, and whether the work-off rate is increasing. From this data, you can determine your likely acceptance date. In addition, you can determine whether you are on track or if some intervention is called for. For example, you may want to review the must-fix process or find out what is impeding the work-off rate.

Customer Communication

Here are some points to help you manage customer communications during this phase. You will be in frequent contact during the phase, exchanging test reports, problem reports, and fixes. Therefore, it is very important for you and your team to maintain discipline and process. The best way to accomplish this is to include your customer in the process. Doing so is reassuring, not interfering. In addition, make it clear to the customer and your team that all commitments are made through the processes—informal agreements do not count.

Customers will be anxious to capture the experience and insights gained in operational testing as new requirements. This is good, as long as they do not derail

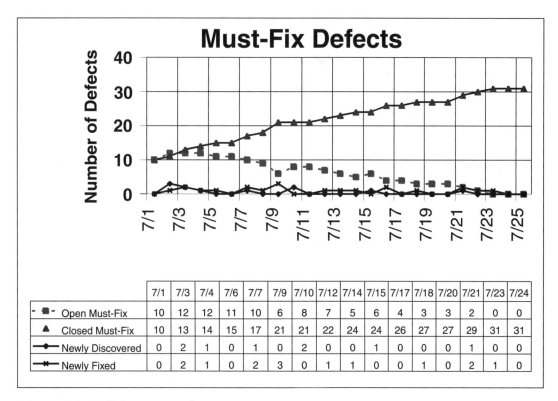

Must-Fix Defects

	7/1	7/3	7/4	7/6	7/7	7/9	7/10	7/12	7/14	7/15	7/17	7/18	7/20	7/21	7/23	7/24
Open Must-Fix	10	12	12	11	10	6	8	7	5	6	4	3	3	2	0	0
Closed Must-Fix	10	13	14	15	17	21	21	22	24	24	26	27	27	29	31	31
Newly Discovered	0	2	1	0	1	0	2	0	0	1	0	0	0	1	0	0
Newly Fixed	0	2	1	0	2	3	0	1	1	0	0	1	0	2	1	0

Figure 8.3 *A defect status chart.*

the completion of the build. Capture any new operational and functional requirements in the change request database for consideration for inclusion in the next build.

If any functional deficiencies emerge during operational testing, do not place blame; instead, agree on a mutually acceptable recovery plan in as mature a manner as possible.

Transition Phase Exit Criteria

The transition phase is complete when the build is *accepted*. Furthermore, the phase does not end until you have confirmed that your system artifacts are in good shape. Not only do you want to deliver the code, you also want to ensure that the intellectual content of your system has been captured—that the system is an asset that can be maintained and extended. Ideally, the packages and subsystems are in good enough shape to be reused in future development.

Customer Acceptance of the Simulator

The system is finally installed. The instructors are trained how to create the mission scenarios. Everyone is encouraged when the first student pilot takes the stick, and operational testing of the shipped functionality starts in earnest.

Three challenging must-fix defects are found in the first two weeks of acceptance testing:

- The system's performance degrades slowly so that it is unusable after about an hour of flight.

- The mission scenario database becomes corrupted when it is saved, restored, modified, and saved more than a few times.

- The pilots complain that the instrument readings are inconsistent at some points of the flight.

The last problem raises the emotional temperature. Some of the students refuse to use the system, saying it interferes with their training, that it actually damages their reflexes with the wrong input.

No one panics. You immediately put together a tiger team to address the first problem. They add some system calls to the implementation to determine where the system is spending its time. After a week of monitoring, they trace the problem to an implementation design error. The class that registers the entities in the system is repeated, and so the same entity is registered millions of times. The time is taken by the list traversal. Changes in a few lines of code fix the problem.

The second problem is assigned to the trainer workstation team, which traces the problem to a misuse of the underlying database. You send the pilot you hired as a consultant to the customer site to monitor the tests and to sit with the student pilots. He comes back with a detailed understanding of the problem. He reviews the data with the instrument team. They eventually trace the problem to an incorrect sign in one of the methods. A value is returned as positive when it should be negative. This problem was not discovered at unit test because the developer was confused about the sign. With this fix, the problem goes away.

There are a series of other must-fix problems, all of which can be traced to subtle implementation errors within the classes. The customer accepts the build! You and your team turn your attention to completing the inception phase of the second build.

At the end of the phase, it is a good idea to have your team check that:

- The code adheres to your project's standard.
- The design and code are in synchronization.
- All of the system's artifacts have been updated.

From Here

This chapter completes the discussion of how to manage your program through a complete build. We have covered a lot of ground. I have showed you how to plan your object-based program, organize your team, choose a lifecycle model, manage through the phases, and finally, deliver a complete build of the system. In the next chapter, I explain how to keep your program on track.

Part three

MEASURING PROGRESS AND SUCCESS

9 TRACKING AND OVERSIGHT

> *"I know not anything more pleasant, or more instructive, than to compare experience with expectation, or to register from time to time the difference between idea and reality. It is by this kind of observation that we grow daily less liable to be disappointed."*

> Samuel Johnson (1709–84) lexicographer, author

Up to now, we've explored communicating and working with your team. We've looked at the importance of establishing a development plan to communicate how you intend to deliver the program to the customer. This chapter focuses on communicating and working with your management. I will show you how to achieve an overall assessment of the health and stability of your project and how to share your assessment in a useful way. I will also show you how to track your progress against the plan and the baseline. Later in this chapter, I propose a monthly program status review format that includes a tracking and oversight activity consisting of preparing and presenting the monthly reviews.

This chapter comprises three topics:

Budget tracking. How to determine whether your spending is according to plan and the projected program costs.

Development metrics. Measures of the size, progress, and stability of your development effort.

Monthly review format. The sequence of charts that succinctly communicate your program's health and status.

Budget Tracking

The development plan tells you how much money you plan to spend and how much work you expect to have completed at any given point in time. Budget tracking is a way to assess whether the amount you have spent at any point in the project is in line with your plan. The tracking techniques in this section provide two views on the financial status:

Variances. The difference between actual and planned spending.

Projected costs. Estimates of the actual cost of the project based on the current rate of spending.

Become familiar with the following terms in order to understand and communicate budget tracking:

- Budgeted cost of work scheduled (BCWS)
- Budget cost of work performed (BCWP)
- Earned value (EV)
- Actual cost of work performed (ACWP)
- Percent complete (PC)
- Cost variance (CV)
- Cost variance index (CVI)
- Schedule variance (SV)
- Schedule variance index (SVI)
- Cost performance index (CPI)
- Estimate at complete (EAC)
- Variance at complete (VAC)

Each of these terms is explained next.

Although this may seem to be an extensive list of terms, they enable us to establish a standard and effective vocabulary for reporting financial status. Use them and you will be able to communicate your budget status with your customer and management with confidence and precision.

TIP

Take the time to become familiar with the language of budget tracking.

Tracking these measures also gives you the view of the program you need to control your spending. The variances tell you whether you are spending money faster than you should for the amount of work accomplished. The completion estimates, EAC and VAC, can help you determine whether your budget is adequate or adjustments are needed.

In Chapter 4, I described how to create a time-phase budget—a plan of how you expect to spend money during the phases of each of the builds. This is the *budgeted cost of work scheduled* (BCWS), sometimes called *planned cost*. To determine the BCWS at a given date, go to your Gantt chart to see how much of the project you planned to have completed and add up the cost of the planned budget items done to that point. These costs generally include the labor, the staff assigned to the effort, hardware and software, and others, such as planned travel and meeting costs. For example, if on July 1, you planned to be at the end of the elaboration phase of build 2, the BCWS for July 1 is the planned budget for build 1, plus the budget for the inception and elaboration phases of build 2.

The BCWS does not measure value of the actual work performed. The accepted way to measure the planned and accomplished work is to assign a dollar value, called the *earned value*, to the scheduled work. Conceptually, if at any point in the program you can determine how much of the budget should have been spent to accomplish the amount of completed work, you have a basis of comparison for deciding if you are ahead or behind in your budget. If you have spent more than you expected to reach this point, you are behind budget; if you have spent less, you are ahead of budget. The earned value of the work is measured by the *budgeted cost of work performed* (BCWP). Compute the BCWP by assessing how far along you are in the development—the amount of work complete—and by computing the budget for that amount of work. Using the same example, suppose on July 1 you are still in the inception phase of build 2. The BCWP is the sum of the budget for build 1, the budget for the inception phase of build 2, and some fraction of the budget for the elaboration phase of build 2. Note that, in this case, since you are behind schedule, the BCWP is less that the BCWS.

FOR FURTHER READING

See Harold Kerzner's textbook, *Project Management*, published by Van Nostrand Reinhold for more detail on budget tracking and cost control. A less detailed discussion is found in James Lewis', *Fundamentals of Project Management*, published by the American Management Association in 1997. Also keep in mind that standard project management tools can help you track the various indices and variances.

How do you compute the BCWS and BCWP values when you are between phases? Generally, the phases are long enough to incur value in approximating these figures. For object-oriented programs, I suggest you adopt the following methods:

BCWS. Assume a linear model of expenditure throughout the phase; that is, that you will spend the phase's budget at a constant rate. This is probably how your plan was set in the beginning. This is an approximation, but is preferable to the 50/50 method (half at start, half at completion) often adopted.

BCWP. For the first three phases, use the percent of completed items on your microschedule as the measure. For example, if during the inception phase, you plan to develop 350 use cases and have completed 175, claim the BCWP for that phase is 50 percent of the BCWS of the phase. Adopt a 50/50 strategy for the transition phase—half the value at the beginning, half at the end.

BCWS and BCWP are views of your budget, *not your spending*. With BCWS and BCWP, you have a view of how much money you expected have spent at a given point in time (BCWS) and how much you expected to spend for the amount of work actually accomplished (BCWP). To complete the picture, you need to track how much money you actually spent. You might be right on schedule—in which case, BCWS and BCWP are equal—but still have spent more or less than planned.

The *actual cost of work performed* (ACWP) is the amount of money spent to date. It is computed by adding up the project's expenditures. Your accounting department usually provides the information. The other financial measures are computed from the BCWS, BCWP, and the ACWP. Each of the calculations provides a useful measure for assessing how well you are tracking the budget.

The next two measures are variances. Variances are differences between actual and planned values. The *cost variance* (CV) is the difference between planned and actual cost for the accomplished effort.

CV = BCWP − ACWP

It measures the difference between what you planned to spend and what you actually spent to do the amount of work done to date. If the CV is negative, you have a cost overrun; if it is positive, you have spent less then you expected to get the work done—you are ahead of budget.

CV = BCWP − ACWP

The *schedule variance* (SV) is the difference between the cost of the work accomplished to date and the cost of the work scheduled to date.

SV = BCWP − BCWS

It measures the difference in the value of the work done and the work you expected to be done. If the value of the work actually done is less than you planned at a given point in time, the SV is negative and you are behind schedule. On the other hand, a positive SV means your team has done more work that you expected for this point in time, and so you are ahead of schedule.

The *percent complete* (PC) is the percentage of the scheduled work to date that is actually completed.

$$PC = 100 \times BCWP / BCWS$$

The PC provides a view of the same information as the SV, normalized by the size of budget. It illustrates the importance of the SV. An SV of –$100,000 is less serious in a $10,000,000 BCWS than in a $1,000,000 BCWS. The same SV in the first case results in a PC of 1 percent and 10 percent in the second. Communicating the PC immediately conveys the seriousness of your variance independent of project size.

In addition to the PC, two other normalized values are of interest: CV and SV, normalized by the appropriate view of the budget. The *cost variance index* (CVI) is the cost variance normalized by the budgeted cost of work performed.

$$CVI = CV/BCWP = (BCWP - ACWP)/BCWP$$

The *schedule variance index* (SVI) is the schedule variance normalized by the budgeted cost of work scheduled.

$$SVI = SV/BCWS = (BCWP - BCWS)/BCW$$

The CVI and SVI are used in the same way as the CV and SV, respectively. They measure whether the work done and money spent is on budget. By normalizing the variances with respect to the budgets, the CVI and SVI provide a comparison of the size of the variance and the budget. The quotients put the size of the variances in perspective.

Understanding the Variances

SV and CV are independent quantities. Knowing one will not enable you to compute the other. For example, it is possible to be ahead of schedule but over budget. Table 9.1 covers all the possibilities.

Your budget status is your variances (or variance indices) and the percent complete. Use these values to report the status. A simple cost and variance report is given in Figure 9.1. The data comes from our simulator example (discussed in the sidebars) and contains the budget measures in tabular form. The rows should be rolled up like WBS items—project builds and the like. As mentioned earlier, your project management tool should be able to produce the reports.

Table 9.1 Possible Combinations Of Cost And Schedule Variance

	SV $\geq$ 0	SV < 0
CV $\geq$ 0	**On or under budget and on or ahead of schedule:** At this point in time, the amount of work performed is greater than or equal to the amount planned. In addition, you have not spent more than planned for work performed. This situation occurs when the planned resource gets the work done early or exactly on time.	**On or under budget and behind schedule:** At this point in time, the amount of work accomplished is less than planned. However, you have not spent more than planned for the work. This situation may arise if not all of your planned staff has been available. The smaller staff has performed well, but they cannot keep up with the schedule.
CV < 0	**Over budget and on or ahead of schedule:** At this point in time, you have spent more than planned for the work accomplished. However, that work was done before the planned date. This situation may arise if you have more staff than planned working the problem; however, that staff brought in the work ahead of schedule.	**Over budget and behind schedule:** At this point in time, you have spent more than planned for the work accomplished and that work is behind schedule. This situation may arise if your planned staff does not get the work done as rapidly as planned. They have charged the project at the planned rate, but the amount of work accomplished is less than expected. In this situation, the cost of the work accomplished is greater than planned.

Tracking the values over time on a graph helps to determine budget trends—whether the variances are growing over time. This lets you see whether your variances are getting better or worse. See Figure 9.2 where the ACWP, BCWS, and BCWP are graphed. The difference between the lines is variance. If the project were going exactly according the plan, the graphs would line up. The vertical line shows the completion. The horizontal line at the top is the final budget. If the project goes exactly as planned, the graphs will cross where the completion date and the BAC line intersect. The graph gives you a visual representation of the budget trends. If the gaps between the lines is growing, then so are your variances. If it appears the graphs will cross the vertical line above the BAC line, then you are over budget.

Another measure of the spending trend is the *cost performance index* (CPI), the ratio of the earned value to the actual cost. It can be computed as follows:

CPI = BCWP / ACWP

	BCWS	BCWP	ACWP	SV	SVI	CV	CVI
Program (Product)	3,829,828	3,470,180	3,864,528	(359,647)	(0.09)	(394,348)	(0.11)
Development	3,829,828	3,470,180	3,864,528	(359,647)	(0.09)	(394,348)	(0.11)
Build 1	3,829,828	3,470,180	3,864,528	(359,647)	(0.09)	(394,348)	(0.11)
Inception	1,900,000	1,900,000	1,900,000	0	0.00	0	
Elaboration	3,026,210	2,736,500	3,130,848	(289,710)	(0.10)	(394,348)	(0.14)
Construction	0	0	0	0		0	
Transition	0	0	0	0		0	
Build 2							
Fixed Costs	623,438	553,500	553,500	(69,938)	(0.11)	0	

Figure 9.1 *A Stealth simulator variance report.*

If the CPI < 1.0, then the actual cost is greater than the earned value. If the project continues at that rate, it will not finish on budget.

You can use the CPI to project your project's estimated final cost. This estimate is called *estimate at complete* (EAC), clearly a useful number. It tells you in advance the most likely final cost of the project if the current trends continue. The EAC is computed as follows:

$$EAC = \frac{BAC}{CPI} = \frac{BAC \times ACWP}{BCWP}$$

where BAC is the *budgeted at completion*, the budget for the project. An alternate useful formula for EAC is given as:

$$EAC = \frac{ACWP}{BCWP} \times BCWP + RC$$

where BCWP is the earned value at the end of the current phase and RC is the *remaining cost*, the budget for the rest of the project. Note that *rebaselining* consists of setting the BAC to the current EAC.

The *variance at completion* (VAC), the projected overrun, is given by:

$$VAC = EAC - BAC$$

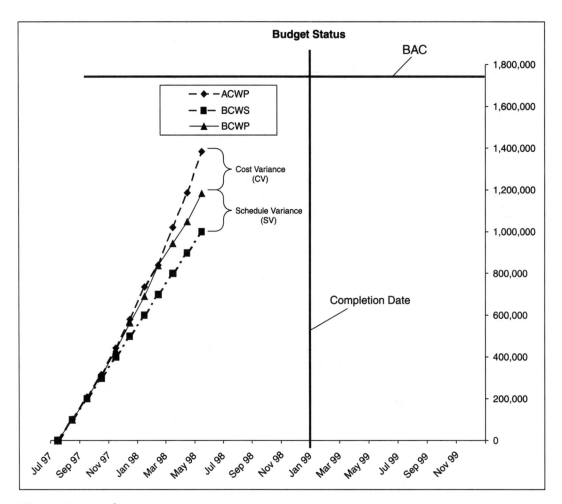

Figure 9.2 Budget status reporting.

If your VAC > 0, make adjustments. The EAC for the example given in Figure 9.1 is shown in Figure 9.3. In this instance, the project is running with a CPI of .9 with a projected overrun of almost $2.5M.

Do not try to maintain the data yourself. Identify an administrative support person who can produce it for you.

Development Metrics

There are two questions to answer in assessing and reporting the state of program development:

	BCWS	BCWP	ACWP	PC	CPI	EAC	BAC	VAC
Program (Product)	3,829,828	3,470,180	3,864,528	91%	0.90	23,793,253	21,365,320	2,427,933
Development	3,829,828	3,470,180	3,864,528	91%	0.90	19,972,803	17,934,720	2,038,083
Build 1	3,829,828	3,470,180	3,864,528	91%	0.90	10,735,034	9,639,600	1,095,434
Inception	1,900,000	1,900,000	1,900,000	100%	1.00	1,927,920	1,927,920	0
Elaboration	3,026,210	2,736,500	3,130,848	90%	0.87	3,462,307	3,026,210	436,097
Construction	0	0	0		0.90	3,915,108	3,523,597	391,511
Transition	0	0	0		0.90	1,290,969	1,161,872	129,097
Build 2							8,295,120	
Fixed Costs	623,438	553,500	553,500	89%	1.00	1,350,000	2,700,000	(1,350,000)
Maintenance						472,080	472,080	0

Figure 9.3 An EAC report.

Progress. How much of the planned development is in place?

Stability. How much change has there been in your project's requirements and size estimate?

For software programs, measure the progress and stability of requirements, the design, and code development. For object-oriented development, this amounts to tracking use cases, classes, and lines of source code. For each of these artifacts, track:

Original sizing. Expected number of items (use cases, lines of code) when the schedule and budget were first set up.

Current sizing. Current expected number of items; this will most likely differ from the original scope.

Implementation plan. Plan for when items will be developed.

Currently implemented. Numbers of items actually generated and accepted (tested and/or reviewed).

Changes in the current scope over time are an indication of instability in the program. Comparing the implementation plan with the currently implemented value shows how the development is progressing.

Figure 9.4 is an example of an *artifact chart*, a graph that tracks each of the four variables, each a line on the graph. In the figure, the stability and progress of

Stealth Simulator Budget Tracking

Every month your administrative assistant prepares a project-earned value report. You review this chart at the monthly program meeting and with your manager at his business unit review. Figure 9.1 shows the variance report for the end of the elaboration phase of build 1. Figure 9.3 shows the earned-value report. The effort was on budget through the inception phase, so the PC for that effort is 100 percent, and the SV, CV, and VAC for the inception activity are 0. However, at the planned end of the elaboration phase, it is only 85 percent complete. Not only that, you have spent more money than expected through the planned time period; that is you have spent more than planned and accomplished less. Both the CV and SV are negative. You are also spending fixed-cost items faster than you should. All of this is bad news. Nevertheless, as shown in Figure 9.2, your estimated cost of completion is about $24M. Recall that your actual budget is $25M; you left 12 percent in reserve. So at the going rate, you will come within budget by using the reserve.

Still, the numbers give you cause for concern. First you look into the schedule slip in the elaboration phase. You wonder why the productivity is lower than expected. When will the phase really end? Is there a logjam that you can clear? Are the variances just the expected errors in the estimates or is there something you can do to improve the team's productivity? Your questions uncover a problem with the core services team lead. You start to explore whether he needs to be replaced.

the project's use cases are tracked. In this example, the initial estimate of use cases was 320. In October, some additional requirements were placed on the project, raising the number of planned use cases to 345. More requirements were added in November. This instability in the number of requirements is a cause for concern. Note, though, that the development is on track. The implementation plan lines up with the number of use cases currently implemented.

Update your project's artifact charts on a monthly basis and have them presented in the monthly program review.

Monthly Status Report

On a monthly basis, the development lead or project manager assembles and presents a status report at the monthly program review. In addition, the next level of

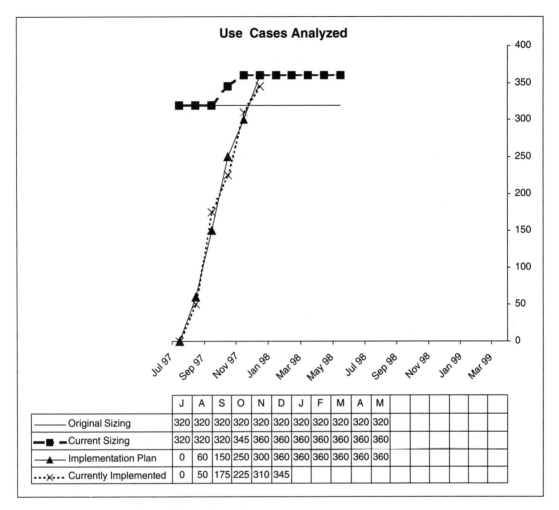

Figure 9.4 *A sample artifact status chart.*

	J	A	S	O	N	D	J	F	M	A	M						
—— Original Sizing	320	320	320	320	320	320	320	320	320	320	320						
—■— Current Sizing	320	320	320	345	360	360	360	360	360	360	360						
—▲— Implementation Plan	0	60	150	250	300	360	360	360	360	360	360						
··×·· Currently Implemented	0	50	175	225	310	345											

management in your organization conducts a monthly review of all of the programs in his or her organization. The report is designed to assess the overall status, progress, and stability of the development. The report serves two functions:

- Early detection and assessment of program risks.
- An opportunity to communicate the risks early so that the customer and upper management has a chance to help and/or respond.

The format is designed to enable you to maintain control of your program. The format tracking includes mechanisms that give sufficient feedback to allow for timely adjustments to the teams' activities or to the plan. In addition, the format has a mechanism to communicate status and risk to other stakeholders: upper management, other teams, and the customer.

As you will see, the format communicates the project's progress, stability, and risk status. One of the strengths of object-oriented techniques is that they provide tangible, demonstrable items against which to track progress and stability. They are measured in terms of use cases accepted, detailed, and integrated.

The monthly status report format is a sequence of charts, designed to quickly convey the current risk status of your program from a variety of views. Cost, schedule, and customer satisfaction risks are addressed. The report is designed so that it can be presented in 15 minutes. Follow this outline when presenting the report:

1. Title Page
2. News
3. Risk Assessment
4. Earned Value Analysis
5. Schedule Tracking and Stability
6. Development Tracking and Stability
7. Other Metrics
8. Review of action items

These reports can be generated in a presentation tool. In my organization, we maintain them in a set of spreadsheets linked as HTML pages so they can be easily maintained, viewed by anyone on our corporate network, and projected at review meetings. We do not pass out hard copies.

You as program manager *own* the responsibility of assembling the monthly status review. However, as a competent program manager, you should *delegate the effort*. Your administrative assistant should assemble the earned value analysis charts. The schedule development charts should be assembled by the development lead.

The following details the contents of each of the outlined sections:

Title Page. The title page identifies the project, the month, and the program manager. An example is given in Figure 9.5. You might want to use this chart to give your program some identity—perhaps add a logo or a slogan.

News. This chart is a simple bullet list used to convey any information that may be of interest and is not covered elsewhere. Use it to convey information that you think should be brought forward. For example, major changes in personnel, changes in customer personnel, or competitive announcements might be reported on this chart. Figure 9.6 is an example.

The Fighter Simulator Program

Status as of July 31, 1999

Carmine Jones, Program Manager

Figure 9.5 *Monthly review title page.*

Risk Assessment and Status. This key chart, shown in Figure 9.7, summarizes the overall risk status of the program. This is your opportunity to assess the project's overall status in simple terms that even an executive can understand: red, yellow, and green. Add up or down arrows to report the trend—such as whether the risk items are getting worse or improving. More important, identify any causes for concern and report how these concerns are being handled. Use this chart to ask for help or to reset expectations. For example, if the cause of the slip is a missed dependency from another organization in your company, your manager can raise the issue with his or her peer. Using this chart efficiently can help you enlist your manager as partner in the effort.

- Customer visit planned for 8/15.

- Jessica Quinn named Core Services team lead on 7/15.

Figure 9.6 *Program news.*

Risk Assessment Summary

RISK AREA	RYG	↑↓	CAUSE	ACTION
Schedule	Y	*	Staffing shortfall	Two new developers start next week.
Cost	Y	↓	Low productivity due to compiler bug	Contacted vendor, looking for fix or workaround.
Customer Satisfaction	G	*		

	G	On track
	Y	At risk, special attention required
	R	Mitigation required
	↑	Improving
	*	No change
	↓	Worsening

Figure 9.7 Program risk summary chart.

Be candid and straightforward when presenting this chart—tell the whole truth. For example, if you decide to put off reporting the bad news by reporting *green* up to the month before delivery, and then in the last month move everything to *red*, your manager has every right to be annoyed, and you will have lost credibility.

Earned Value Analysis. This section consists of the tables shown in Figures 9.1 and 9.3 with the most recent data. I also suggest you include a current variance trend graph like that in Figure 9.2. The charts add detail to the risk assessment. In particular, the variances quantify the cost and schedule risk identified in the previous chart.

Schedule Tracking and Stability. The schedule tracking and stability section of the review consists of two charts. The first is a summary Gantt. The Gantt chart, as shown in Figure 9.8, shows the summary tasks and the program milestones. You can choose to show some detailed tasks if you want to discuss their progress during the review, but keep the detail to a minimum.

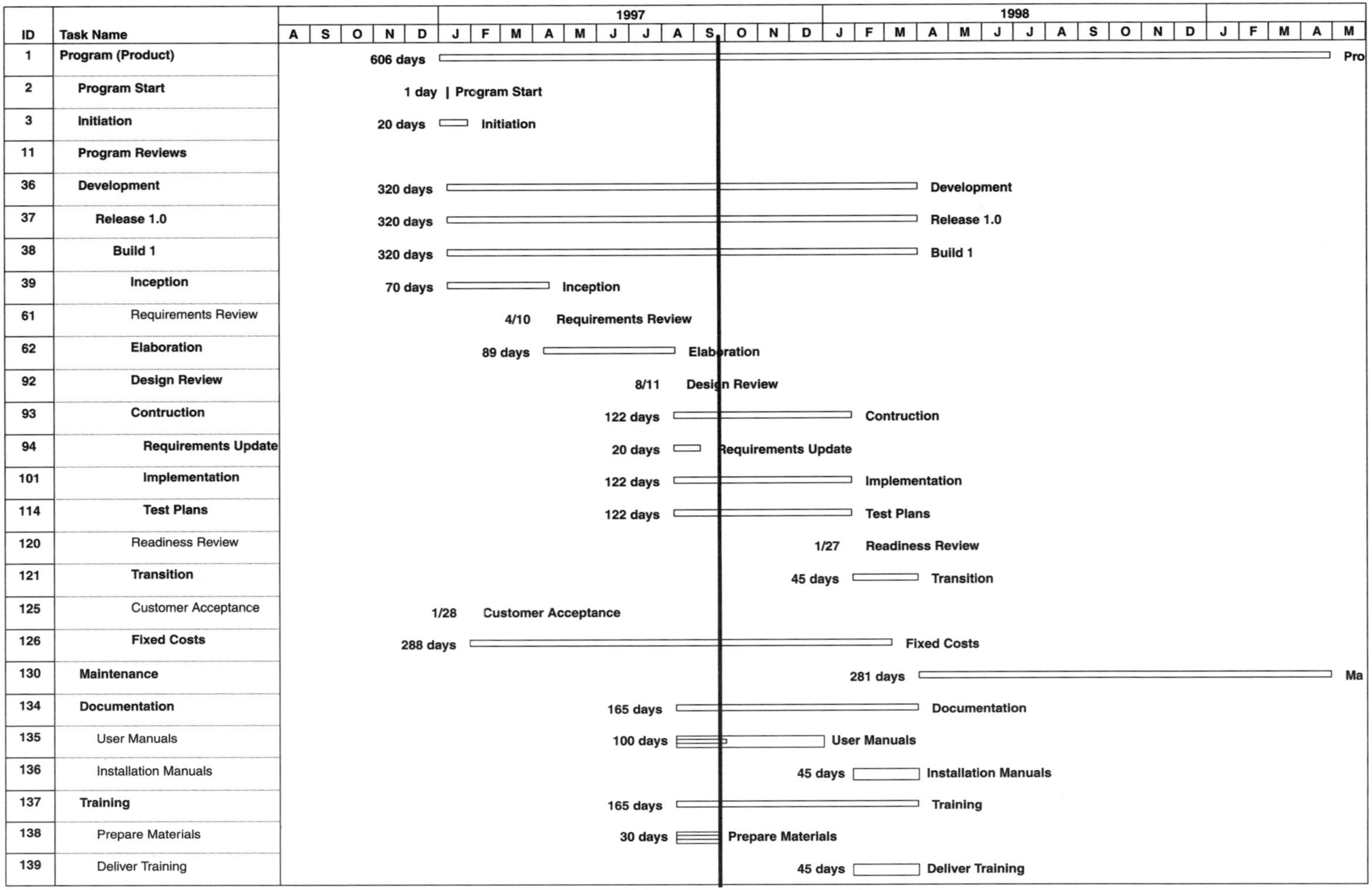

ID	Task Name	Duration
1	Program (Product)	606 days
2	Program Start	1 day / Program Start
3	Initiation	20 days / Initiation
11	Program Reviews	
36	Development	320 days / Development
37	Release 1.0	320 days / Release 1.0
38	Build 1	320 days / Build 1
39	Inception	70 days / Inception
61	Requirements Review	4/10 / Requirements Review
62	Elaboration	89 days / Elaboration
92	Design Review	8/11 / Design Review
93	Contruction	122 days / Contruction
94	Requirements Update	20 days / Requirements Update
101	Implementation	122 days / Implementation
114	Test Plans	122 days / Test Plans
120	Readiness Review	1/27 / Readiness Review
121	Transition	45 days / Transition
125	Customer Acceptance	1/28 / Customer Acceptance
126	Fixed Costs	288 days / Fixed Costs
130	Maintenance	281 days / Ma
134	Documentation	165 days / Documentation
135	User Manuals	100 days / User Manuals
136	Installation Manuals	45 days / Installation Manuals
137	Training	165 days / Training
138	Prepare Materials	30 days / Prepare Materials
139	Deliver Training	45 days / Deliver Training

Figure 9.8 Review Gantt Chart

317

WORK ITEM/ MILESTONE	CHANGE	REASON	IMPACT
Design Review	Move from 8/15 to 8/22.	Customer Schedule.	None.
Construction	Ending moved from 11/15 to 12/10.	Subcontractor reset deliveries.	Can contain one week of change; end date of build moved out to 6/30.

Figure 9.9 Sample schedule delta chart.

The second, the schedule delta chart (delta is tech-speak for "difference"), is a simple table explaining how the schedule has changed since the last review (see Figure 9.9). The first column is the WBS item or milestone, the second column is the schedule change, the third is the reason for the change, and the fourth is its impact.

Development Tracking and Stability. This portion of the report consists of a series of artifact status charts in the format of Figure 9.4. Include the following charts:

- *Use cases detailed.* Original and current number of planned use cases, along with the plan for and status of each step fully delineated. This chart measures progress during the inception phase, but may need to be updated during all of the phases if requirements change.

- *Development-level use cases detailed.* Original and current number of planned development use cases, along with the plan for and status of each step fully delineated. This chart measures progress during the elaboration phase, but may need to be updated during the construction and transition phases.

- *Classes specified.* Original and current number of planned object classes in the system design, along with the plan for and status of each of the classes' attributes and methods specified. This chart measures progress during the elaboration phase, but may need to be updated during all of the phases if requirements change. Track only the initial specification: do not be concerned with the inevitable changes.

- *Use cases integrated.* Original and current number of planned use cases, along with the plan for and status of their functionality as tested in system integration. This chart measures progress during the construction phase, but may need to be updated during the transition phase if requirements change.

- *Methods integrated.* Original and current number of planned class methods, along with the plan for and status of their implementation as tested in a system integration. This chart measures progress during the construction phase, but may need to be updated during the transition phase if requirements change.

- *Lines of code integrated.* Original and current number of lines of source code, along with the plan for and status of developing and testing in a system integration. This chart measures progress during the construction phase, but may need to be updated during the transition phase if requirements change.

Do not use all of the charts. Use only those that provide useful information for your particular project. I suggest Use Cases Detailed, Classes Specified, Use Cases Integrated, and Lines of Code Integrated as a minimal set of charts.

Other Metrics. This section includes any other charts that would give insight into your status. Some examples include:

- *Staffing curves.* Staff onboard versus staff planned

- *Defect analysis.* The charts from Chapter 8

- *System and operational test status.* Number of system tests written and number successfully executed

Review of Action Items. The final chart is a review of the status of the action items generated during previous reviews. It should include the action item, its date, its status (open or closed), and the outcome. It can be maintained as a table; Figure 9.10 is an example.

DATE	ITEM	STATUS	OUTCOME
7/1/98	Schedule review with subcontractor.	Closed	Meeting set for 7/23.

Figure 9.10 Action item review.

From Here: Principles for Success

Using the techniques you've learned from this book, you can deliver a project on schedule that meets the customer needs while enhancing the lives of your team. Keep these principles in mind as you go forward:

- *Look after your team.* Your role is to enable and empower them to do their work. You provide the context; they make it happen. Respect them as individuals. Celebrate their strengths and make allowances, if possible, for their shortcomings. Trust them and earn their trust. Take responsibility for making their lives better by working on your projects.

- *Maintain focus and momentum.* Strive to meet the planned phase transition dates. If they slip, your project slips. Defend the schedule from new requirements and latecomer *good ideas.* The opportunity for new requirements and design changes diminishes with each succeeding phase:

    Inception. Fold the new requirement into the project's priorities.

    Elaboration. Control impact of new requirements.

    Construction. Address new requirements only if they are critical.

    Transition. It is too late to include new requirements. They must be prioritized in the next build.

Finally, hold the course; protect your team from the high-frequency noise generated by your management.

- *Stay disciplined.* Discipline is the key to all successful development. The flexibility allowed by the use of iteration requires even more focus than some other models. Remember to use the microschedules; use the design tools and configuration management tools to control design integrity; and meet each completion criterion at the end of each phase transition.

Your learning should not stop here. Throughout the book and in the Bibliography I have listed other sources on the topics covered in the text. More pertinent advice is to find a project to manage. Try out what you learned. You will find it very rewarding.

APPENDIX

THE WEB PAGE

I invite you to visit www.wiley.com/compbooks/cantor, the book's accompanying Web site. There you will find material useful for applying some of the techniques in the book, among which is a collection of downloadable files including:

- A sample project file for the simulator example that includes a work breakdown structure (WBS) in .mpx (version 4) and .mpp formats, staff loadings, and the basis for the time-phased budget. You will need either Microsoft Project 98 or another project management tool that can import .mpx format to use the file.

- A database template for managing use cases described in Chapter 5 in Microsoft Access format. The template includes the table definitions and an input form for maintaining the project's use cases. Of course, either Access or a database manager that imports the Access format is required.

- A spreadsheet workbook for creating and maintaining the Svedlow diagram found in Chapter 7 for tracking development during the construction phase. This file is in Microsoft Excel format, so you will need either Excel or another spreadsheet program that can read Excel files.

- A spreadsheet file that can be used to create development artifact status graphs like that shown in Figure 9.4. This file contains a chart linked to a set of cells for easy update. The same format can be used for reporting the status of all the development metrics (use cases, classes, lines of code, etc.) discussed in Chapter 9. This file is also in Excel format.

These files are intended as a starting point. You may want to modify one or more to meet your project's particular needs. (Of course, these files are provided as is as a convenience to the user without warranty or support of any kind.)

The Web page also has links to other Web sites you might find useful. In addition to those mentioned in the body of the book, you will find links to various software tool providers and to other relevant online articles. Finally, you will find my e-mail address so you can send me comments and suggestions and share your experiences.

The site will be updated on an ongoing basis. I plan to add more sample files (including some sent in by readers), update the sample files as needed, keep the links current, and add links to useful articles and other material.

BIBLIOGRAPHY

Beck, K. and W. Cunningham. "A Laboratory for Teaching Object-Oriented Thinking," *SIGPLAN Notices*, vol. 24(10), 1989, 1–6.

Bellin, David and Susan S. Simone. *The CRC Card Book* (Addison-Wesley Series in Object-Oriented Software Engineering). (Menlo Park, CA: Addison-Wesley), 1997.

Bennatan, E. *On Time, Within Budget*, 2nd ed. (New York: John Wiley & Sons, Inc.), 1995.

Blair, Gerald. "Groups that Work," *Engineering Management Journal*, vol. I, no. 5, October 1991, 219–293.

Boddie, John. *Crunch Mode: Building Effective Systems on a Tight Schedule*. (Englewood Cliffs, NJ: Prentice-Hall), 1987.

Boehm, Barry. "A Spiral Model of Software Development and Enhancement," *IEEE Computer*, May 1988, 61–67.

Boehm, Barry. *Software Engineering Economics*. (Englewood Cliffs, NJ: Prentice-Hall) 1981.

Boehm, Barry and Philip N. Papaccio. "Understanding and Controlling Software Costs," *IEEE Transactions on Software Engineering*, vol. 14, no. 10, 1988, 1462–1477.

Boehm, Barry, Bradford Clark, Ellis Horowitz, and Chris Westland. "Cost Models for Future Software Life Cycle Processes: COCOMO 2.0," *Annals of Software Engineering*. vol. 1, pp. 57–94, 1995.

Booch, Grady. *Object Solutions*. (Menlo Park, CA: Addison-Wesley), 1996.

Booch, Grady. *Object-Oriented Analysis and Design with Applications* 2nd ed. (Menlo Park, CA: Addison-Wesley), 1994.

Brooks, Fredrick P. and Fredrick P. Brooks Jr. *The Mythical Man-Month*, Anniversary Edition. (Menlo Park: CA: Addison-Wesley), 1995.

Card, David N. and Robert L. Glass. *Measuring Software Design Quality*. (Englewood Cliffs, NJ: Prentice-Hall), 1990.

Clausing, Don. *Total Quality Development*. (New York: ASME), 1994.

Cockburn, Alistar. *Surviving Object-Oriented Projects, a Manager's Guide*. (Reading, MA: Addison-Wesley), 1998.

COCOMO II Software Project, University of Southern California, *COCOMO II Estimation Model*, sunset.usc.edu/COCOMOII/Docs/manual14.pdf.

Cotterell, M. and B. Hughes. *Software Project Planning*. (New York, NY: Chapman & Hall), 1995.

De Santis, Richard M, John Blyskal, Assad Moini, and Mark Tappan. *Evolutionary Rapid Development*, Software Productivity Consortium, http://www.software.org/pub/darpa/erd/erdpv010004.html, (Herndon, VA) 1997.

Donald, Scott and Stanley Siegel. *Cultivating Successful Software Development*. (Upper Saddle River, NJ: Prentice-Hall), 1997.

Dymond, Kenneth. *A Guide to the CMM*. (Annapolis, MD: Process Inc US), 1995.

Eriksson, H. E. and Magnus Penker, *UML Toolkit*. (New York: John Wiley & Sons, Inc.), 1998.

Feuer, Alan. *The C Puzzle Book*. (Englewood Cliffs, NJ: Prentice-Hall), 1982.

Fowler, Martin. *Analysis Patterns: Reusable Object Models*. (Menlo Park, CA: Addison-Wesley), 1997.

Fowler, Martin with Kendall Scott. *UML Distilled*. (Menlo Park, CA: Addison-Wesley), 1997.

Frame, J. Davidson. *The New Project Management*. (San Francisco: Jossey-Bass), 1994.

Gamma, Erich and Richard Helm, Ralph Johnson, John Vlissides. *Design Patterns, Elements of Reusable Object-Oriented Software*. (Menlo Park, CA: Addison-Wesley), 1995.

Gibbs, Wayt. "Software's Chronic Crises," *Scientific American Magazine*, September 1994, 86–95.

Graham, Ian. *Migrating to Object Technology*. (Workingham, England: Addison-Wesley), 1995.

Guttman, Michael and Jason R. Matthews. *The Object Technology Revolution*. (New York: John Wiley & Sons, Inc.), 1995.

Harel, David. *Algorithmics*. (Workingham, England: Addison-Wesley), 1987.

Hersey, Paul and Kenneth Blanchard. *Management of Organization Behavior*. (Englewood Cliffs, NJ: Prentice-Hall), 1979.

Hohmann, Luke, *Journey of the Software Professional*. (Upper Saddle River, NJ: Prentice-Hall PTR), 1997.

Humphrey, Watts. *A Discipline for Software Engineering*. (Reading MA: Addison-Wesley), 1995.

Jacobson, Ivar. *The Object Advantage*. (Workingham, England: Addison-Wesley), 1995.

Jag Sodhi and Prince Sodhi. *Object-Oriented Methods for Software Development.* (New York: McGraw-Hill), 1996.

Jones, Capers. *Applied Software Measurement, Assuring Productivity and Quality,* (New York: McGraw-Hill), 1991.

Jones, Capers. *Applied Software Measurement,* 2nd ed. (New York: McGraw-Hill), 1996.

Jones, Peter. *Handbook of Team Design.* (New York: McGraw-Hill), 1998.

Kerzner, Harold. *Project Management.* (New York: Van Nostrand Reinhold), 1998.

Knuth, Donald. *The Art of Computer Programming V.3, Sorting and Searching.* (Menlo Park, CA: Addison-Wesley), 1973.

Larman, Craig. *Applying UML and Patterns: An Introduction to Object-Oriented Analysis and Design.* (Englewood Cliffs, NJ: Prentice-Hall), 1997.

Lee, Richard C. and William M. Tepfenhart. *UML and C++: A Practical Guide to Object-Oriented Development.* (Englewood Cliffs, NJ: Prentice-Hall), 1997.

Lewis, James. *Fundamentals of Project Management.* (New York: AMACON), 1997.

Love, Tom. *Object Lessons.* (New York: SIGS Books), 1993.

Martin, R. C. *Designing Object-Oriented C++ Applications Using the Booch Method.* (Englewood Cliffs NJ: Prentice-Hall), 1995.

McCabe, Thomas J. "A Complexity Measure," *IEEE Transactions of Software Engineering,* SE-2, no.4, pp. 308–320, December 1976.

McCabe, Thomas J. and Arthur Watson. "Software Complexity," Chapter 8, Addendum B in *Guidelines for Successful Acquisition and Management of Software-Intensive Systems, Version 2.0.* (Department of the Air Force), 1996.

McConnell, Steve. *Rapid Development: Taming Wild Software Schedules.* (Redmond, WA: Microsoft Press), 1996.

McConnell, Steve. *Software Project Survival Guide.* (Redmond, WA: Microsoft Press), 1997.

Metzger, Philip and John Boddie. *Managing a Programming Project.* (Upper Saddle River, NJ: Prentice-Hall), 1996.

Minkiewicz, Arlene. *Estimating Size for Object-Oriented Software,* www.pricesystems.com/foresight/arlepops.htm.

Mowbray, Thomas and Raphael Malveau. *CORBA Design Patterns.* (New York: John Wiley & Sons, Inc.), 1997.

National Air and Space Administration. *Parametric Cost-Estimating Reference Manual,* http://www.jsc.nasa.gov/bu2/COCOMO.html.

Object Management Group. *Unified Modeling Language Notation Guide v. 1.0,* www.omg.org, 1997.

Object Management Group. *Unified Modeling UML Summary v. 1.0,* www.omg.org, 1997.

Parkinson, C. Northcote. *Parkinson's Law.* (Cutchogue, NY: Buccaneer Books), 1957.

Polya, George, *How to Solve It: A New Aspect of Mathematical Method,* 2nd ed. (Princeton, NJ: Princeton University Press), 1957.

Quantini, Terry. *Visual Modeling with Rational Rose and UML.* (Reading, MA: Addison-Wesley), 1998.

Roetzheim, William and Reyna A. Beasley. *Software Project Cost & Schedule Estimating Best Practices.* (Upper Saddle River, NJ: Prentice-Hall), 1997.

Romig, Dennis. *Breakthrough Teamwork.* (Chicago: Irwin), 1996.

Royce, Winston. "Managing the Development of Large Software Systems," in *Proceedings of the 9th Internation Conference on Software Engineering,* Washington, DC: IEEE Computer Society Press, 328-38.

Sabbagh, Karl. *Twenty-First Century Jet, the Making and Marketing of the Boeing 777.* (New York: Scribner), 1996.

Scholtes, Peter. *The Team Handbook.* (Madison, WI: Joiner Associates), 1988.

Software Engineering Process Office, United States Navy Research and Development. *Software Size, Cost, Schedule, Process Estimation Process, Version 2.1,* http://sepo.nosc.mil/docs.html#SOFTWARE PROJECT PLANNING.

Software Technology Support Center (STSC). *Guidelines for Successful Acquisition and Management of Software-Intensive Systems, Version 2.0.* (Department of the Air Force), 1996.

Texel, Putnam and Charles B. Williams. *Use Cases Combined with Booch/OMT/UML: Process and Products.* (Englewood Cliffs, NJ: Prentice-Hall), 1997.

Tian, Jeff and Marvin V. Zelkowitz. "Complexity Measure Evaluation and Selection," in *IEEE Transactions in Software Engineering* vol. 21, no. 8, August 1995, 641–650.

Tuckmann, B. W. and M. A. C. Jensen. "Development Sequence in Small Groups," *Psychological Bulletin*, vol. LXIII, no. 6, 1965, 384-399.

Turing. A. "On Computable Numbers with an Application to the Entscheidungsproblem," in *Proc. London Math Soc.* 42, pp. 230–265, 1936.

Wilkinson, Nancy M. *Using CRC Cards: An Informal Approach to Object-Oriented Development (Advances in Object Technology, No 6).* (Englewood Cliffs NJ: Prentice-Hall), 1995.

Winston, M. R. Chaffer and D. Herrmann. "A taxonomy of Part-Whole Relations," *Cognitive Science*, 11, 417–444, 1987.

Witten, Neal. *Managing Software Development Projects,* 2nd ed. (New York: John Wiley & Sons, Inc.), 1995.

Zachery, Pascal. *Showstopper.* (New York: The Free Press), 1994.

CONTENTS